... WITH MONSTER GIRLS

Volume 9

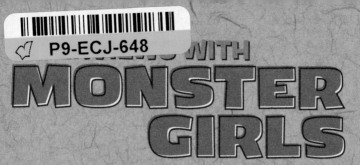

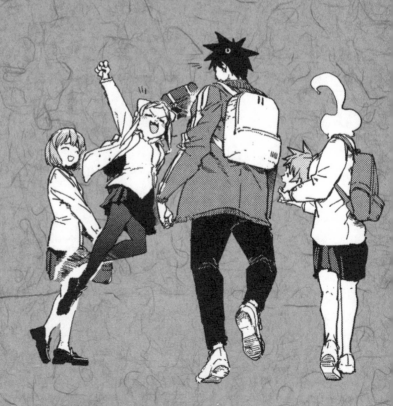

Characters

INTERVIEWS WITH MONSTER GIRLS

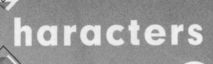

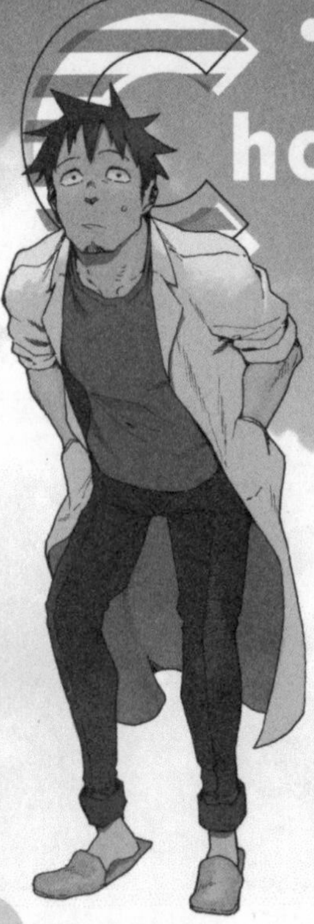

Vampire

Hikari Takanashi

Class 1-B

- Likes liver, tomato juice.
- Enjoys nibbling on arms.
- Receives blood from the government once a month.
- Opinions on romance: plenty; actual experience: none.

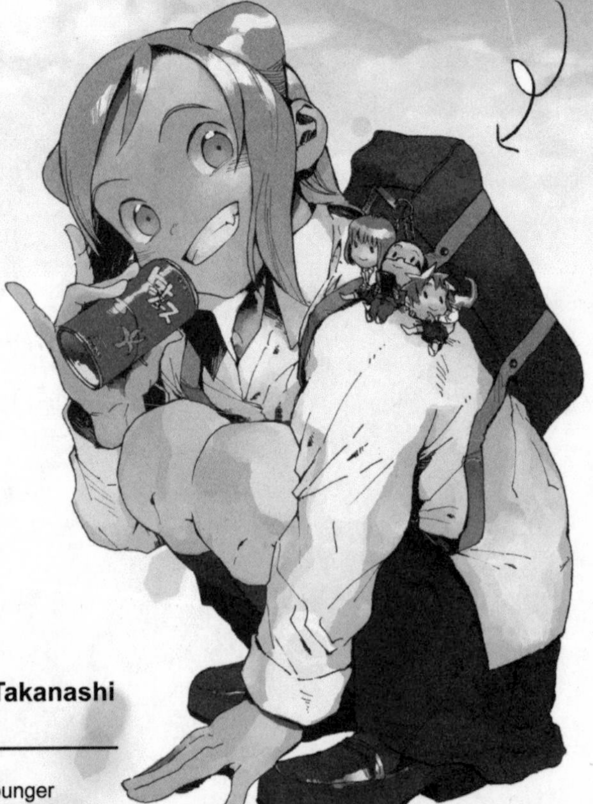

Tetsuo Takahashi

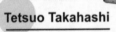

- Biology teacher.
- Fascinated by demi studies since college.
- Tries his best to understand demis.

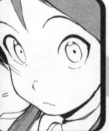

Himari Takanashi

Class 1-C

- Human.
- Hikari's younger twin sister.
- Good grades, mature attitude—polar opposite of her sister.

"Demi-humans" are just a little different from us—these days, they go by "demis." Their problems are as adorable as they are.

*DEMIS: SHORT FOR "DEMI-HUMANS."

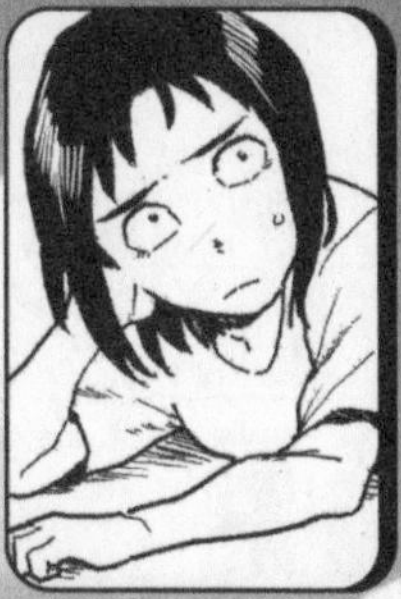

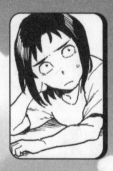

Yoko Takahashi

- Freshman at Musashino University of Science.
- Tetsuo Takahashi's niece.
- Zashiko is her roommate.
- A demi who can see other dimensions.

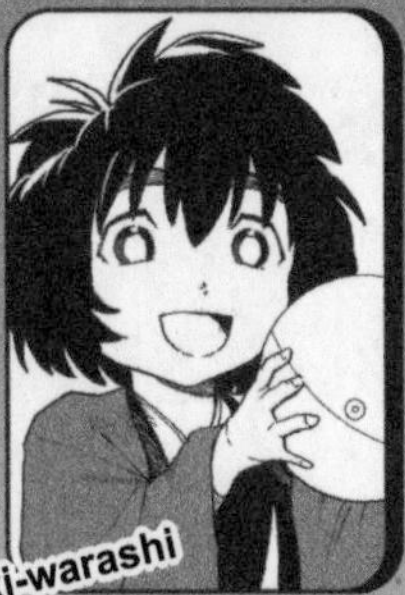

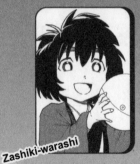

Zashiki-warashi

Zashiko

- A spirit from Tohoku-region legends.
- Said to bring happiness.
- Likes: eating and sleeping.

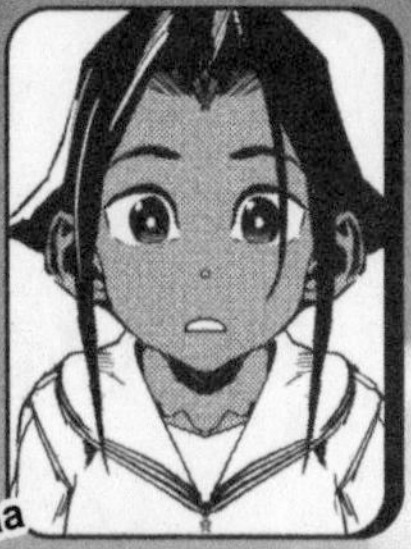

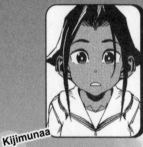

Kijimunaa

Kaoru Higa

- A demi of Okinawan legend that lives in Banyan trees.
- Can tell how people feel by the color of their eyes.
- Scared of dead fish eyes.
- A bit sophomoric.

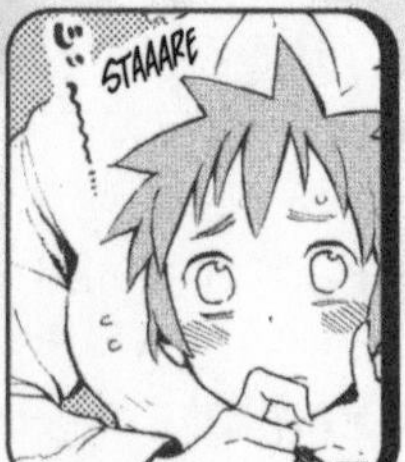
STAAARE

Dullahan

Kyoko Machi Class 1-B

- A demi of Irish legend whose head and body are separate.
- Likes her head to be held.
- In love with Takahashi-sensei.
- Top grades—has even been No. 1 in her class.

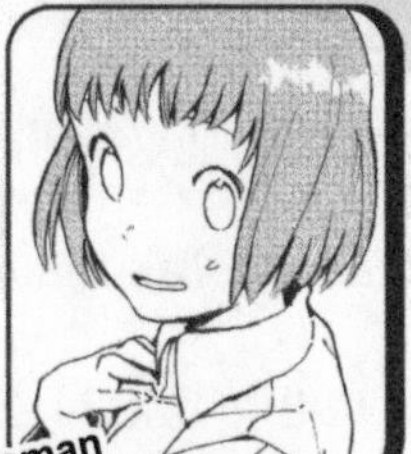

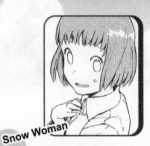

Snow Woman

Yuki Kusakabe Class 1-A

- Exudes cold air and weeps ice under stress.
- Sometimes wishes she could control her powers.
- Embarrassed to admit she likes gag manga; tries to hide it.

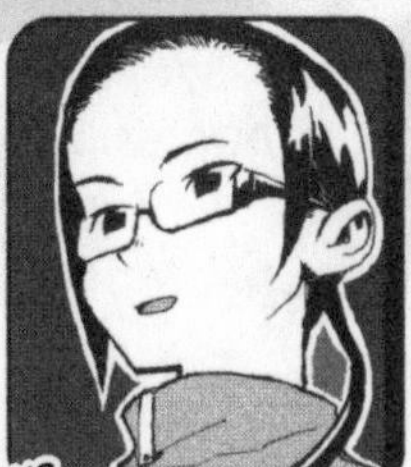

Succubus

Sakie Sato

- Math teacher.
- Lives in an isolated, dilapidated house so as not to unintentionally arouse anyone.
- Has a crush on Takahashi-sensei; has tried to arouse him
- Romantic history: zilch.

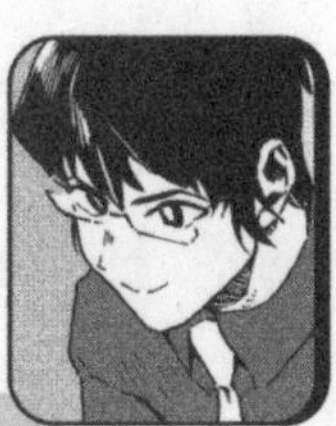

Soma

- Assistant Professor at Musashino University of Science.
- Physicist.
- Takahashi-sensei's college classmate.

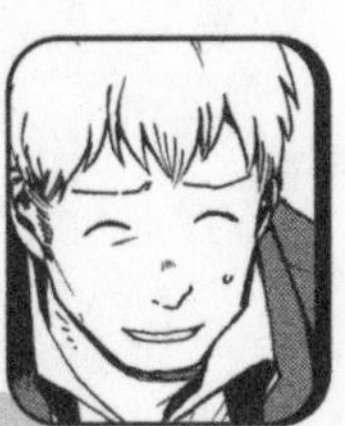

Ugaki

- Detective with the Demi Affairs Dept.
- Father figure to Sato-sensei, a succubus on his beat.
- Encourages Sato-sensei's love for Takahashi-sensei.

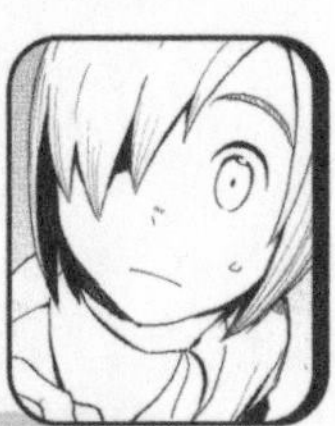

Kurtz

- Ugaki's junior detective.
- Apparently the ultimate anti-succubus weapon.
- Easygoing.

INTERVIEWS WITH MONSTER GIRLS

CONTENTS

9

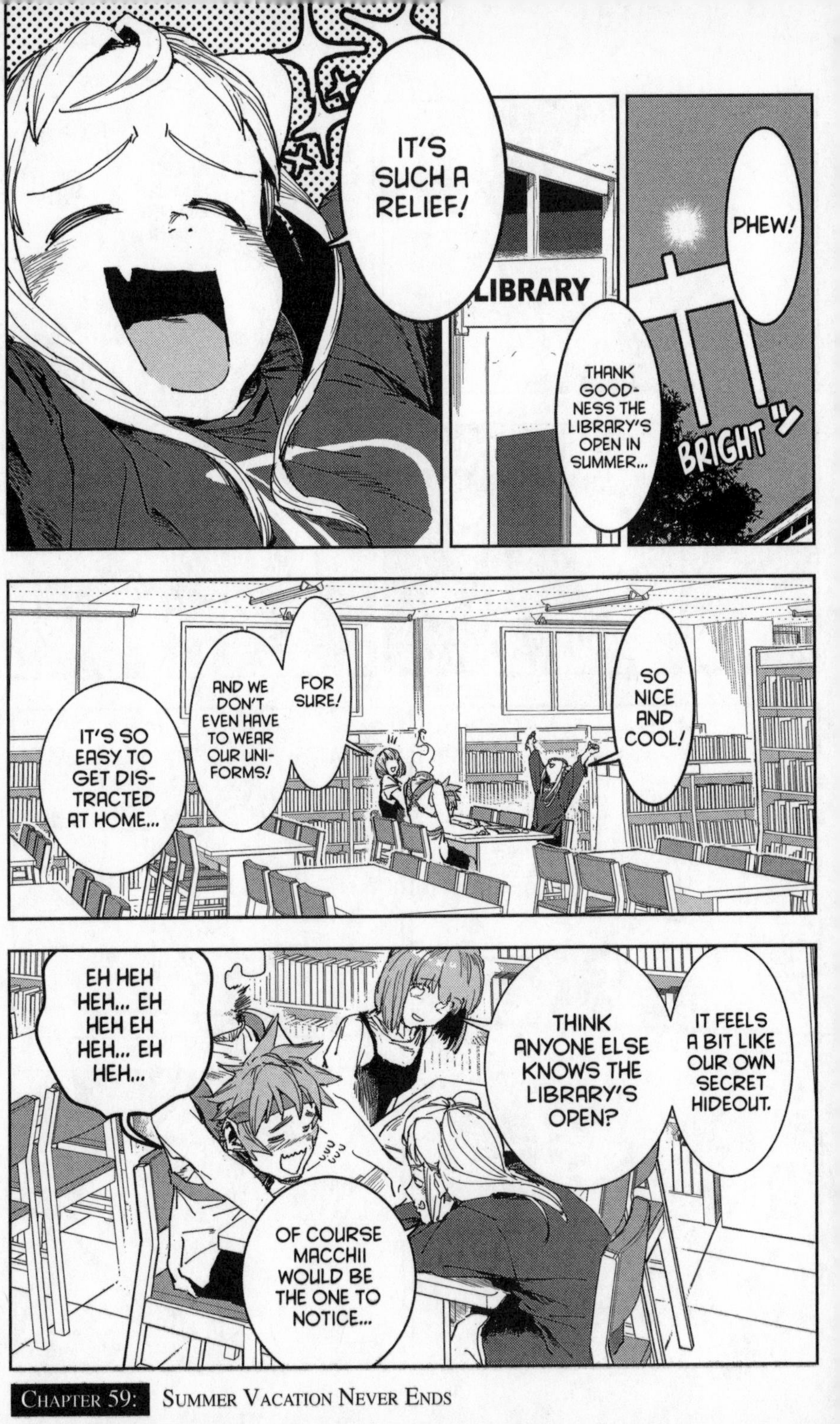
PHEW!
BRIGHT ツ
LIBRARY
THANK GOODNESS THE LIBRARY'S OPEN IN SUMMER...
IT'S SUCH A RELIEF!
SO NICE AND COOL!
FOR SURE!
AND WE DON'T EVEN HAVE TO WEAR OUR UNIFORMS!
IT'S SO EASY TO GET DISTRACTED AT HOME...
IT FEELS A BIT LIKE OUR OWN SECRET HIDEOUT.
THINK ANYONE ELSE KNOWS THE LIBRARY'S OPEN?
OF COURSE MACCHII WOULD BE THE ONE TO NOTICE...
EH HEH HEH... EH HEH EH HEH... EH HEH...

Chapter 59: Summer Vacation Never Ends

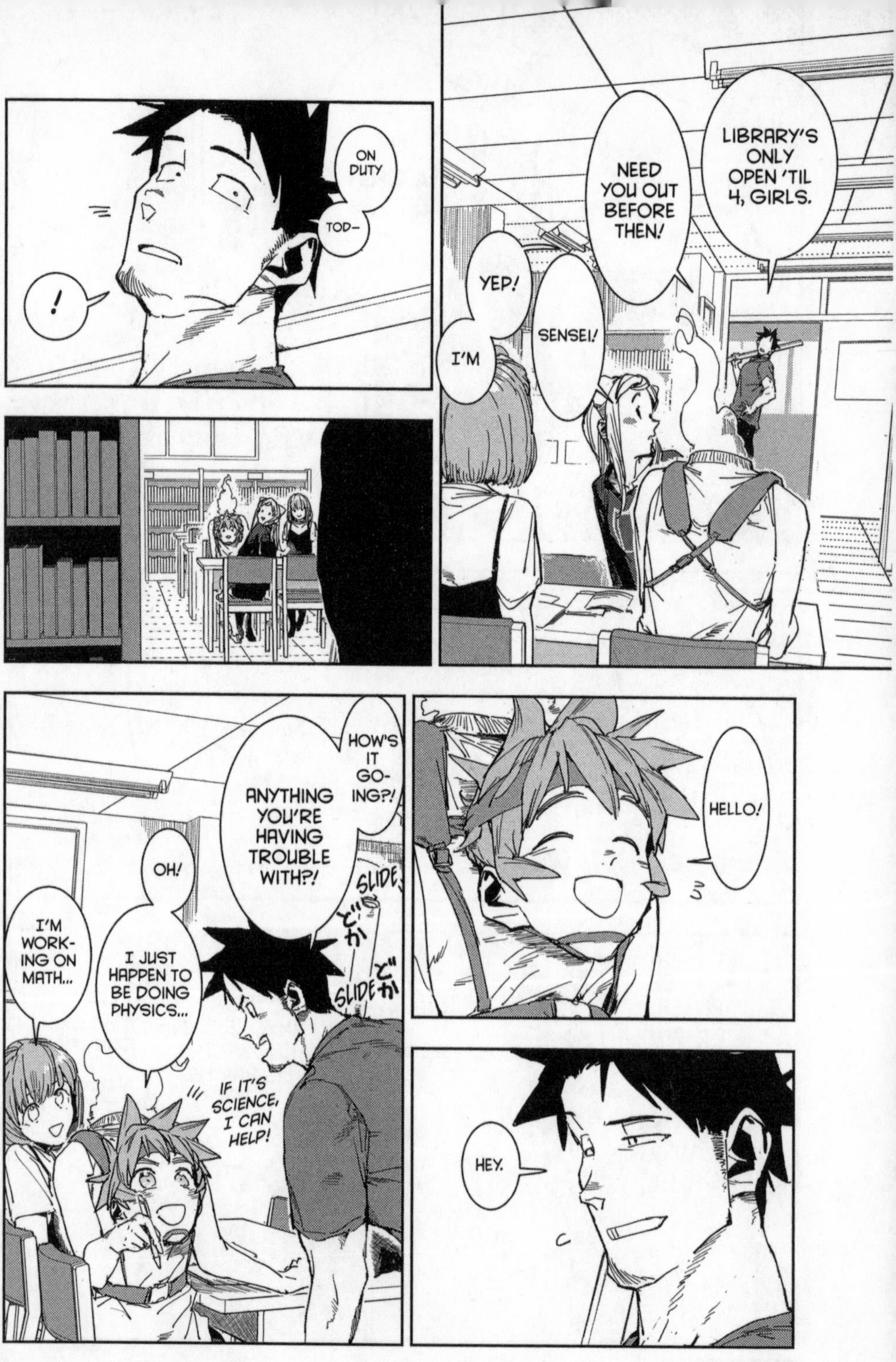
LIBRARY'S ONLY OPEN 'TIL 4, GIRLS.
NEED YOU OUT BEFORE THEN!
SENSEI!
YEP!
I'M
ON DUTY
TOD-
!
HELLO!
HEY.
HOW'S IT GO-ING?!
ANYTHING YOU'RE HAVING TROUBLE WITH?!
SLIDE どか
SLIDE どか
OH!
I JUST HAPPEN TO BE DOING PHYSICS...
I'M WORK-ING ON MATH...
IF IT'S SCIENCE, I CAN HELP!

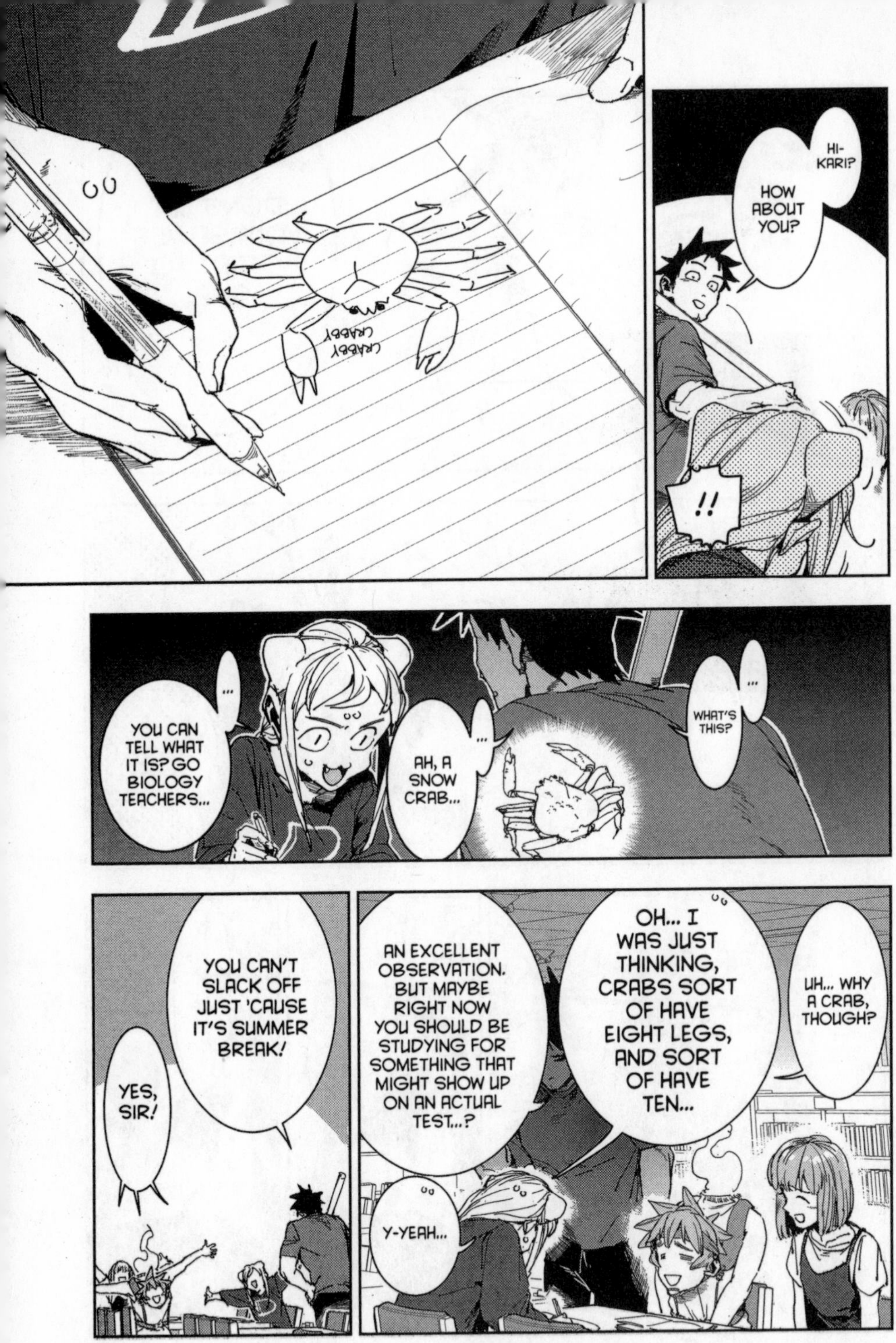
HI-KARI?
HOW ABOUT YOU?
!!
CRABBY CRABBY
...
WHAT'S THIS?
...
AH, A SNOW CRAB...
...
YOU CAN TELL WHAT IT IS? GO BIOLOGY TEACHERS...
UH... WHY A CRAB, THOUGH?
OH... I WAS JUST THINKING, CRABS SORT OF HAVE EIGHT LEGS, AND SORT OF HAVE TEN...
AN EXCELLENT OBSERVATION. BUT MAYBE RIGHT NOW YOU SHOULD BE STUDYING FOR SOMETHING THAT MIGHT SHOW UP ON AN ACTUAL TEST...?
Y-YEAH...
YOU CAN'T SLACK OFF JUST 'CAUSE IT'S SUMMER BREAK!
YES, SIR!

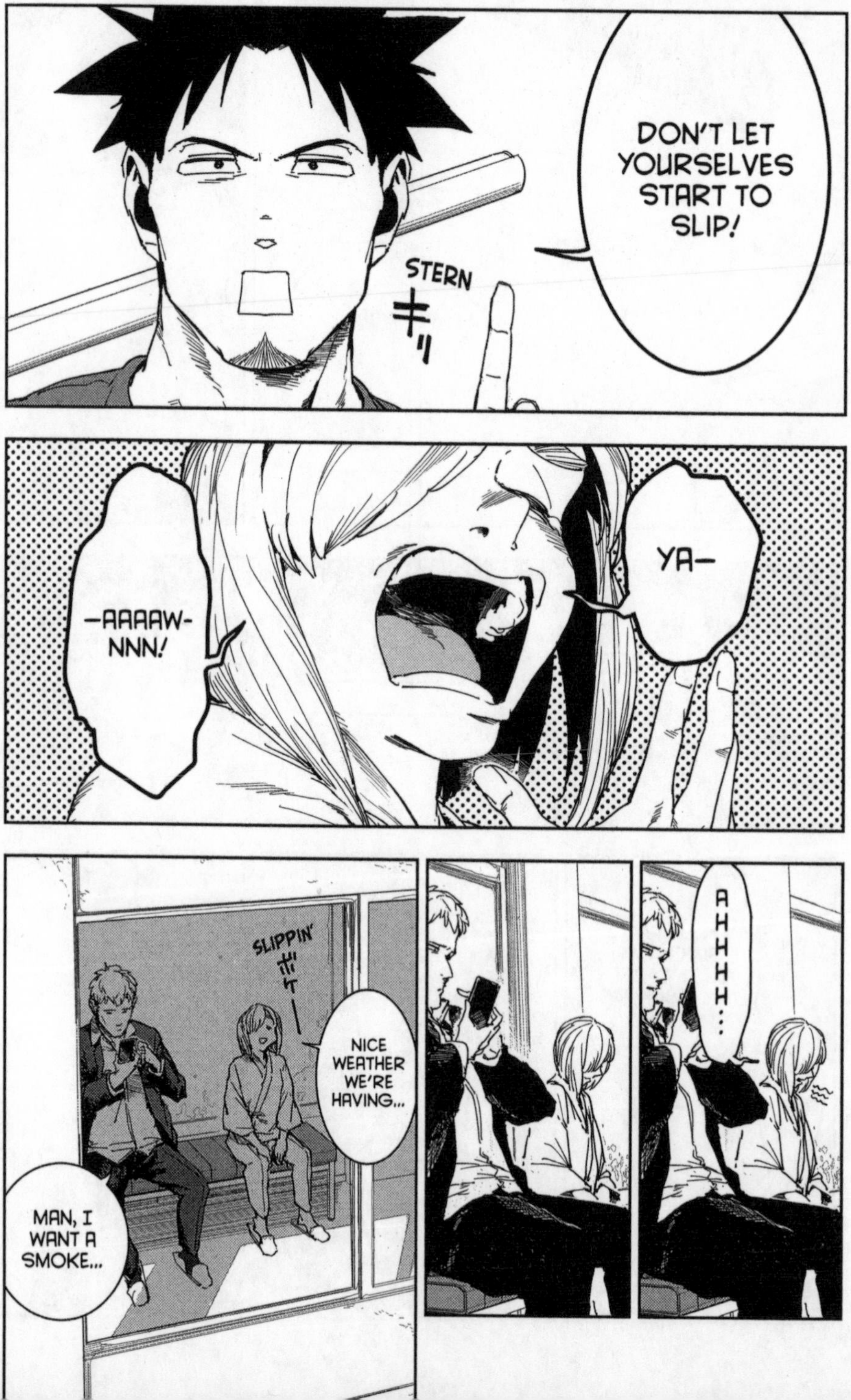
DON'T LET YOURSELVES START TO SLIP!
STERN
キッ
YA—
—AAAAW-NNN!
AHHHH...
SLIPPIN'
ボケー
NICE WEATHER WE'RE HAVING...
MAN, I WANT A SMOKE...

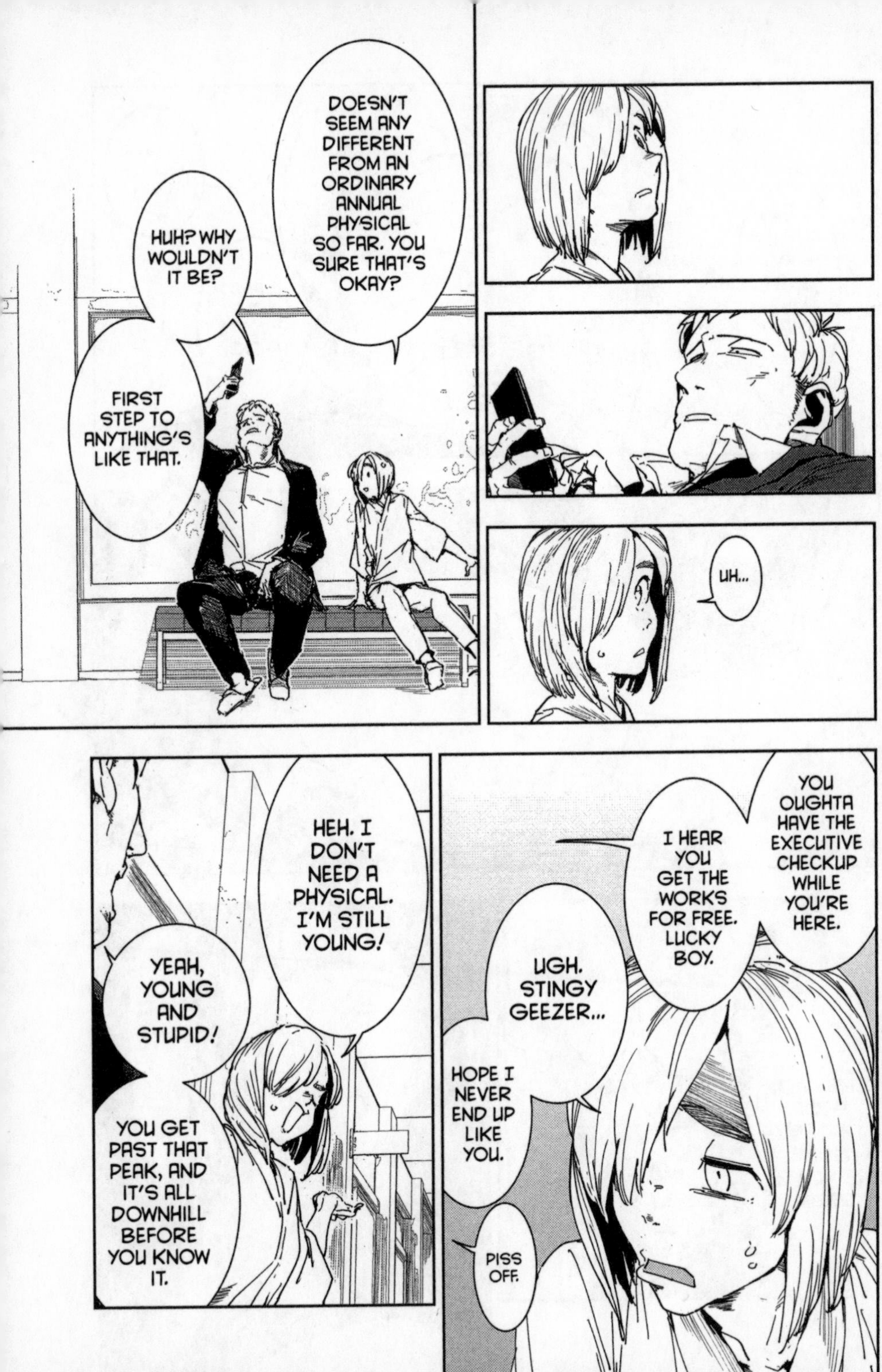
UH...
DOESN'T SEEM ANY DIFFERENT FROM AN ORDINARY ANNUAL PHYSICAL SO FAR. YOU SURE THAT'S OKAY?
HUH? WHY WOULDN'T IT BE?
FIRST STEP TO ANYTHING'S LIKE THAT.
YOU OUGHTA HAVE THE EXECUTIVE CHECKUP WHILE YOU'RE HERE.
I HEAR YOU GET THE WORKS FOR FREE. LUCKY BOY.
UGH. STINGY GEEZER...
HOPE I NEVER END UP LIKE YOU.
PISS OFF.
HEH. I DON'T NEED A PHYSICAL. I'M STILL YOUNG!
YEAH, YOUNG AND STUPID!
YOU GET PAST THAT PEAK, AND IT'S ALL DOWNHILL BEFORE YOU KNOW IT.

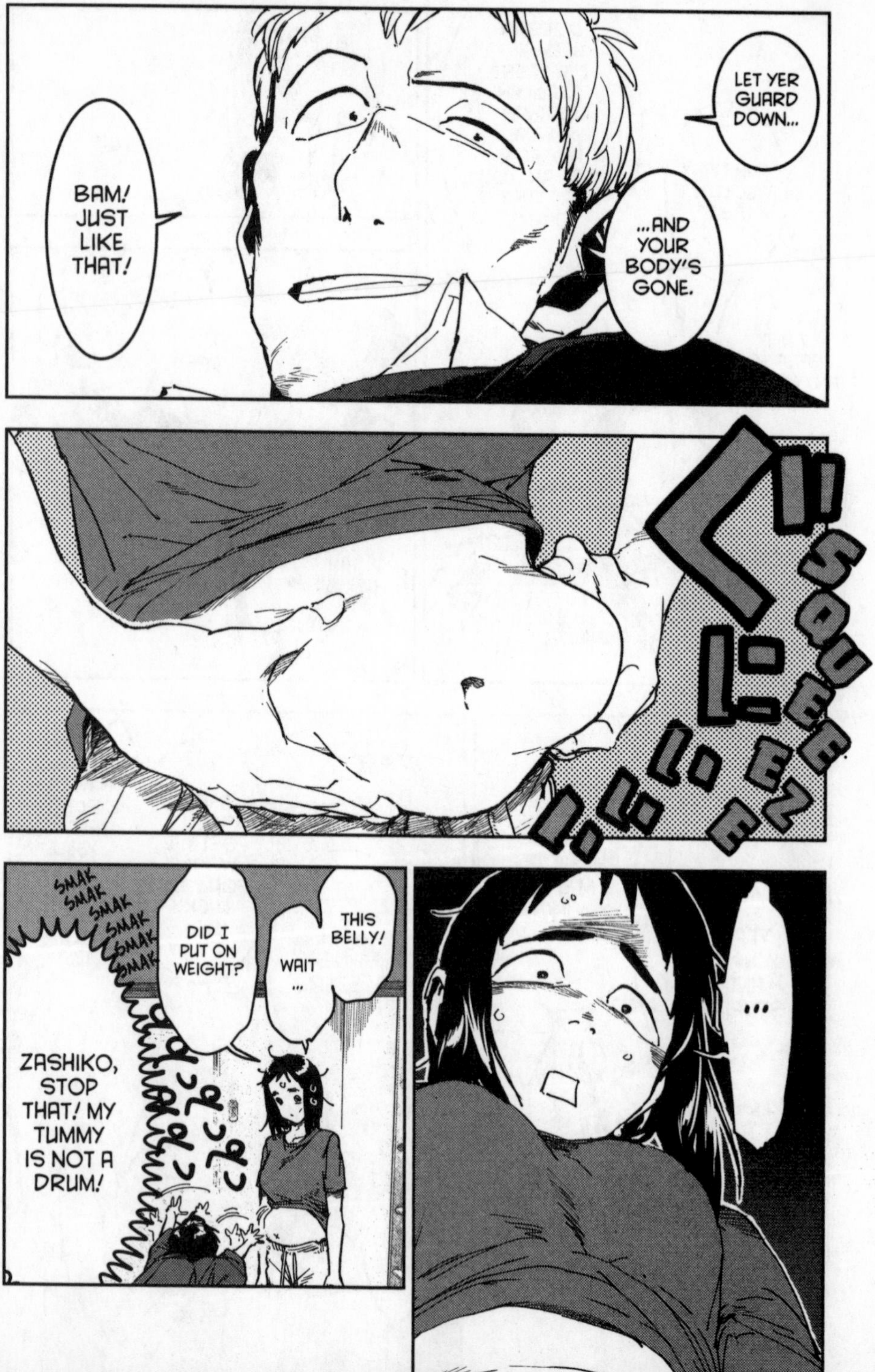
LET YER GUARD DOWN...
...AND YOUR BODY'S GONE.
BAM! JUST LIKE THAT!
SQUEEEZE
...
THIS BELLY!
WAIT ...
DID I PUT ON WEIGHT?
SMAK SMAK SMAK SMAK SMAK SMAK
ZASHIKO, STOP THAT! MY TUMMY IS NOT A DRUM!

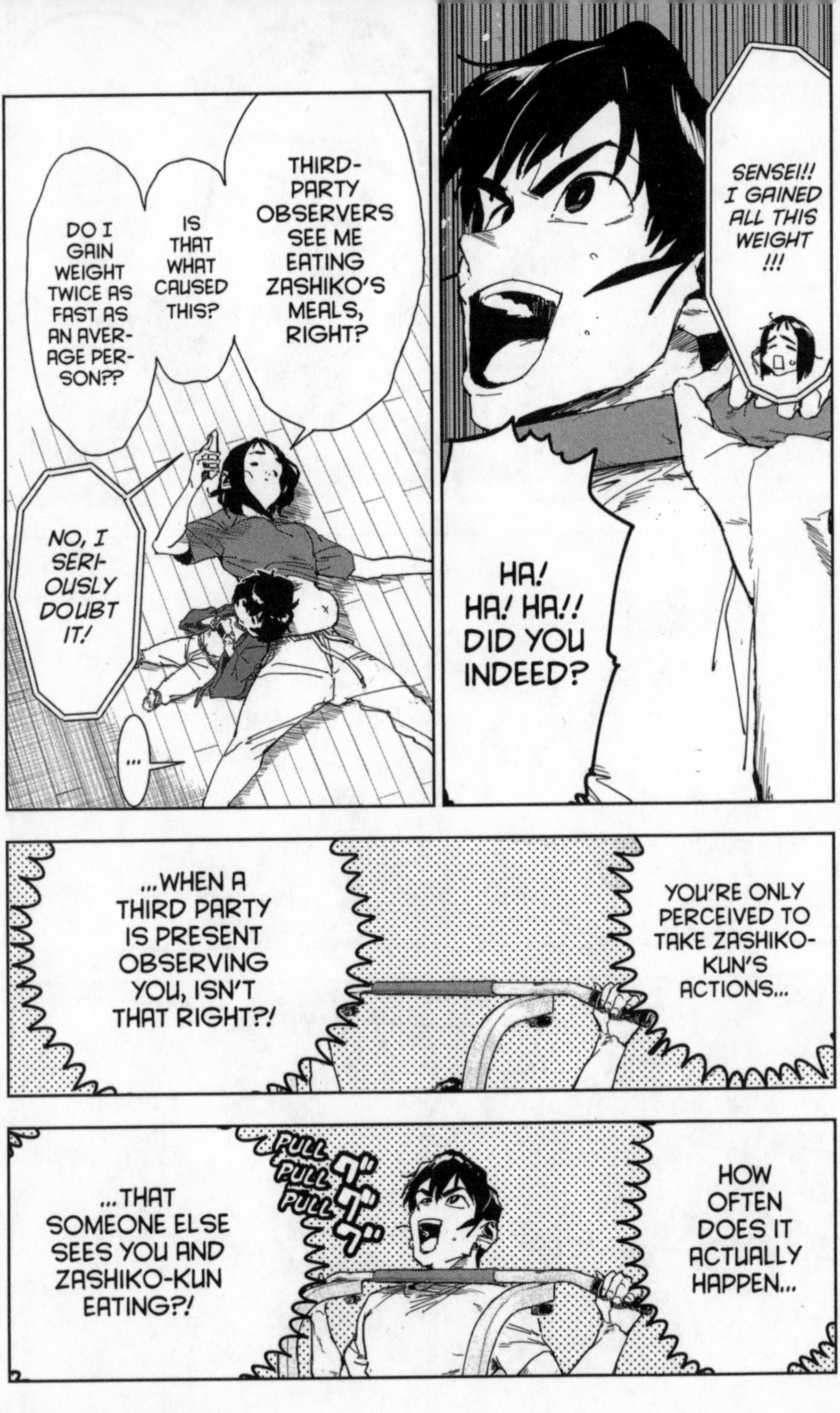
SENSEI!! I GAINED ALL THIS WEIGHT!!!
HA! HA! HA!! DID YOU INDEED?
THIRD-PARTY OBSERVERS SEE ME EATING ZASHIKO'S MEALS, RIGHT?
IS THAT WHAT CAUSED THIS?
DO I GAIN WEIGHT TWICE AS FAST AS AN AVERAGE PERSON??
NO, I SERIOUSLY DOUBT IT!
...
YOU'RE ONLY PERCEIVED TO TAKE ZASHIKO-KUN'S ACTIONS...
...WHEN A THIRD PARTY IS PRESENT OBSERVING YOU, ISN'T THAT RIGHT?!
HOW OFTEN DOES IT ACTUALLY HAPPEN...
PULL PULL PULL
...THAT SOMEONE ELSE SEES YOU AND ZASHIKO-KUN EATING?!

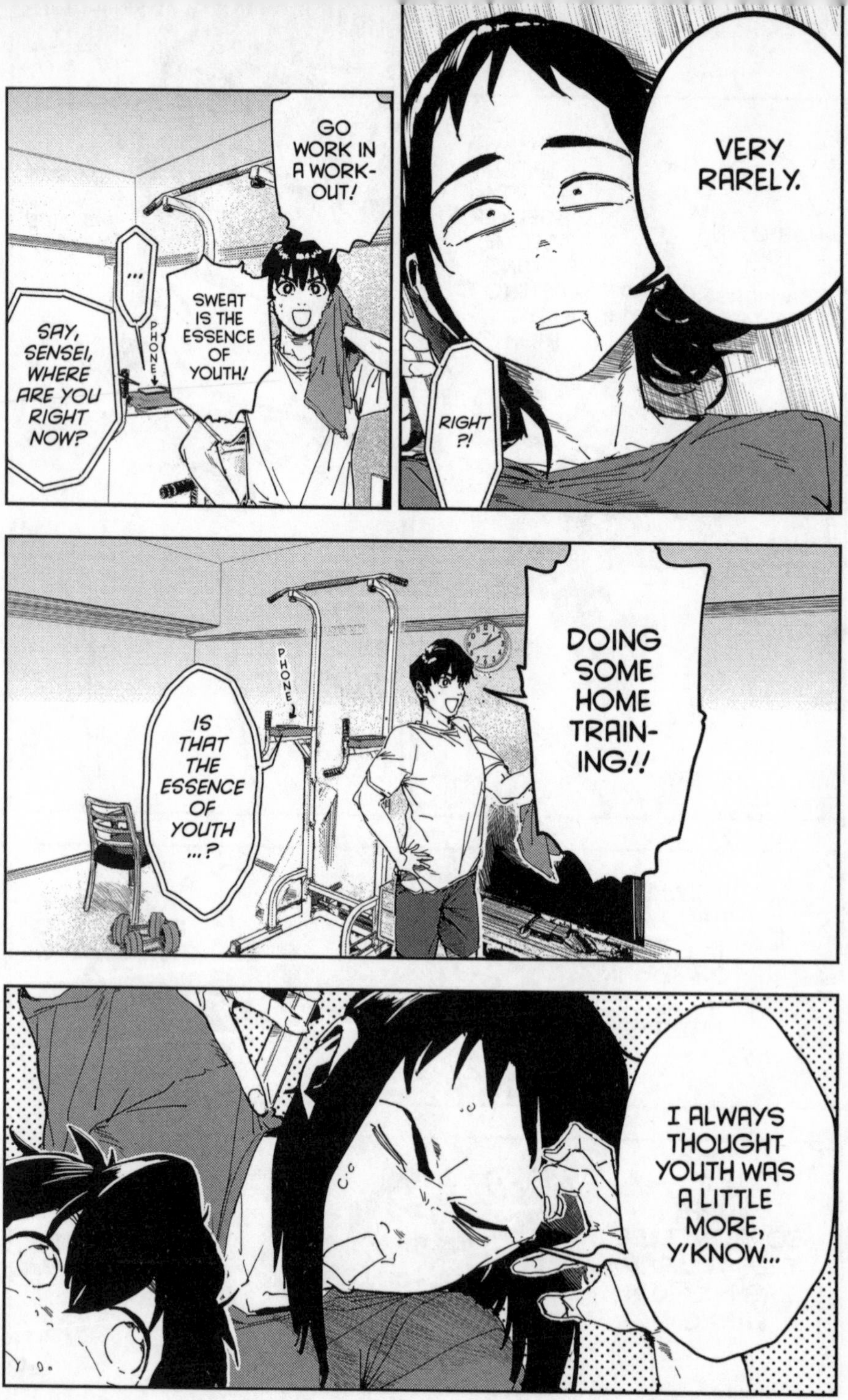
VERY RARELY.
RIGHT?!
GO WORK IN A WORK-OUT!
SWEAT IS THE ESSENCE OF YOUTH!
...
PHONE
SAY, SENSEI, WHERE ARE YOU RIGHT NOW?
DOING SOME HOME TRAINING!!
PHONE
IS THAT THE ESSENCE OF YOUTH ...?
I ALWAYS THOUGHT YOUTH WAS A LITTLE MORE, Y'KNOW...

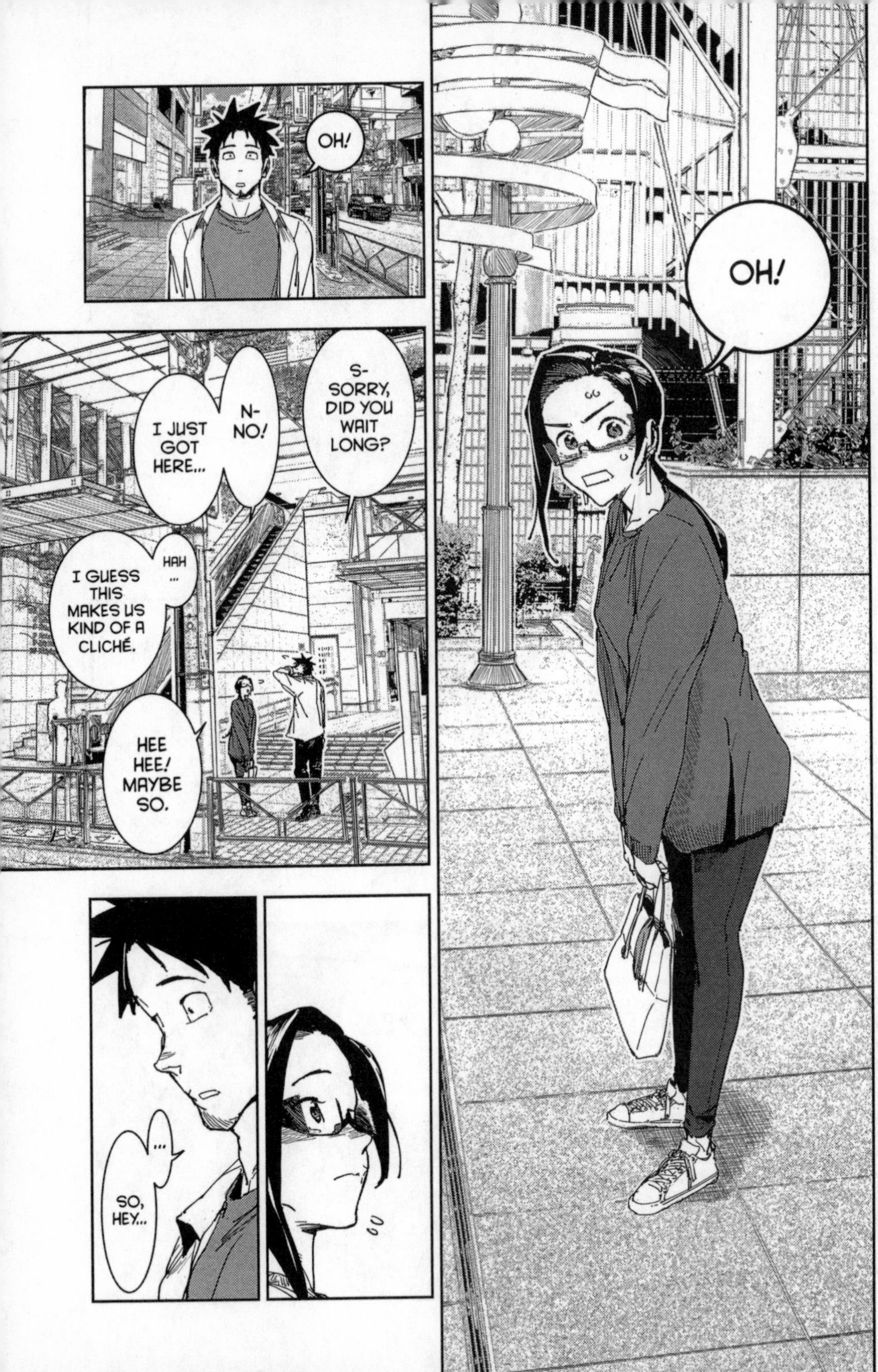
OH!
OH!
S- SORRY, DID YOU WAIT LONG?
N- NO!
I JUST GOT HERE...
HAH ...
I GUESS THIS MAKES US KIND OF A CLICHÉ.
HEE HEE! MAYBE SO.
...
SO, HEY...

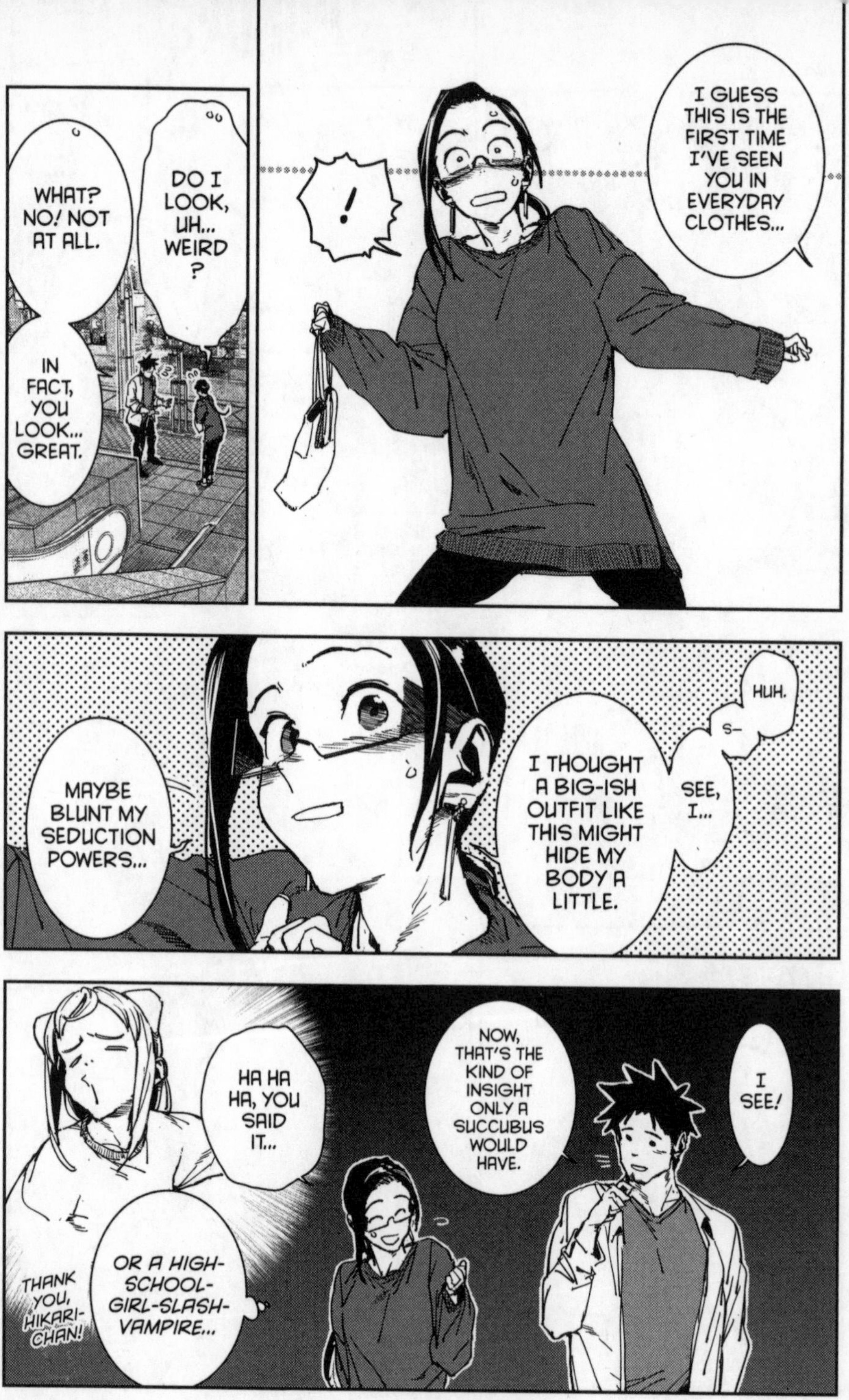
I GUESS THIS IS THE FIRST TIME I'VE SEEN YOU IN EVERYDAY CLOTHES...
!
DO I LOOK, UH... WEIRD?
WHAT? NO! NOT AT ALL.
IN FACT, YOU LOOK... GREAT.
HUH.
S—
SEE, I...
I THOUGHT A BIG-ISH OUTFIT LIKE THIS MIGHT HIDE MY BODY A LITTLE.
MAYBE BLUNT MY SEDUCTION POWERS...
I SEE!
NOW, THAT'S THE KIND OF INSIGHT ONLY A SUCCUBUS WOULD HAVE.
HA HA HA, YOU SAID IT...
OR A HIGH-SCHOOL-GIRL-SLASH-VAMPIRE...
THANK YOU, HIKARI-CHAN!

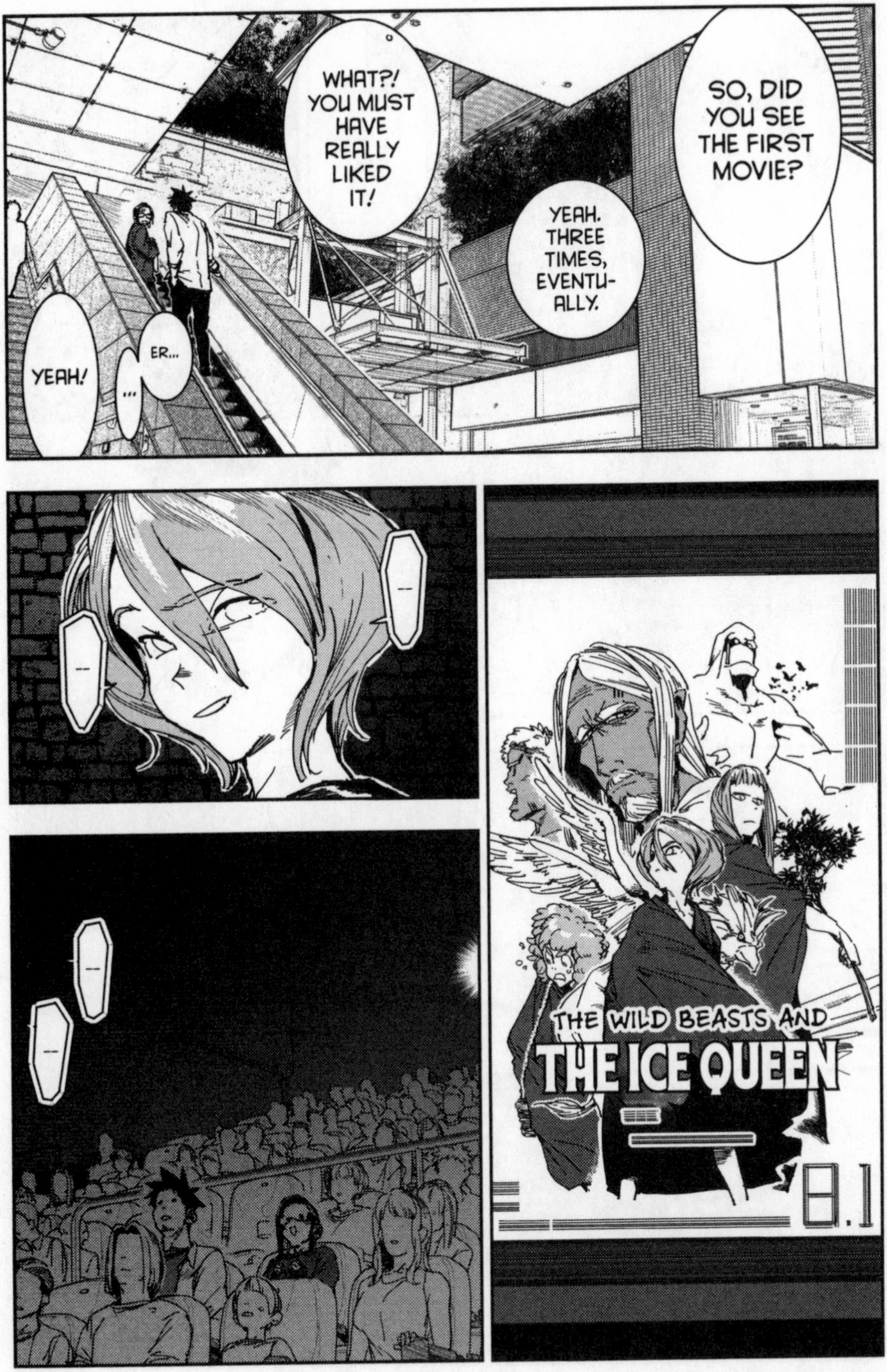
SO, DID YOU SEE THE FIRST MOVIE?
YEAH. THREE TIMES, EVENTU-ALLY.
WHAT?! YOU MUST HAVE REALLY LIKED IT!
ER...
...
YEAH!
THE WILD BEASTS AND
THE ICE QUEEN
--
--
--
--

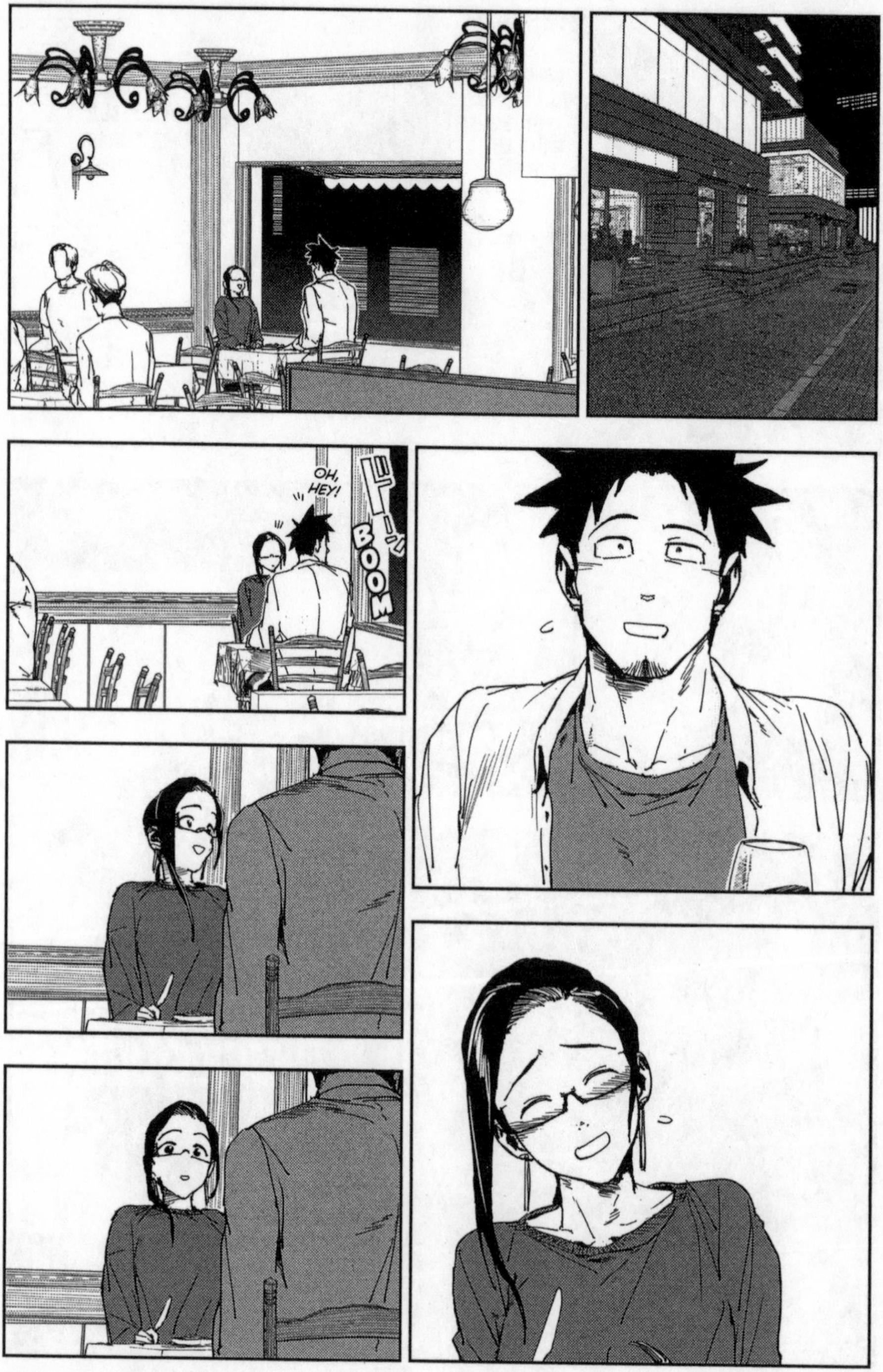
OH, HEY!
BOOM

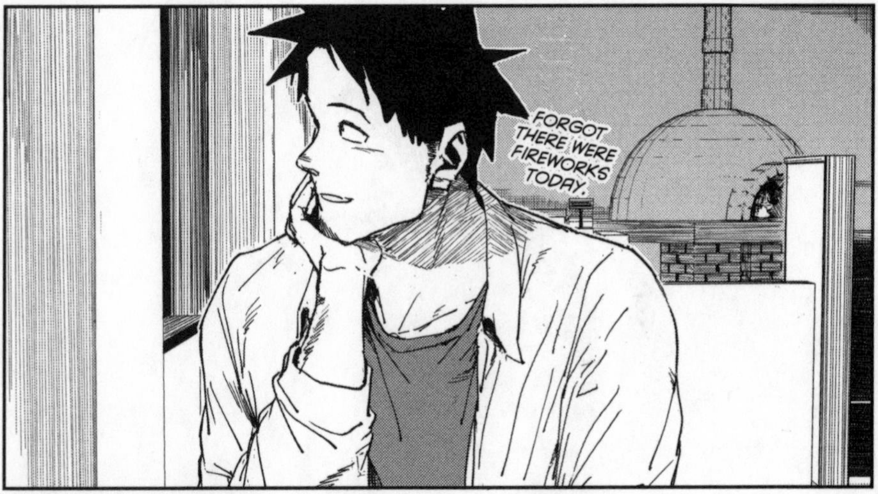
FORGOT THERE WERE FIREWORKS TODAY.

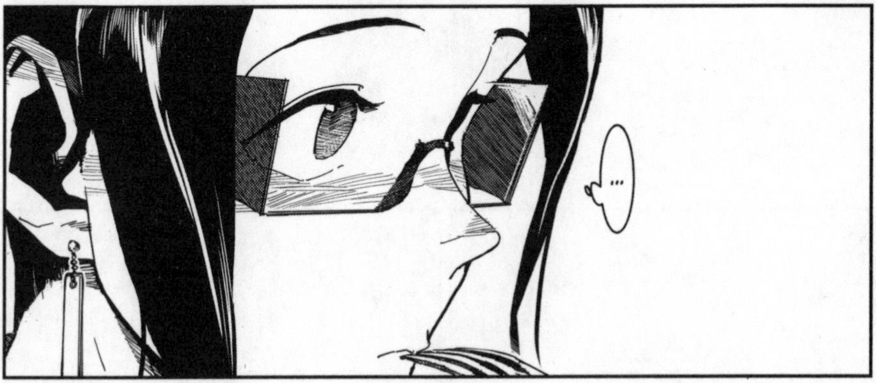
...

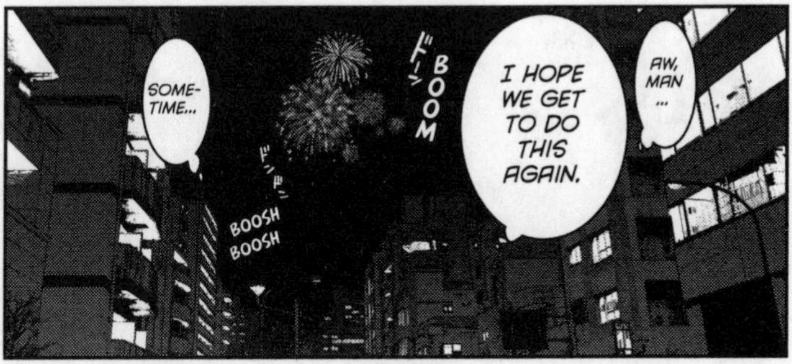
AW, MAN ...
I HOPE WE GET TO DO THIS AGAIN.
BOOM
SOME-TIME...
BOOSH BOOSH

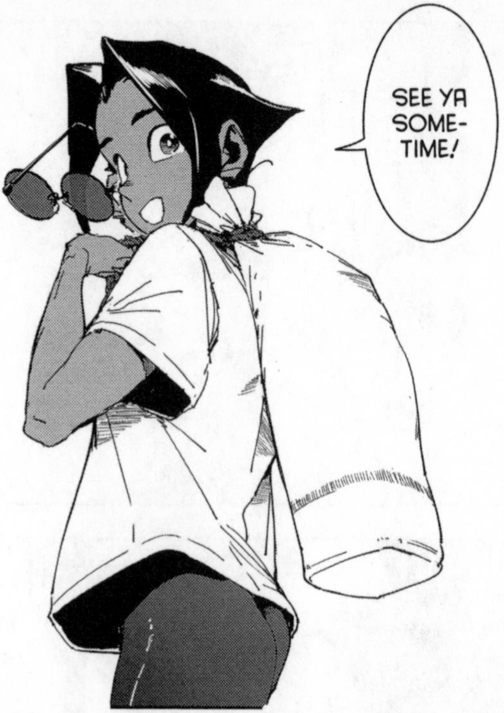
SEE YA SOME-TIME!

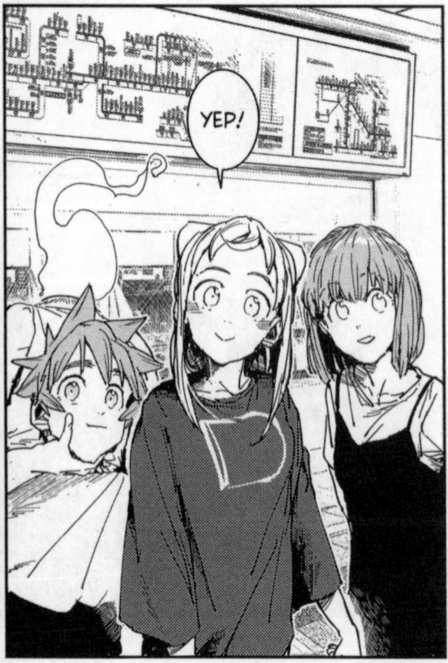
YEP!

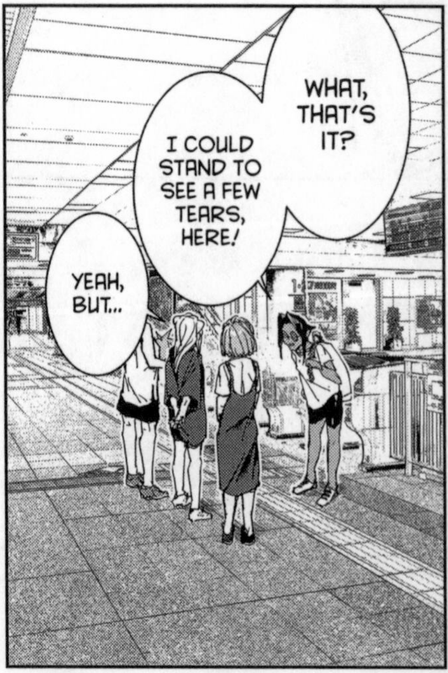
WHAT, THAT'S IT?
I COULD STAND TO SEE A FEW TEARS, HERE!
YEAH, BUT...

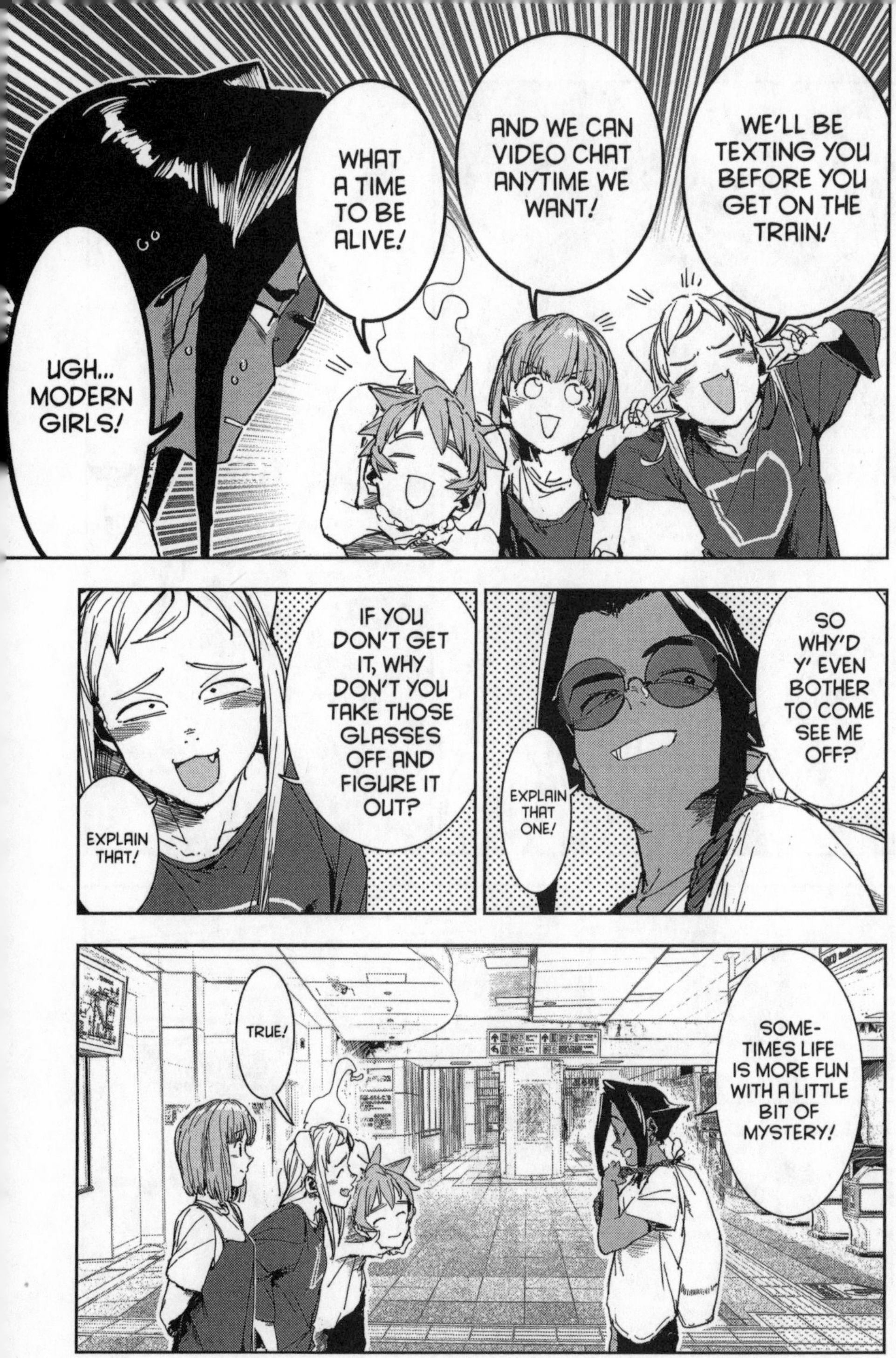
WE'LL BE TEXTING YOU BEFORE YOU GET ON THE TRAIN!
AND WE CAN VIDEO CHAT ANYTIME WE WANT!
WHAT A TIME TO BE ALIVE!
UGH... MODERN GIRLS!
SO WHY'D Y' EVEN BOTHER TO COME SEE ME OFF?
EXPLAIN THAT ONE!
IF YOU DON'T GET IT, WHY DON'T YOU TAKE THOSE GLASSES OFF AND FIGURE IT OUT?
EXPLAIN THAT!
SOME-TIMES LIFE IS MORE FUN WITH A LITTLE BIT OF MYSTERY!
TRUE!

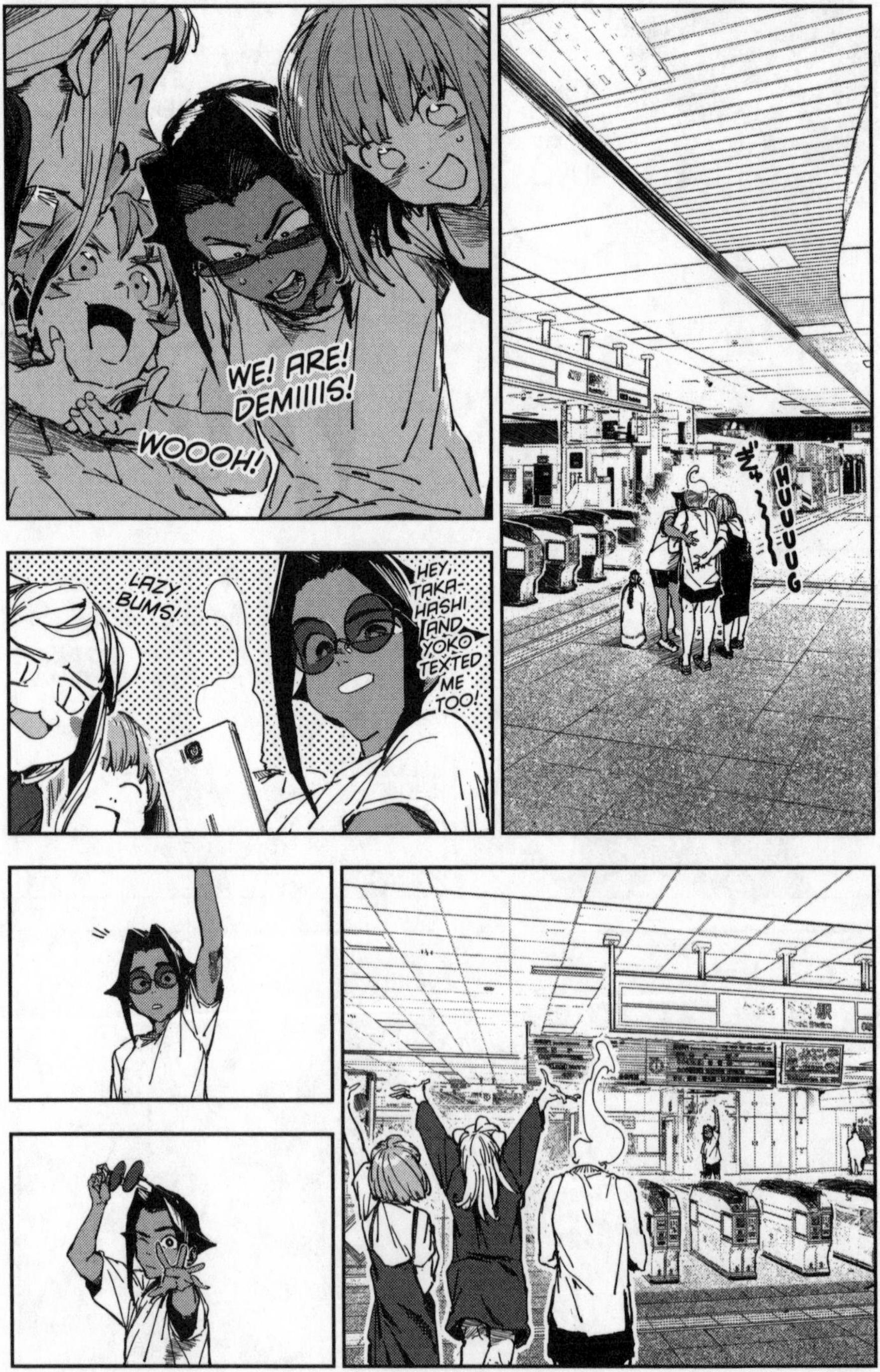
HUUUUG
WE! ARE! DEMIIIIS!
WOOOH!
HEY TAKA-HASHI AND YOKO TEXTED ME TOO!
LAZY BUMS!

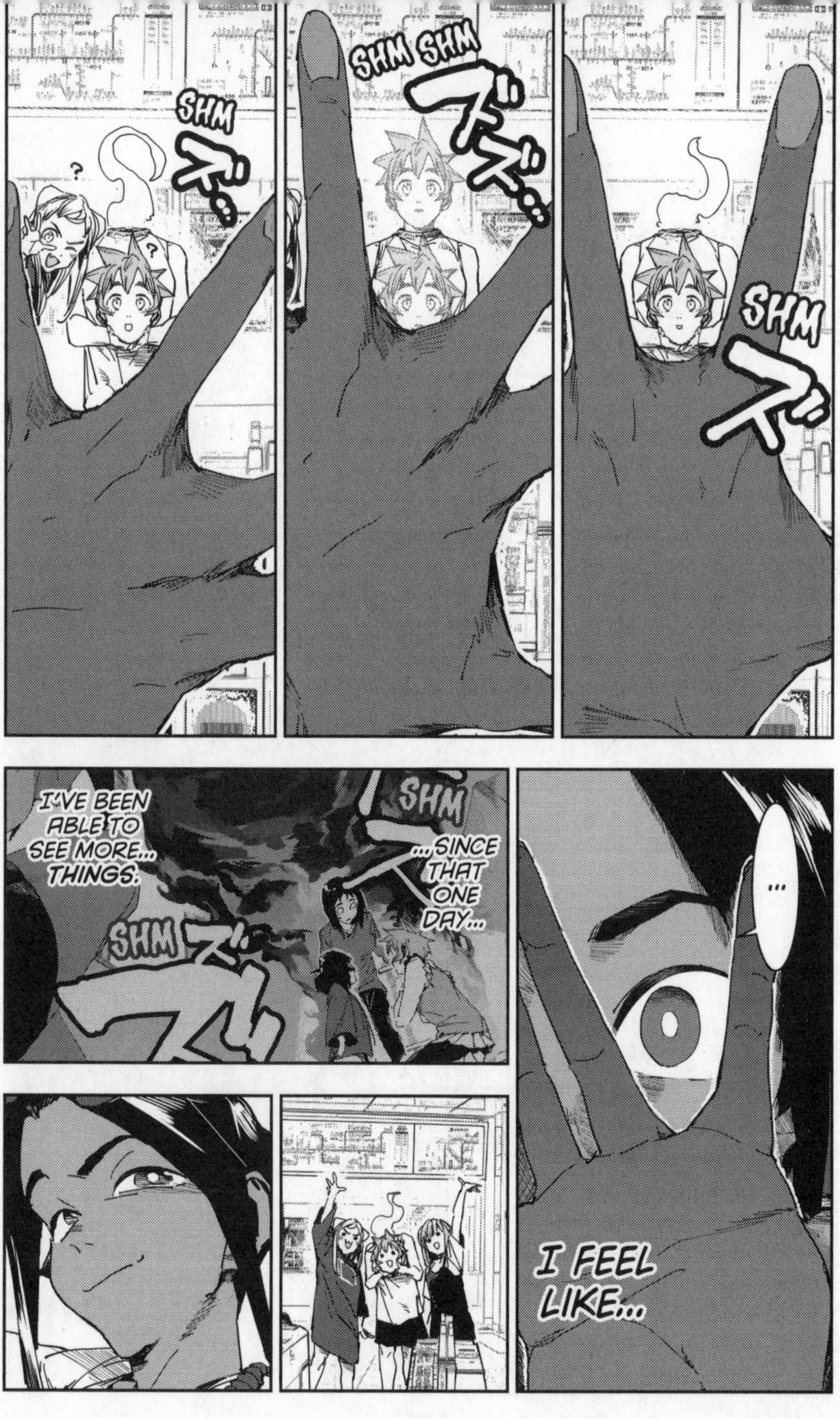
SHM
SHM SHM
SHM
?
?
...
I FEEL LIKE...
I'VE BEEN ABLE TO SEE MORE... THINGS.
SHM
...SINCE THAT ONE DAY...
SHM

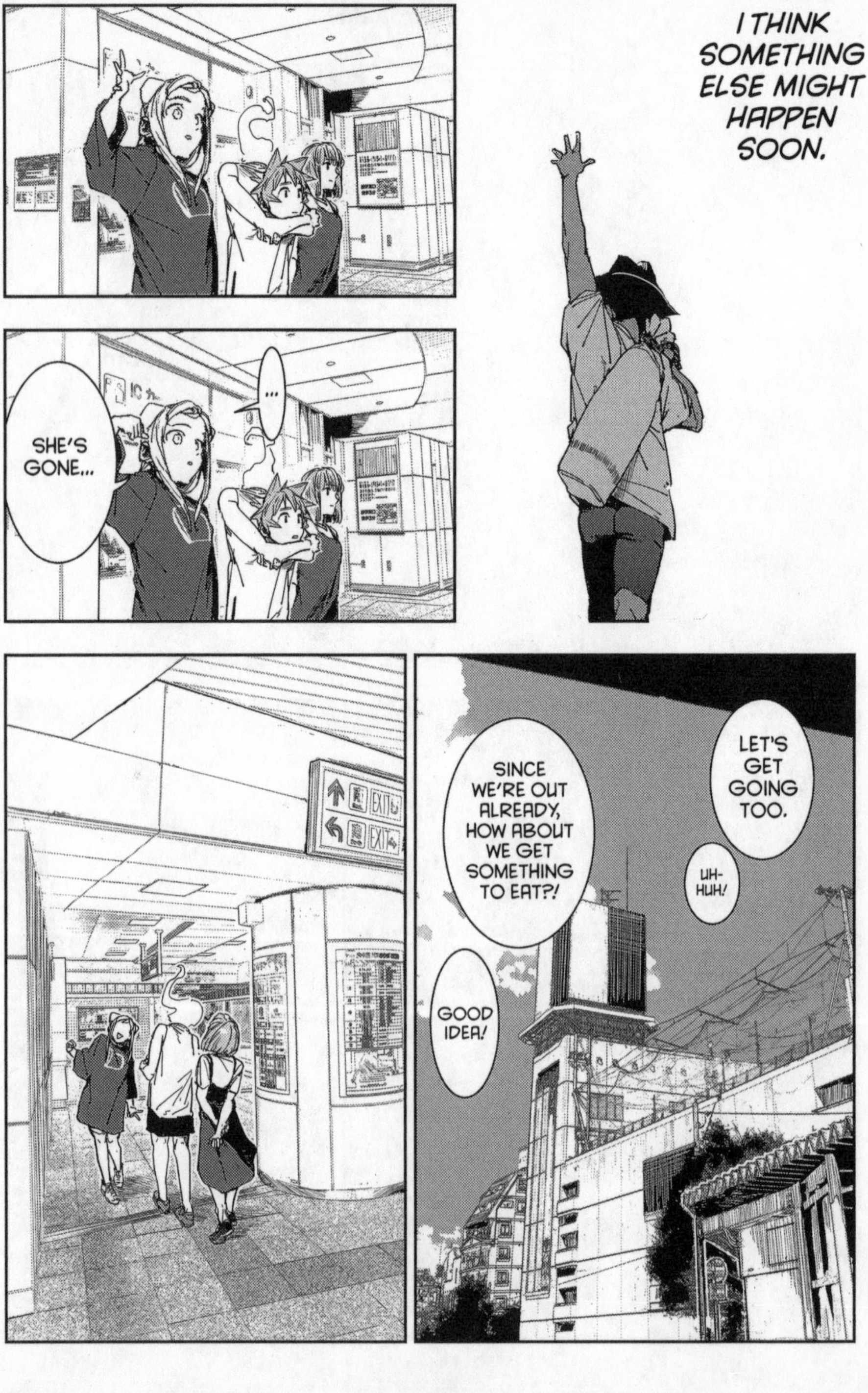
I THINK SOMETHING ELSE MIGHT HAPPEN SOON.
...
SHE'S GONE...
LET'S GET GOING TOO.
UH-HUH!
SINCE WE'RE OUT ALREADY, HOW ABOUT WE GET SOMETHING TO EAT?!
GOOD IDEA!

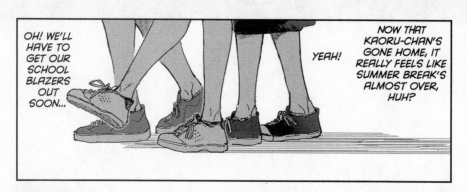

NOW THAT KAORU-CHAN'S GONE HOME, IT REALLY FEELS LIKE SUMMER BREAK'S ALMOST OVER, HUH?
YEAH!
OH! WE'LL HAVE TO GET OUR SCHOOL BLAZERS OUT SOON...
DON'CHA THINK BLAZERS WOULD BE GREAT IN SPRING, TOO? WAY FASHIONABLE!
MAYBE... A LITTLE WARM FOR ME, THOUGH...
YEAH, JAPAN HAS WARM SPRINGS.

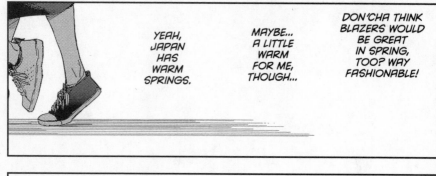

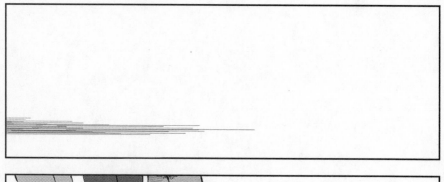

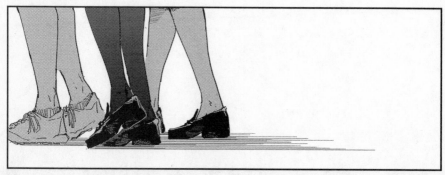

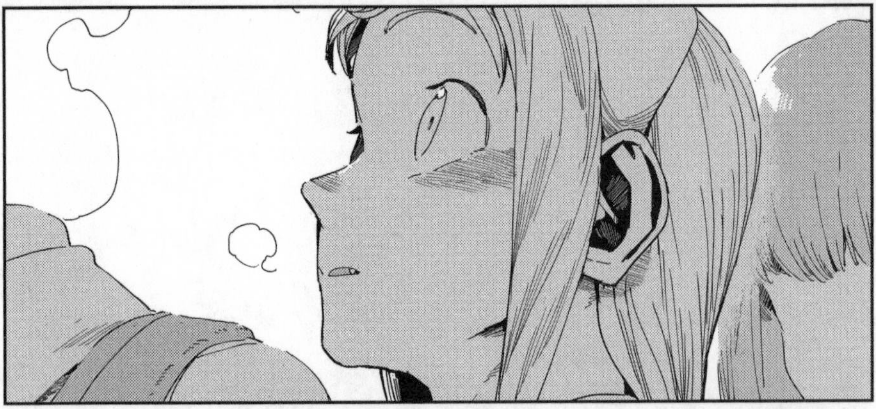

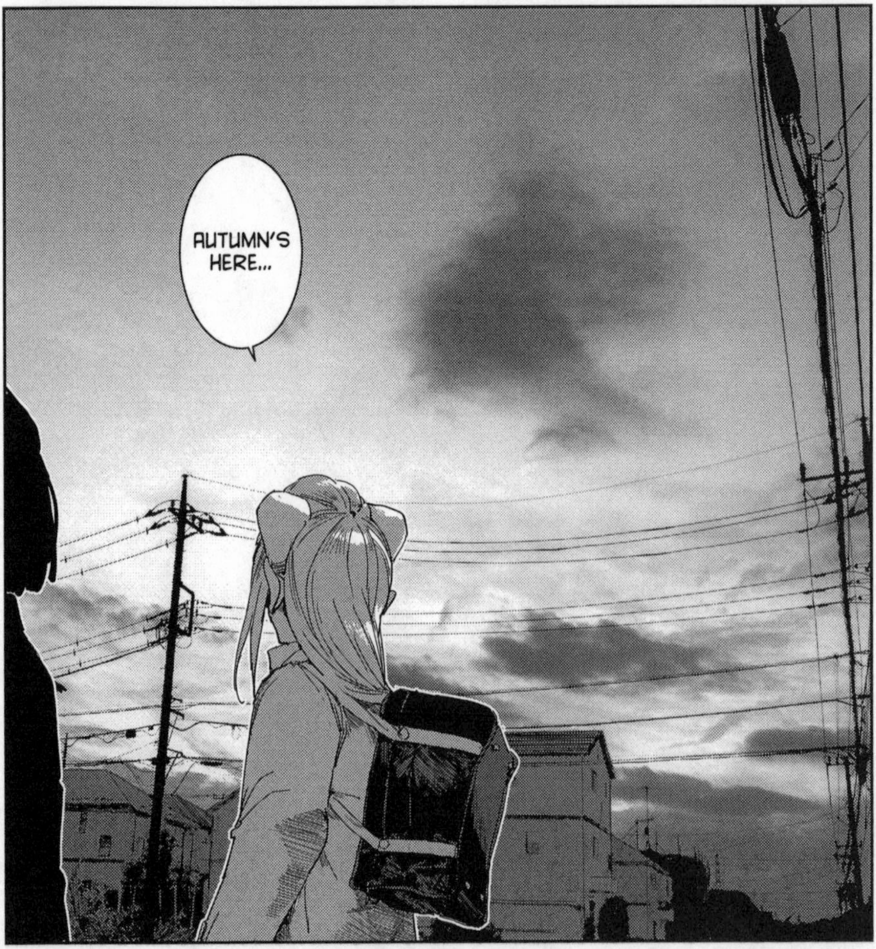
AUTUMN'S HERE...

THE THEATER WAS PRETTY CROWDED. WERE YOU OKAY?
YOUR POWERS...
YEAH. THERE'S ENOUGH SPACE BETWEEN THE SEATS, SO I DIDN'T TOUCH ANYONE.
IT'S NOT LIKE BEING ON A TRAIN FULL OF PEOPLE.
WE SHOULD EXPERIMENT WITH DIFFERENT PLACES!
TO FIND OUT WHERE YOU'RE COMFORTABLE GOING!
YEAH!
LIKE THE ZOO!
NICE, WIDE PATHS.
LET'S TRY IT!
...
...
SHUFFLE SHUFFLE
スタスタ...
GREAT EXCUSE TO GO ON SOME DATES.
PHEW.
PHEW!
WHAT A GREAT EXCUSE TO GO ON SOME DATES!

INTERVIEWS WITH MONSTER GIRLS

CHAPTER 60: THE TALE OF THE TAKANASHI SISTERS (PART 1)

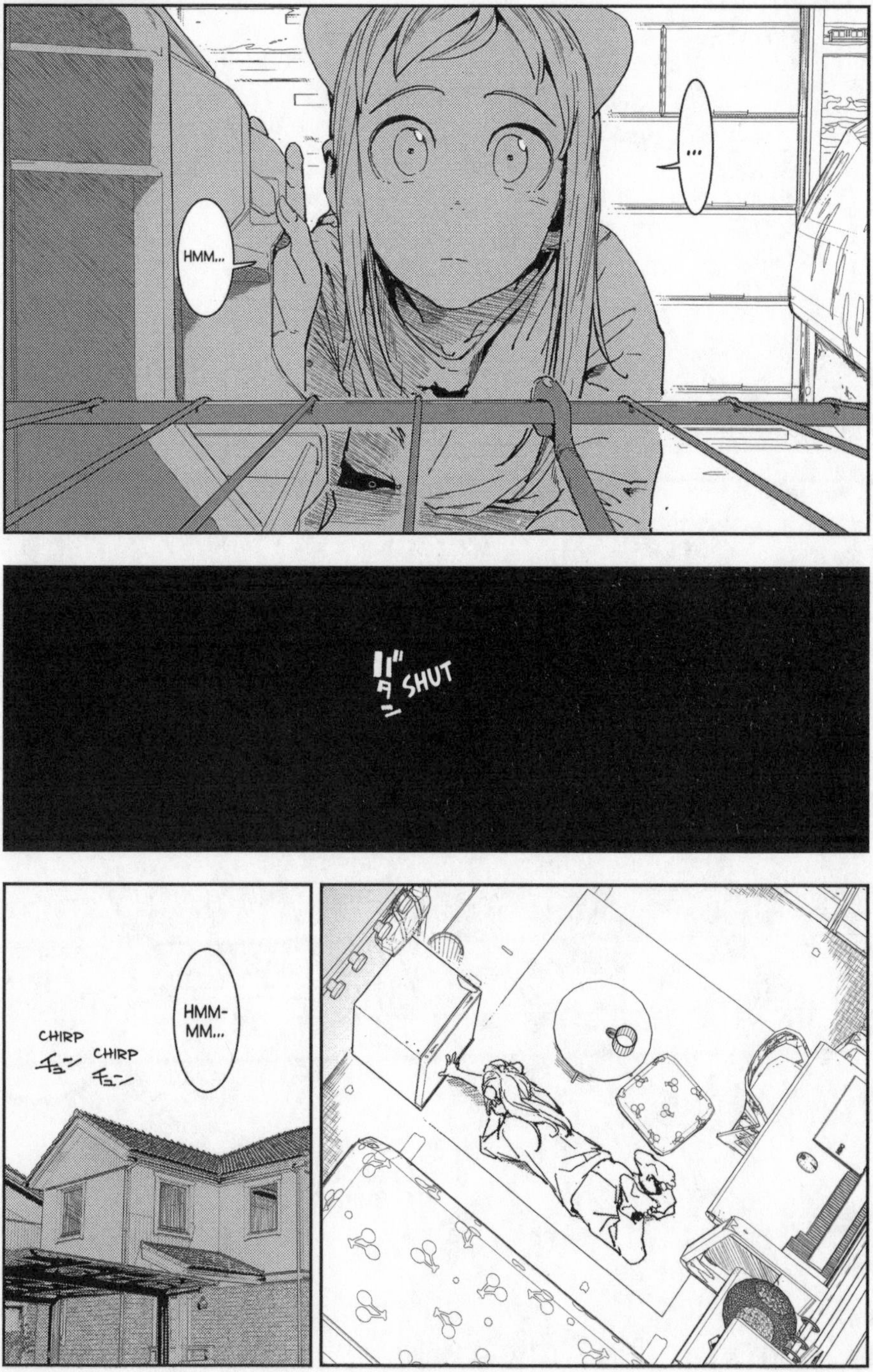
...
HMM...
バタン SHUT
HMM-MM...
CHIRP チュン
CHIRP チュン

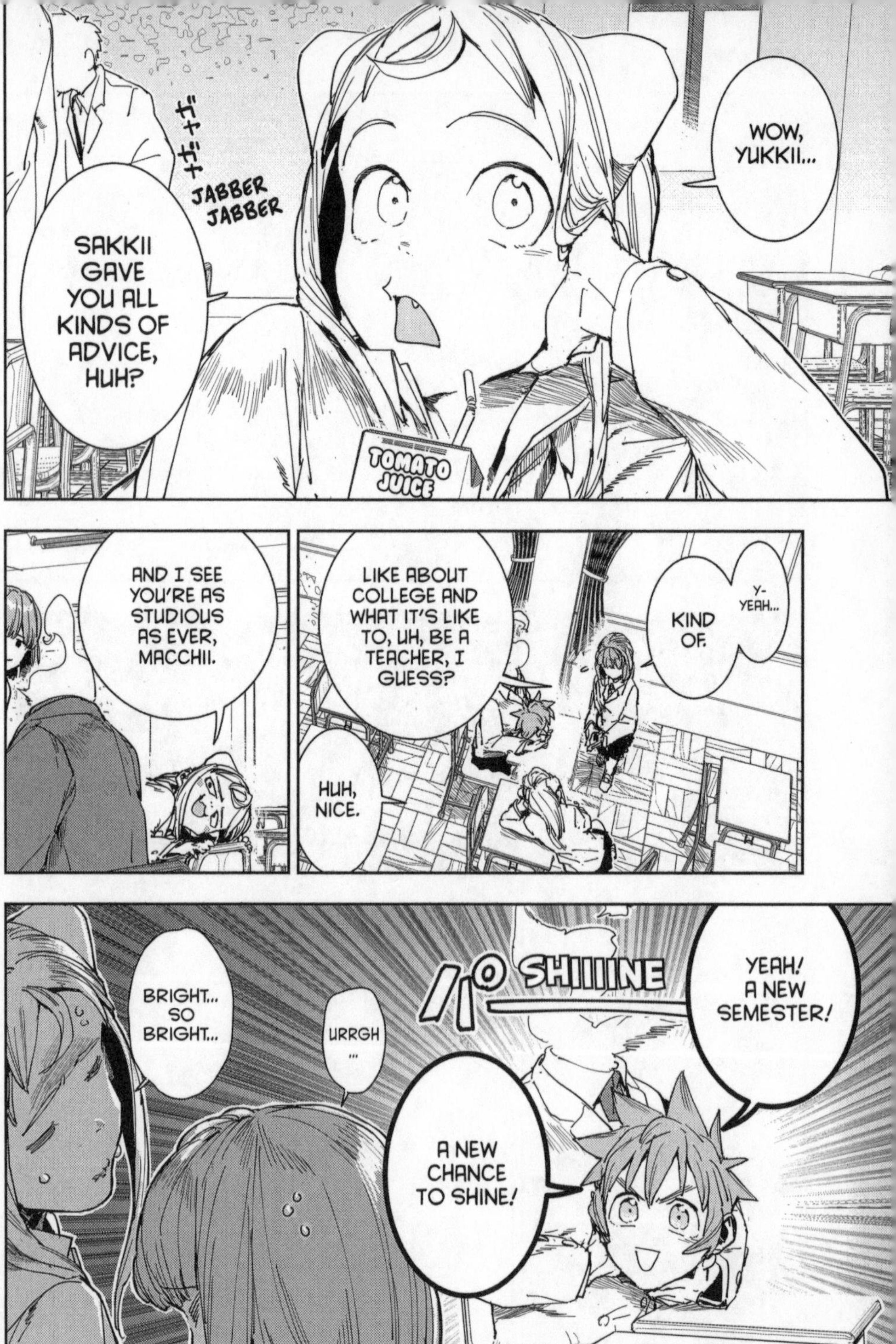
WOW, YUKKII...
ガヤガヤ
JABBER JABBER
SAKKII GAVE YOU ALL KINDS OF ADVICE, HUH?
TOMATO JUICE
Y-YEAH...
KIND OF.
LIKE ABOUT COLLEGE AND WHAT IT'S LIKE TO, UH, BE A TEACHER, I GUESS?
HUH, NICE.
AND I SEE YOU'RE AS STUDIOUS AS EVER, MACCHII.
YEAH! A NEW SEMESTER!
SHIIIINE
A NEW CHANCE TO SHINE!
URRGH ...
BRIGHT... SO BRIGHT...

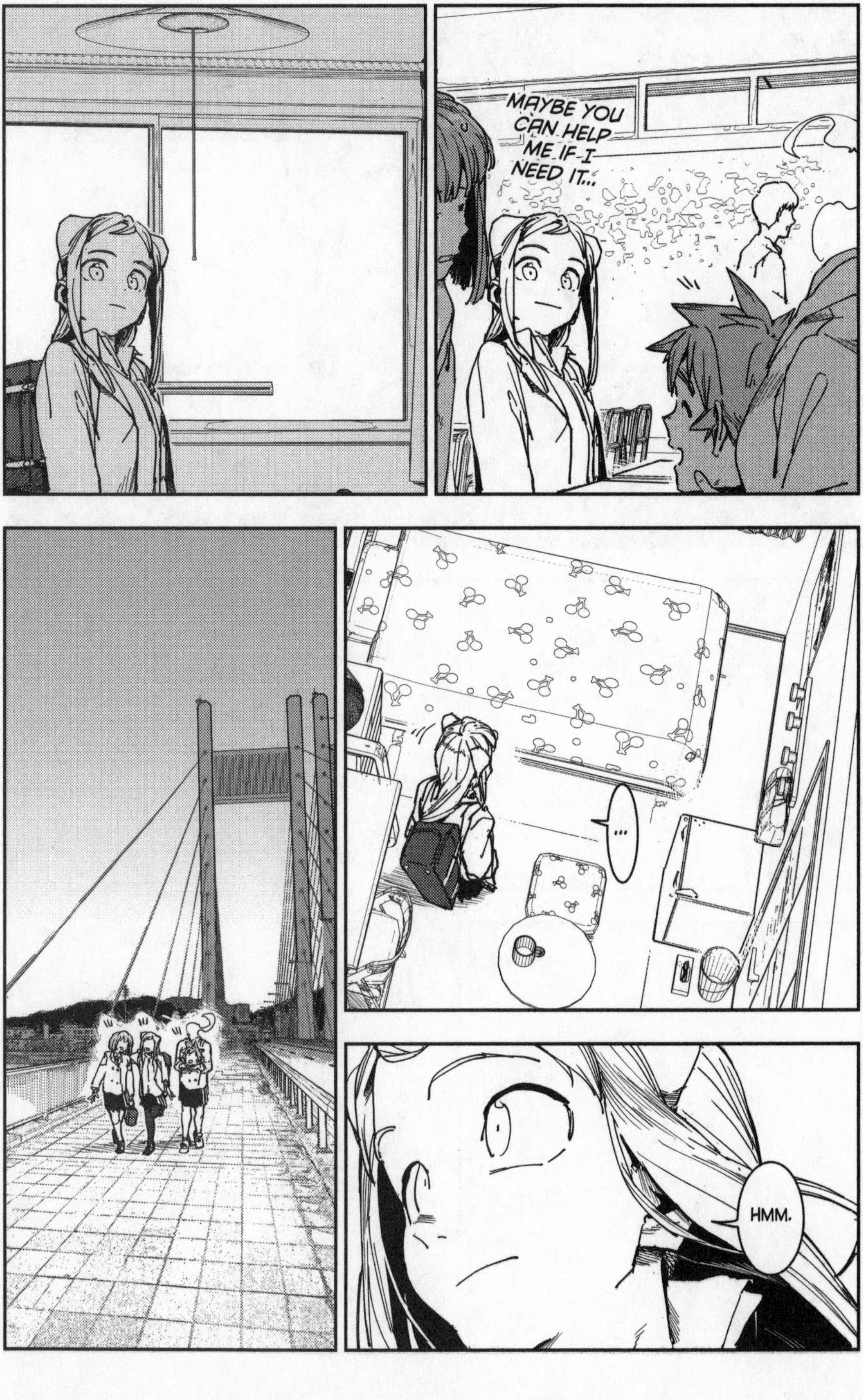
MAYBE YOU CAN HELP ME IF I NEED IT...
...
HMM.

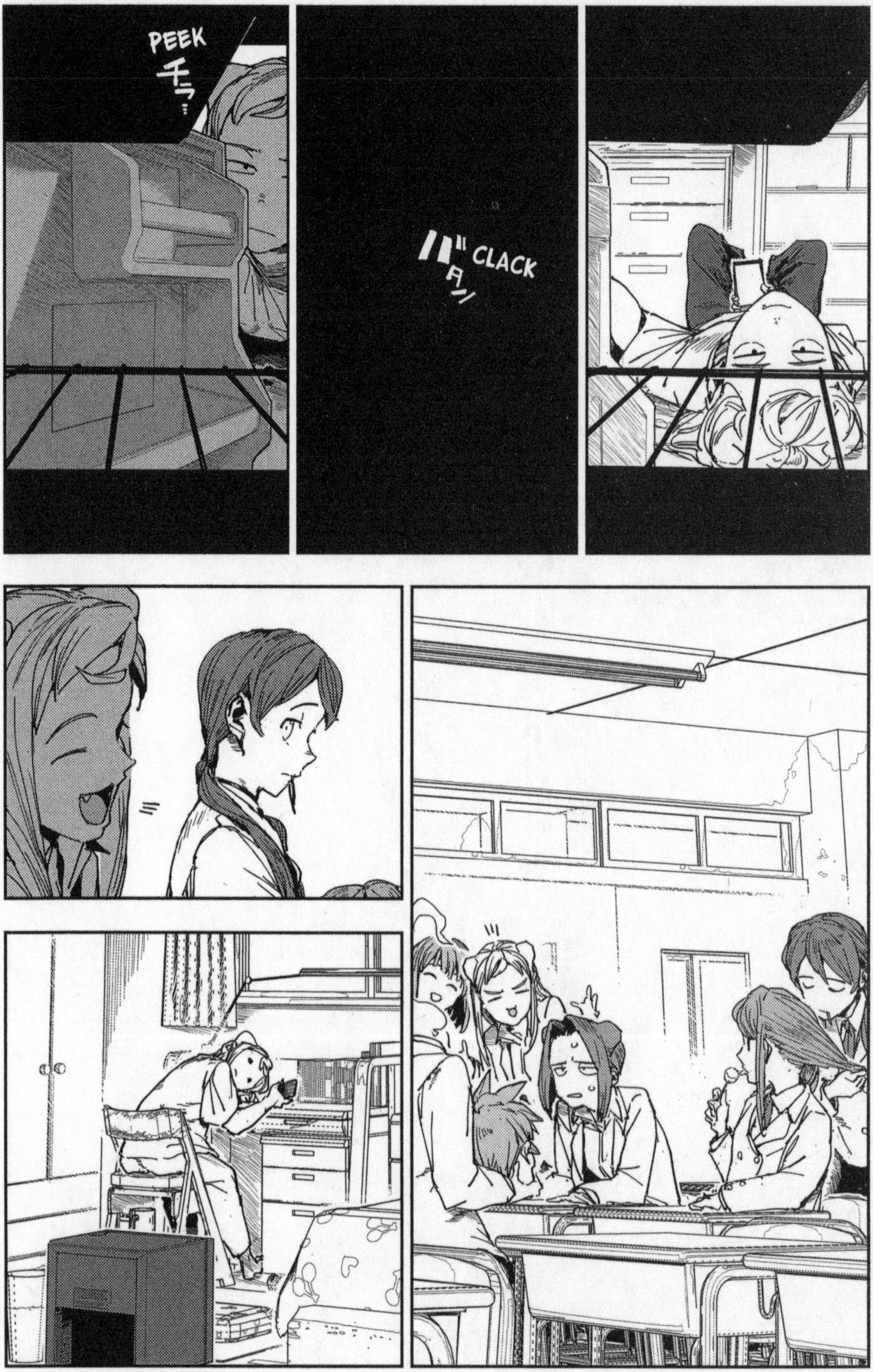
バタン
CLACK
PEEK
チラ…

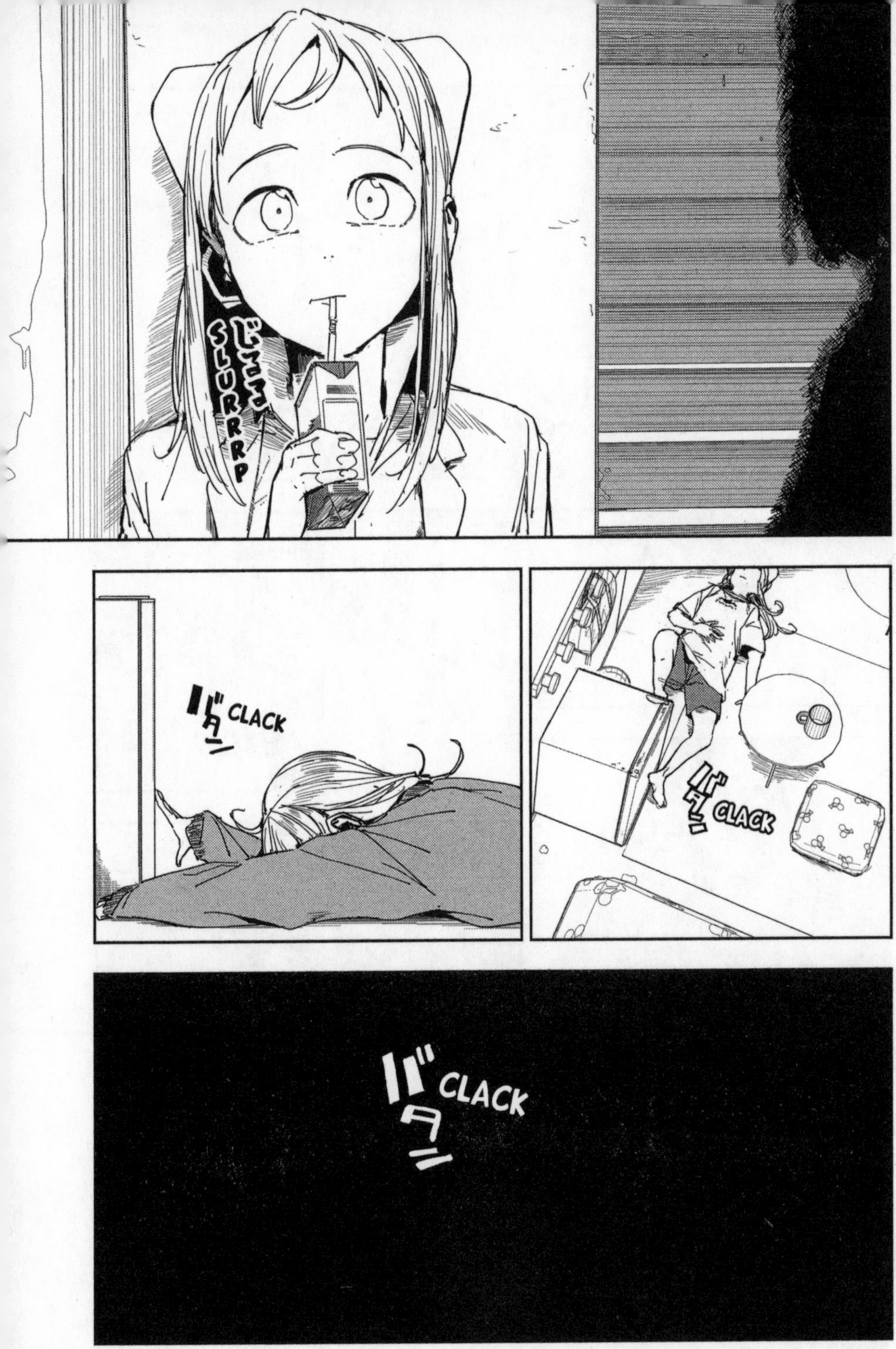
SLURRRP
バタン CLACK
バタン CLACK
バタン CLACK

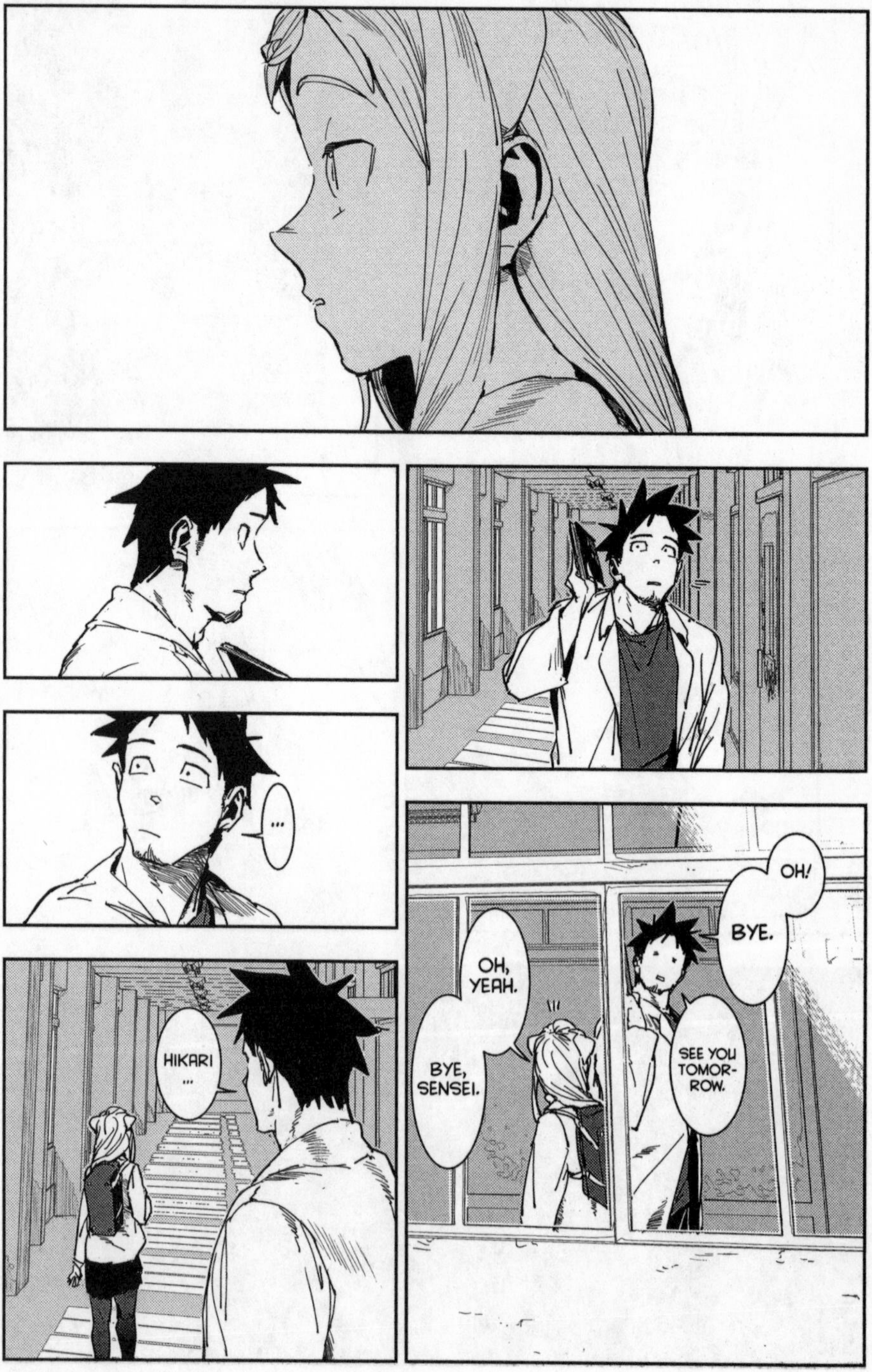

...
HIKARI ...
OH!
BYE.
SEE YOU TOMORROW.
OH, YEAH.
BYE, SENSEI.

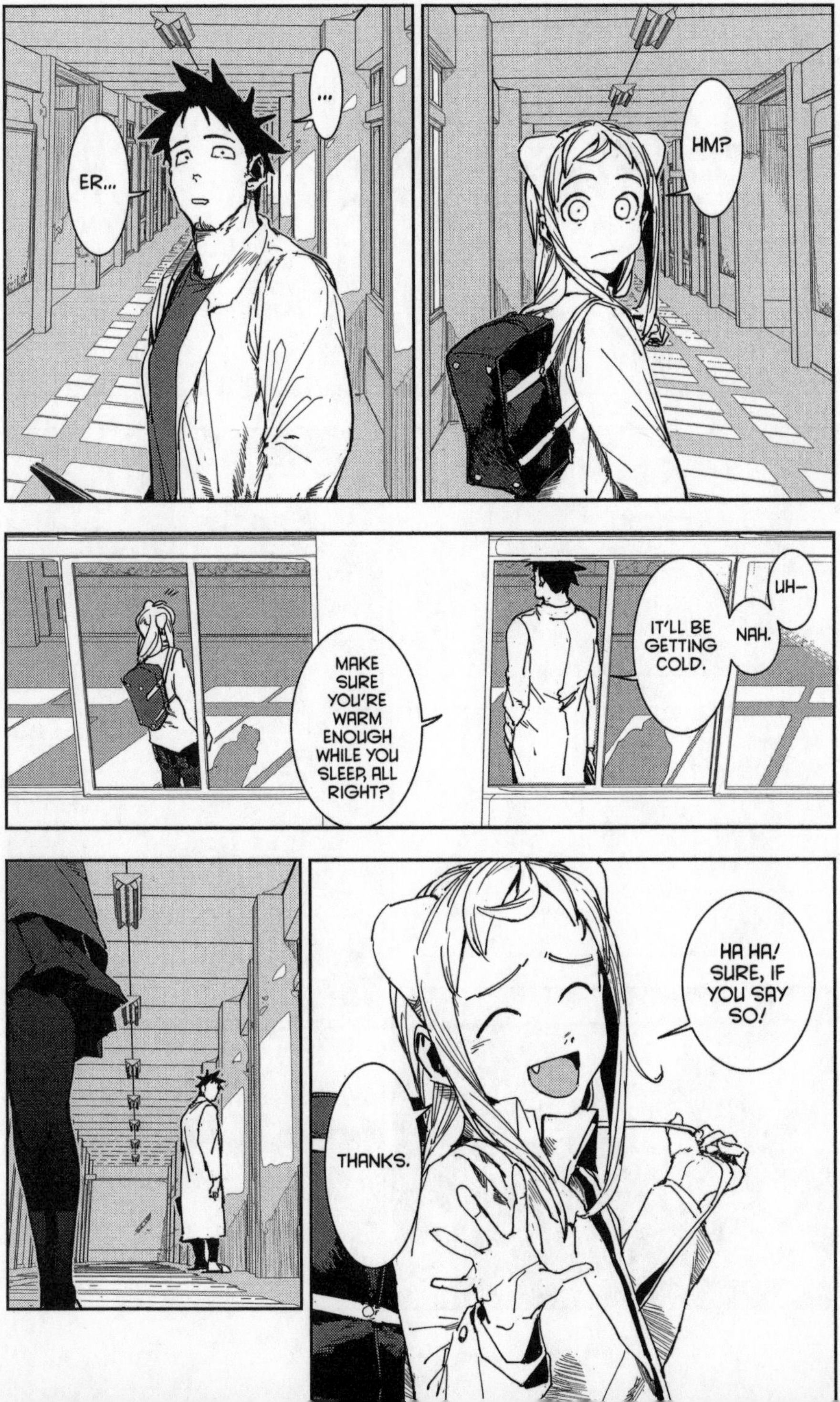
HM?
...
ER...
UH—
NAH.
IT'LL BE GETTING COLD.
MAKE SURE YOU'RE WARM ENOUGH WHILE YOU SLEEP, ALL RIGHT?
HA HA! SURE, IF YOU SAY SO!
THANKS.

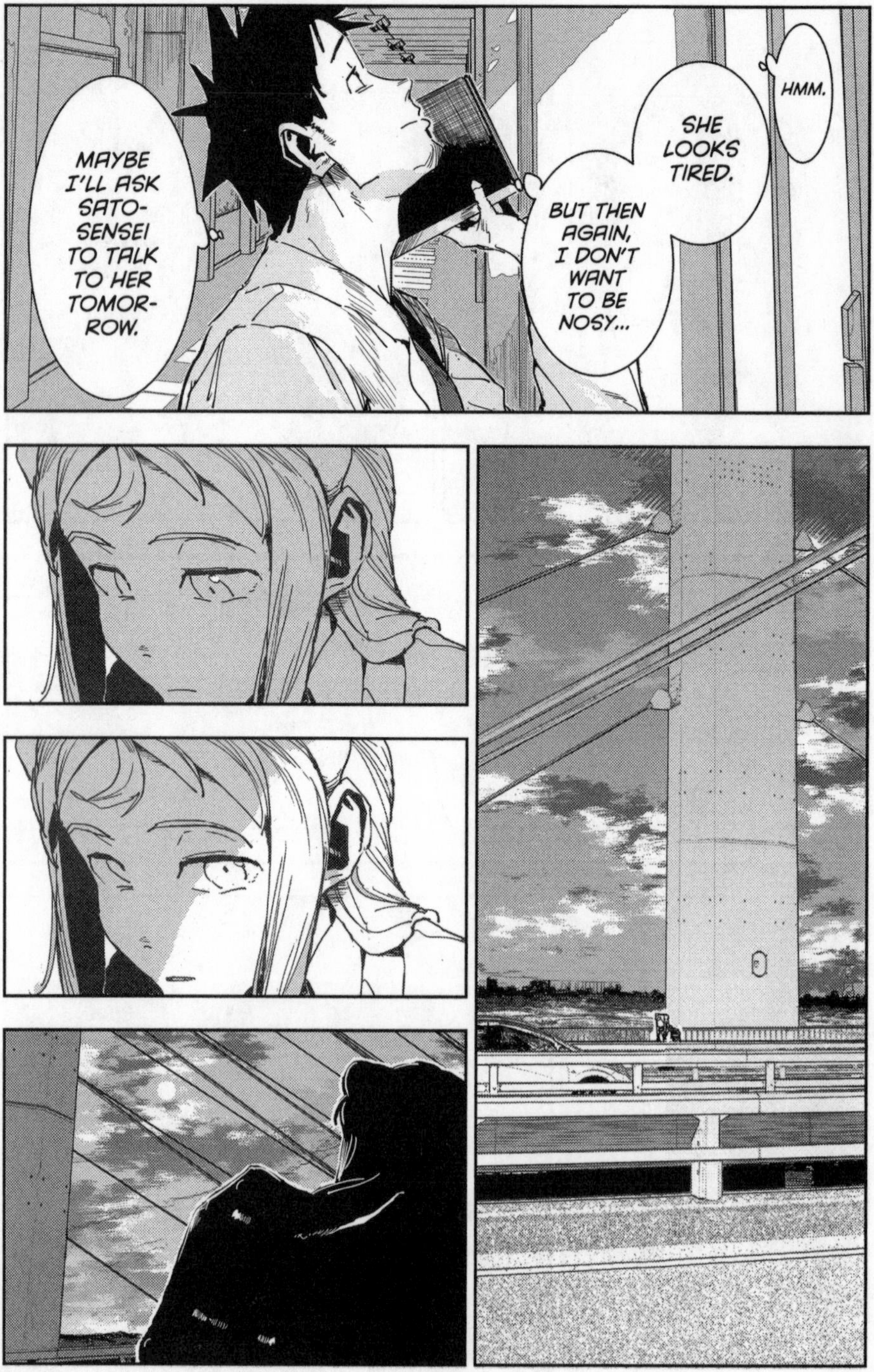
HMM.
SHE LOOKS TIRED.
BUT THEN AGAIN, I DON'T WANT TO BE NOSY...
MAYBE I'LL ASK SATO-SENSEI TO TALK TO HER TOMOR-ROW.

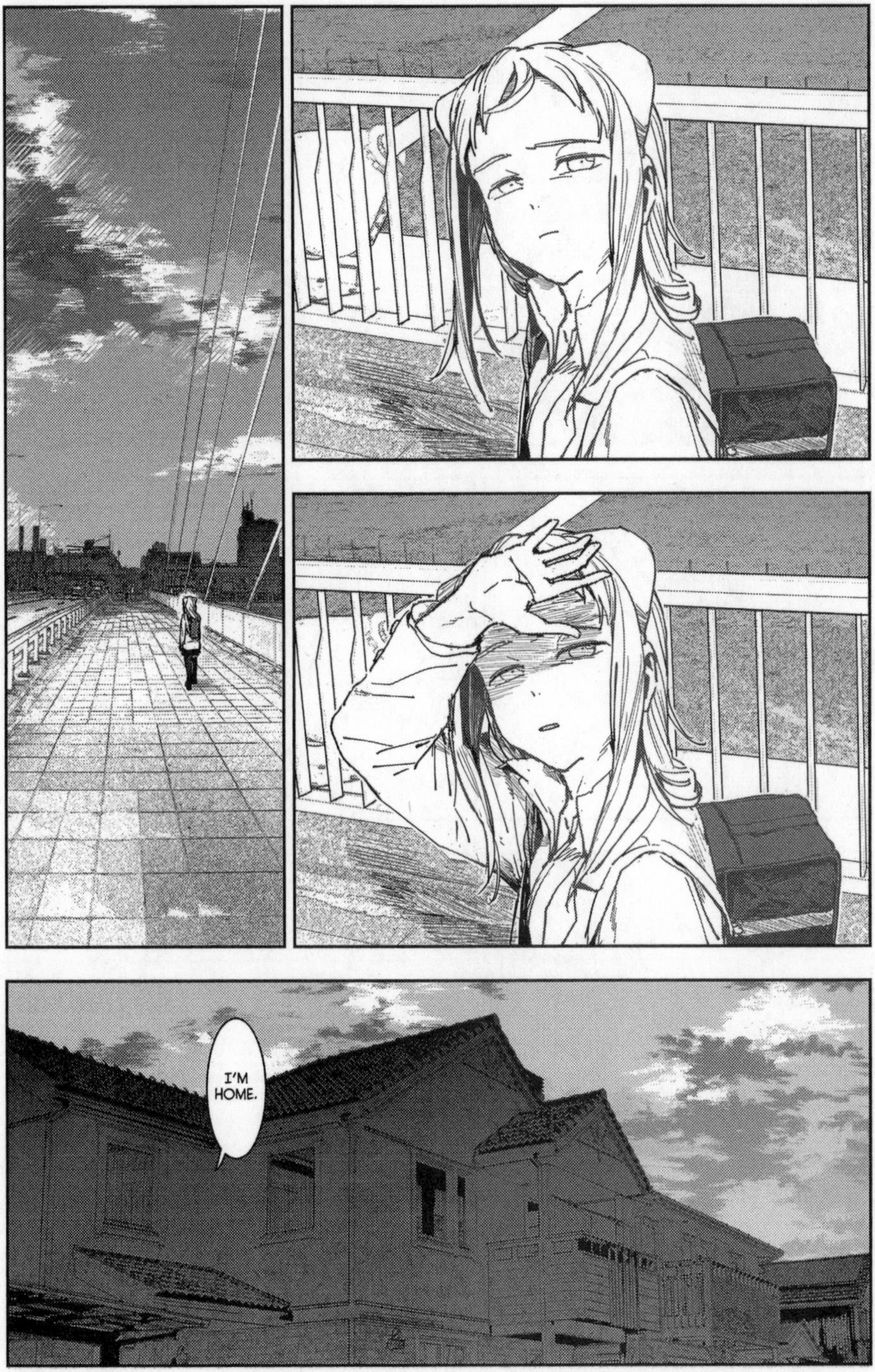
I'M HOME.

HEY,
SIS.

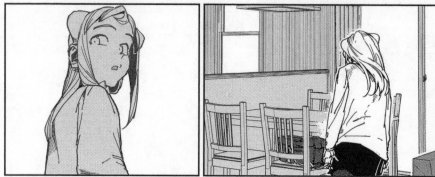

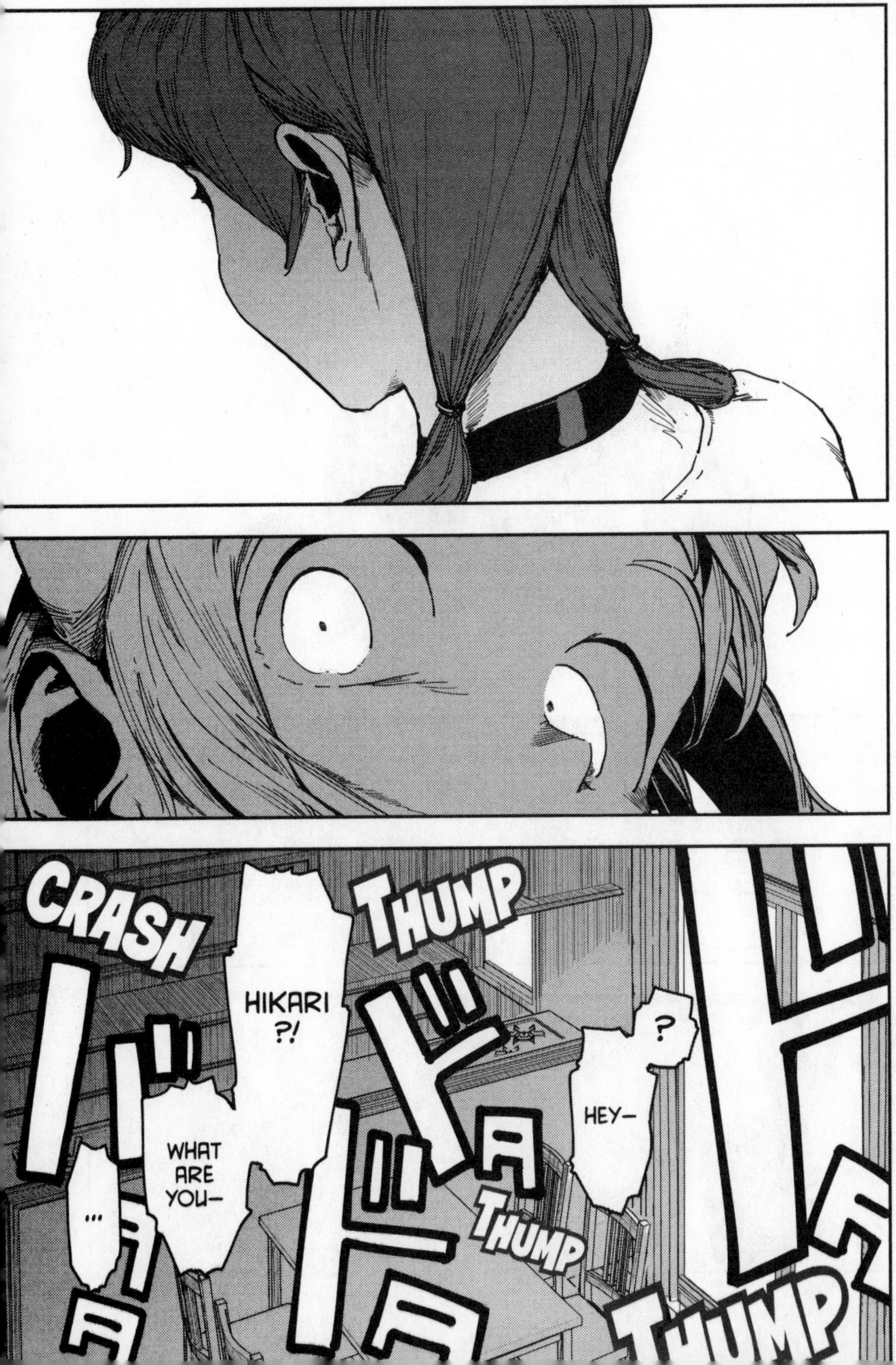
?
HEY—
THUMP
HIKARI ?!
CRASH
THUMP
WHAT ARE YOU—
...
THUMP

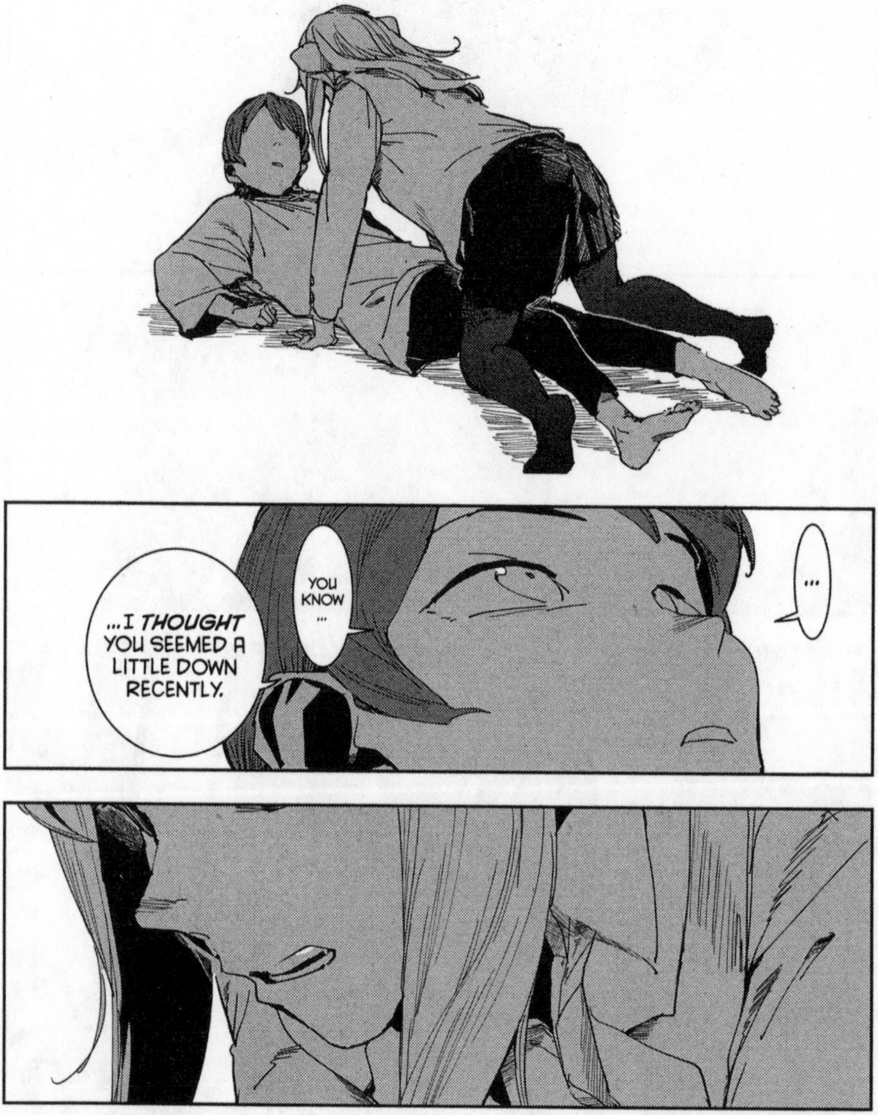
...
YOU KNOW ...
...I *THOUGHT* YOU SEEMED A LITTLE DOWN RECENTLY.

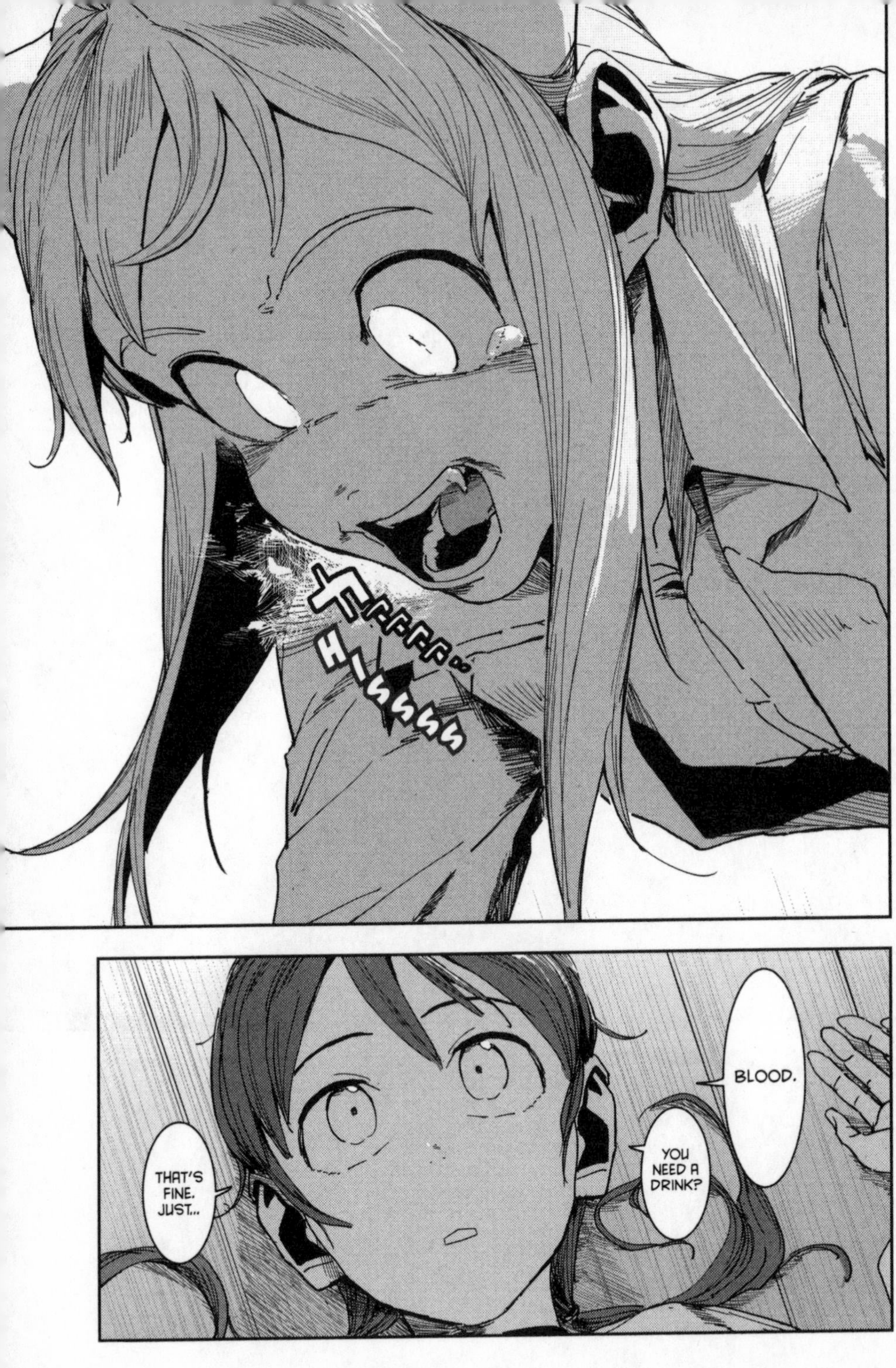
HISSSSS
BLOOD.
YOU NEED A DRINK?
THAT'S FINE. JUST...

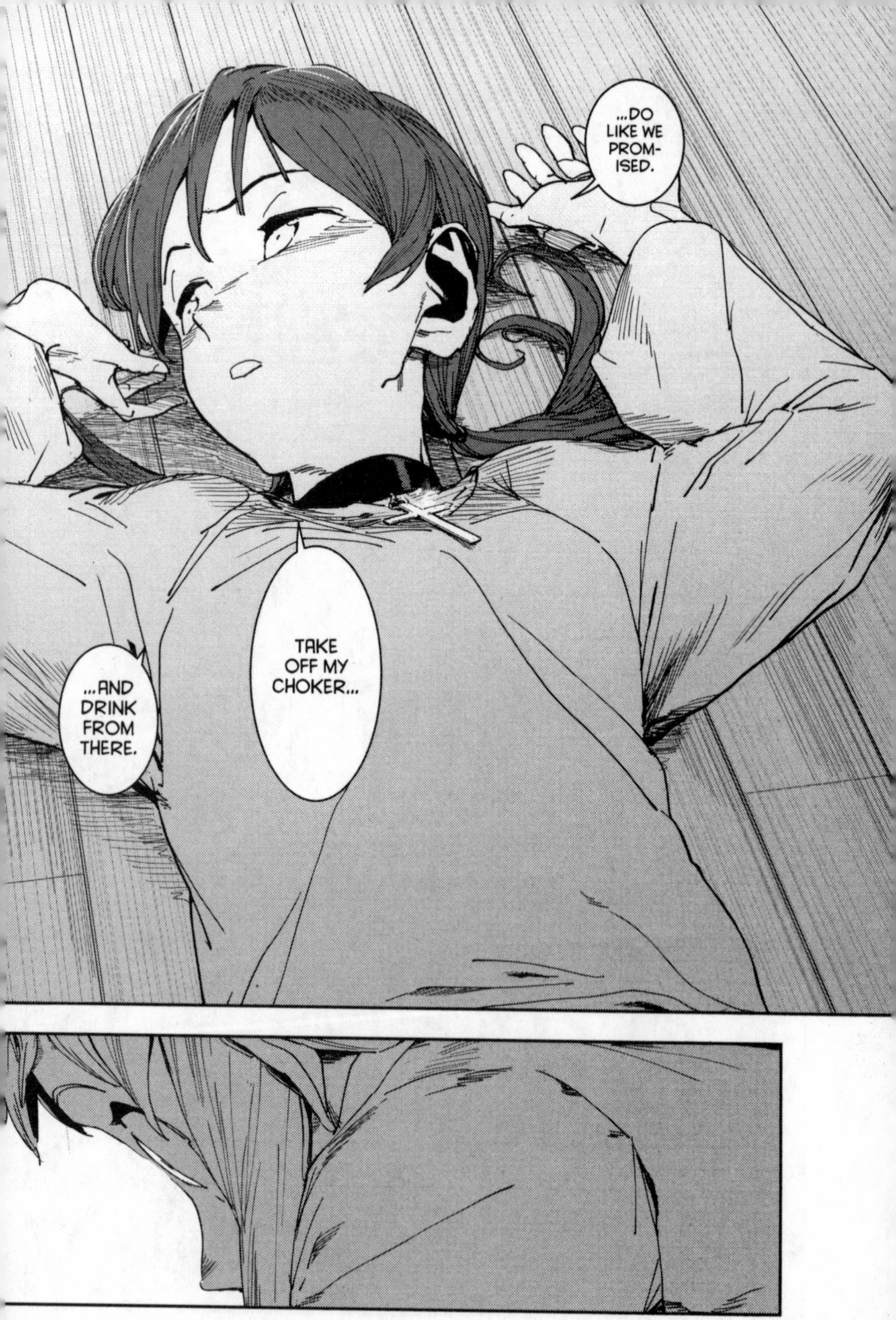
...DO LIKE WE PROMISED.
TAKE OFF MY CHOKER...
...AND DRINK FROM THERE.

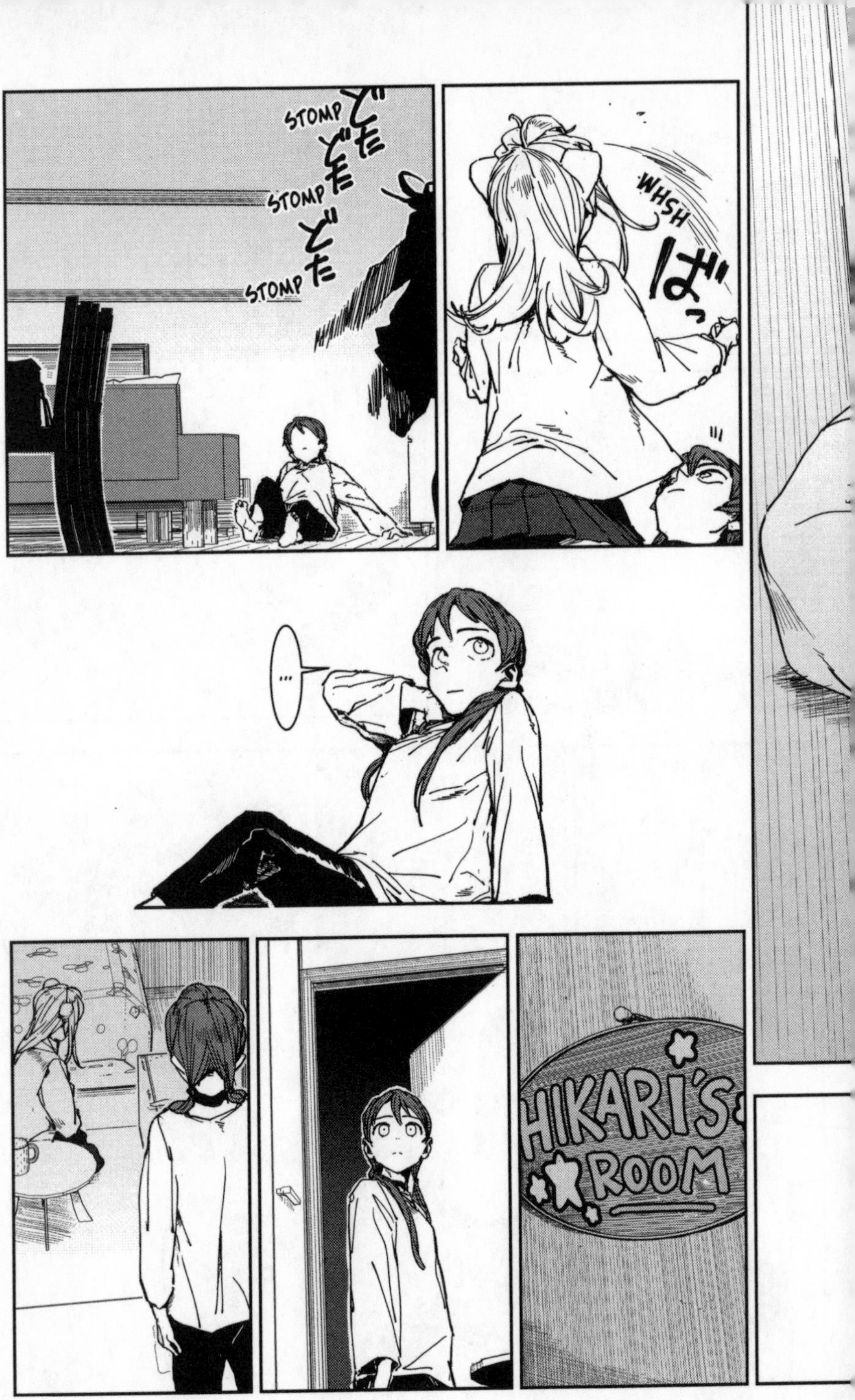

WHSH
ばっ
STOMP
どた
STOMP
どた
STOMP
どた
...
HIKARI'S ROOM

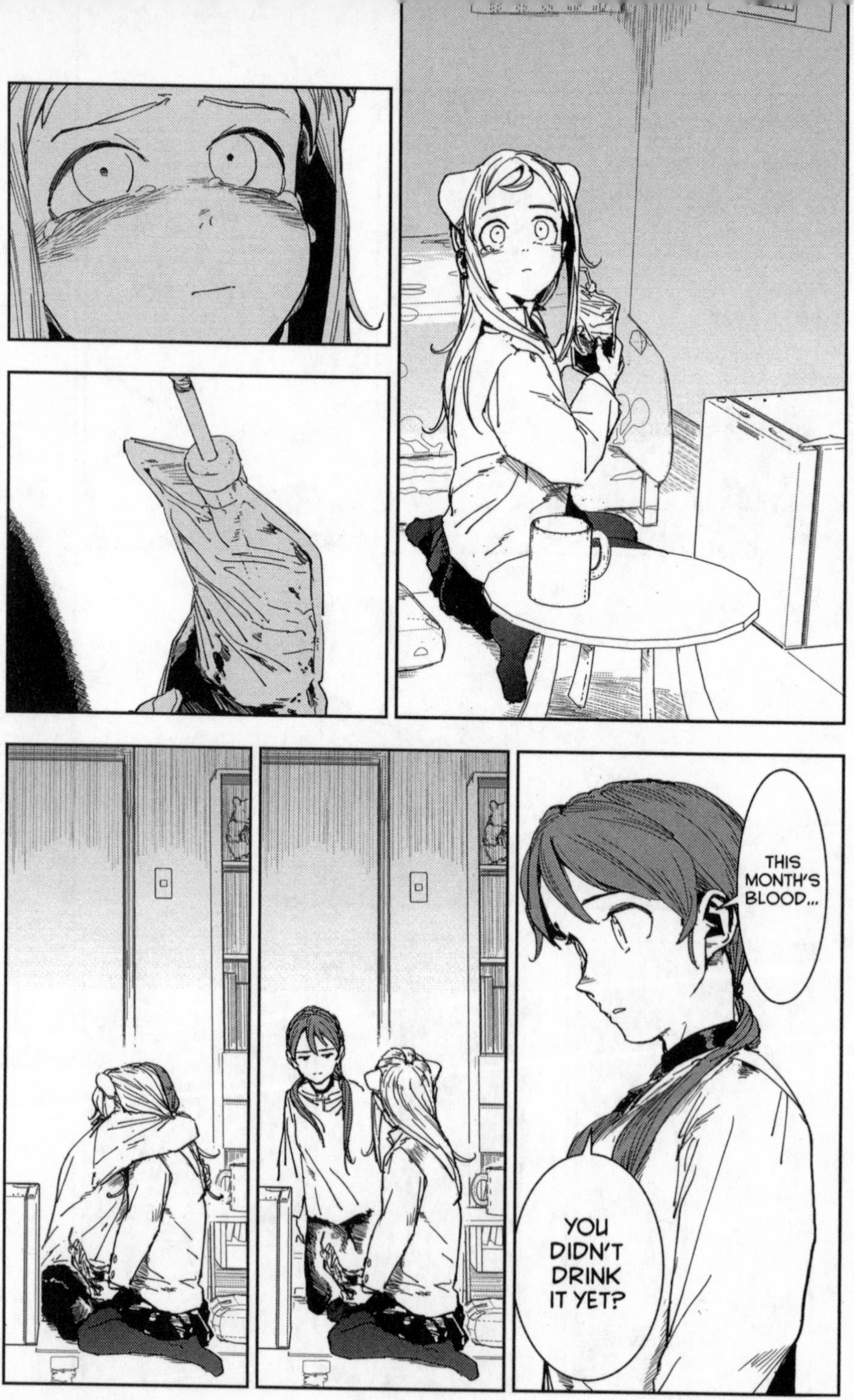
THIS MONTH'S BLOOD...
YOU DIDN'T DRINK IT YET?

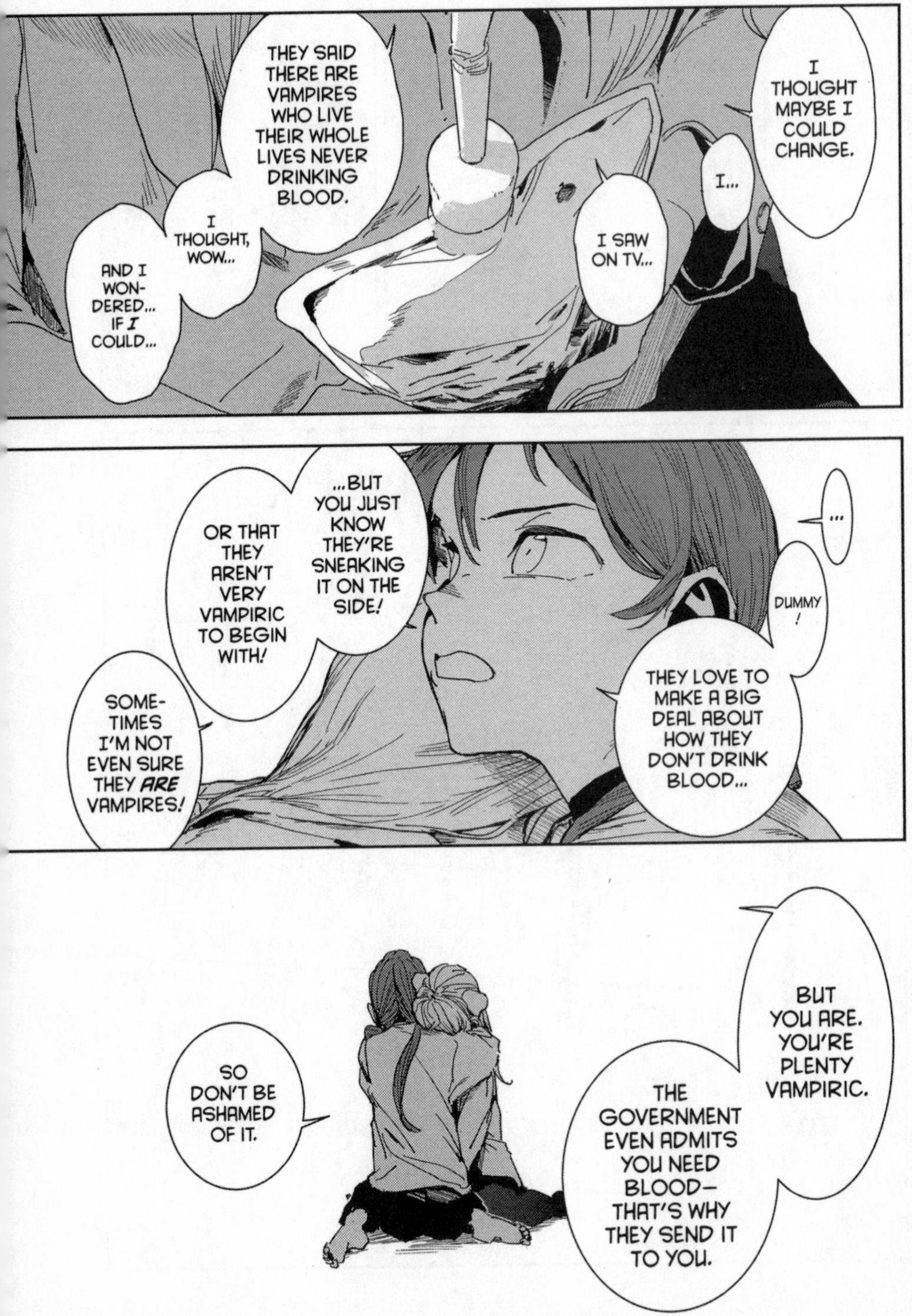
I THOUGHT MAYBE I COULD CHANGE.
I...
I SAW ON TV...
THEY SAID THERE ARE VAMPIRES WHO LIVE THEIR WHOLE LIVES NEVER DRINKING BLOOD.
I THOUGHT, WOW...
AND I WONDERED... IF *I* COULD...
...
DUMMY!
THEY LOVE TO MAKE A BIG DEAL ABOUT HOW THEY DON'T DRINK BLOOD...
...BUT YOU JUST KNOW THEY'RE SNEAKING IT ON THE SIDE!
OR THAT THEY AREN'T VERY VAMPIRIC TO BEGIN WITH!
SOMETIMES I'M NOT EVEN SURE THEY *ARE* VAMPIRES!
BUT YOU ARE. YOU'RE PLENTY VAMPIRIC.
THE GOVERNMENT EVEN ADMITS YOU NEED BLOOD—THAT'S WHY THEY SEND IT TO YOU.
SO DON'T BE ASHAMED OF IT.

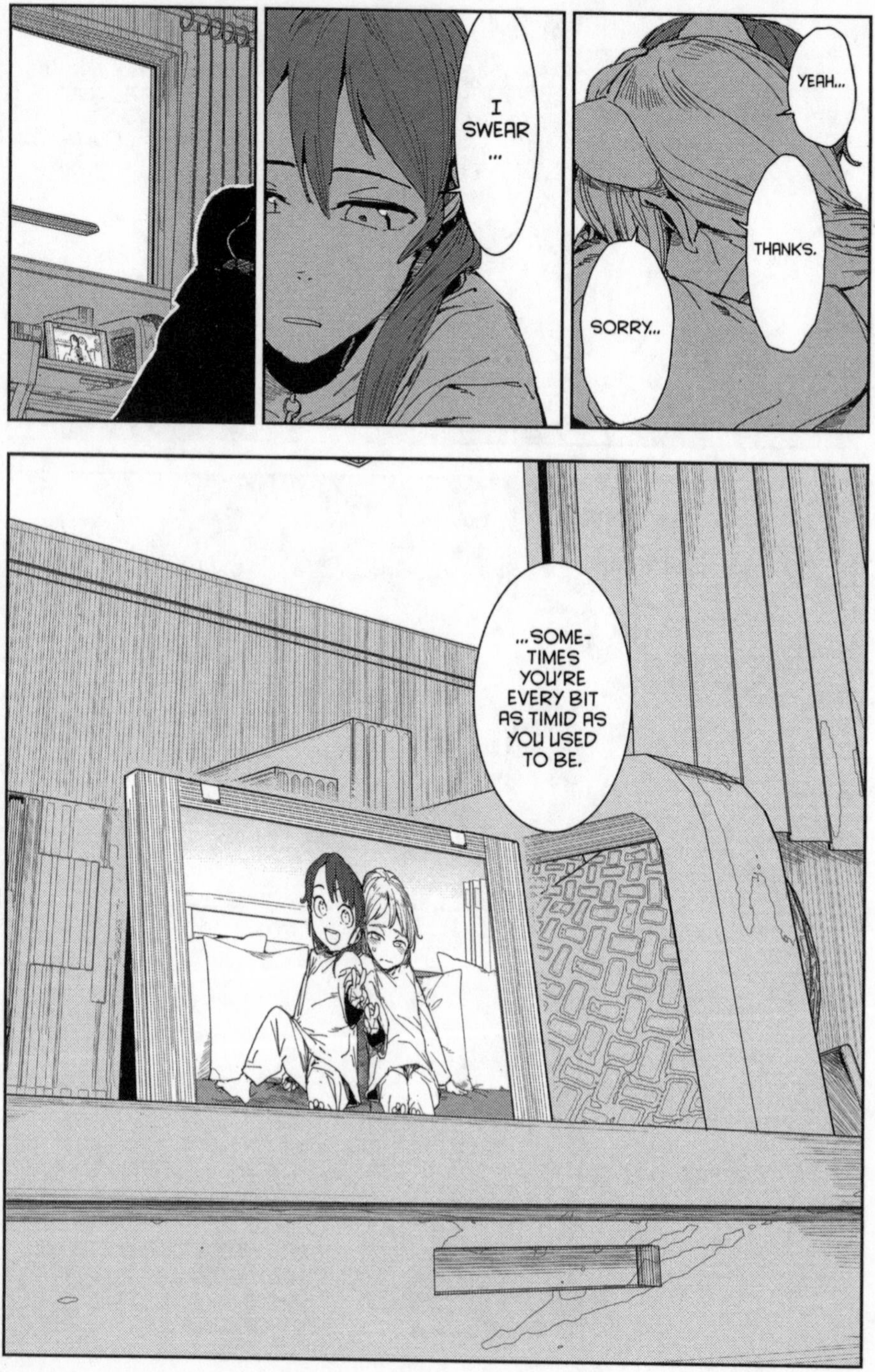
YEAH...
THANKS.
SORRY...
I SWEAR ...
...SOMETIMES YOU'RE EVERY BIT AS TIMID AS YOU USED TO BE.

...
...
DOES HIKARI-CHAN SEEM A LITTLE DOWN?
MAY-BE.
THOSE WHO KNOW... KNOW.

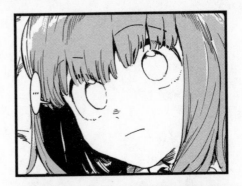

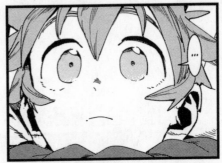

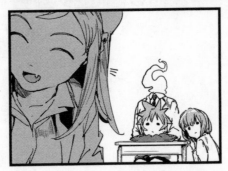

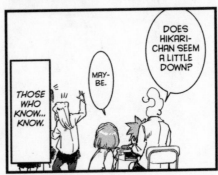

INTERVIEWS WITH MONSTER GIRLS

Chapter 61: The Tale of the Takanashi Sisters (Part 2)

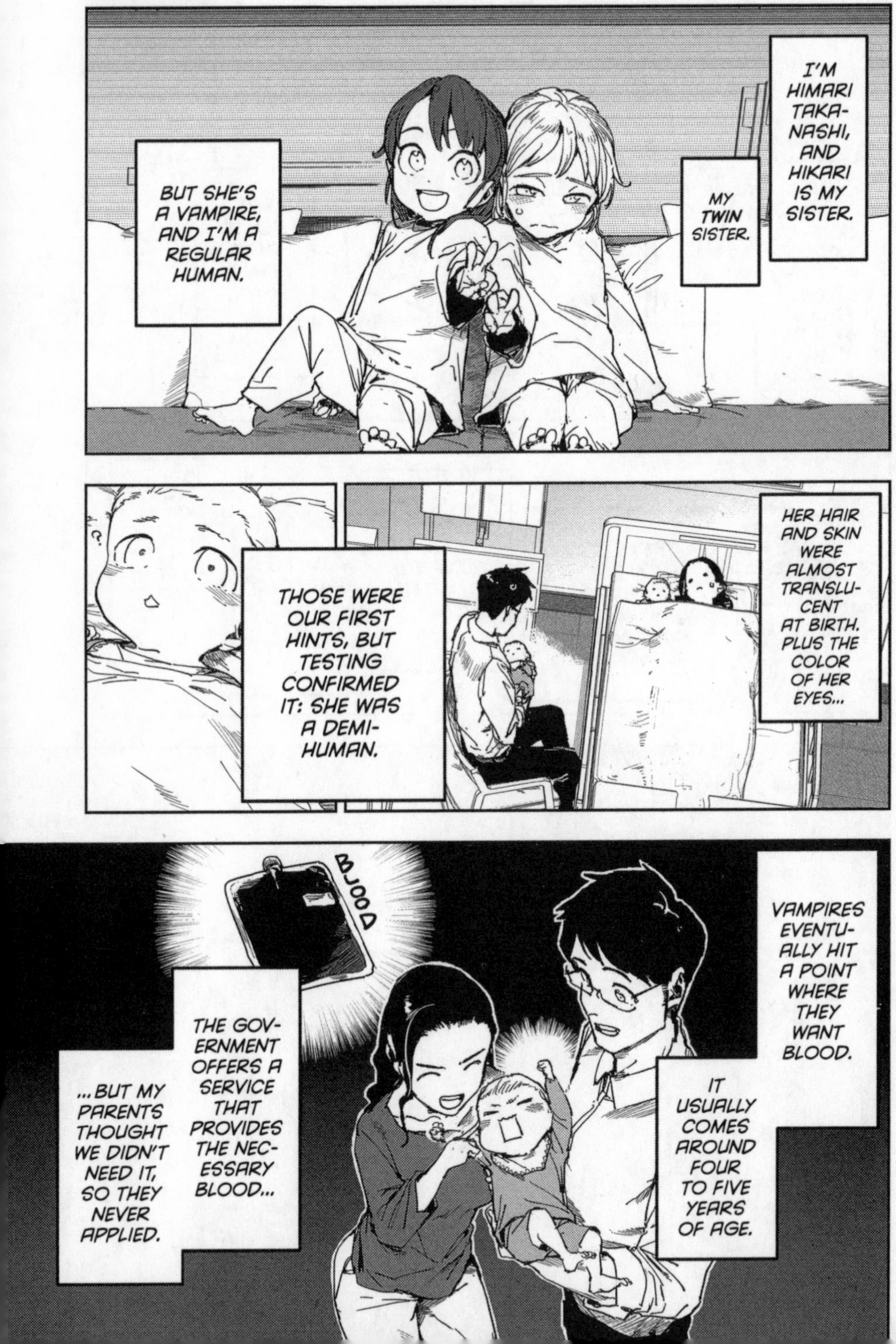
I'M HIMARI TAKANASHI, AND HIKARI IS MY SISTER.
MY TWIN SISTER.
BUT SHE'S A VAMPIRE, AND I'M A REGULAR HUMAN.
HER HAIR AND SKIN WERE ALMOST TRANSLUCENT AT BIRTH. PLUS THE COLOR OF HER EYES...
THOSE WERE OUR FIRST HINTS, BUT TESTING CONFIRMED IT: SHE WAS A DEMI-HUMAN.
?
VAMPIRES EVENTUALLY HIT A POINT WHERE THEY WANT BLOOD.
BLOOD
IT USUALLY COMES AROUND FOUR TO FIVE YEARS OF AGE.
THE GOVERNMENT OFFERS A SERVICE THAT PROVIDES THE NECESSARY BLOOD...
...BUT MY PARENTS THOUGHT WE DIDN'T NEED IT, SO THEY NEVER APPLIED.

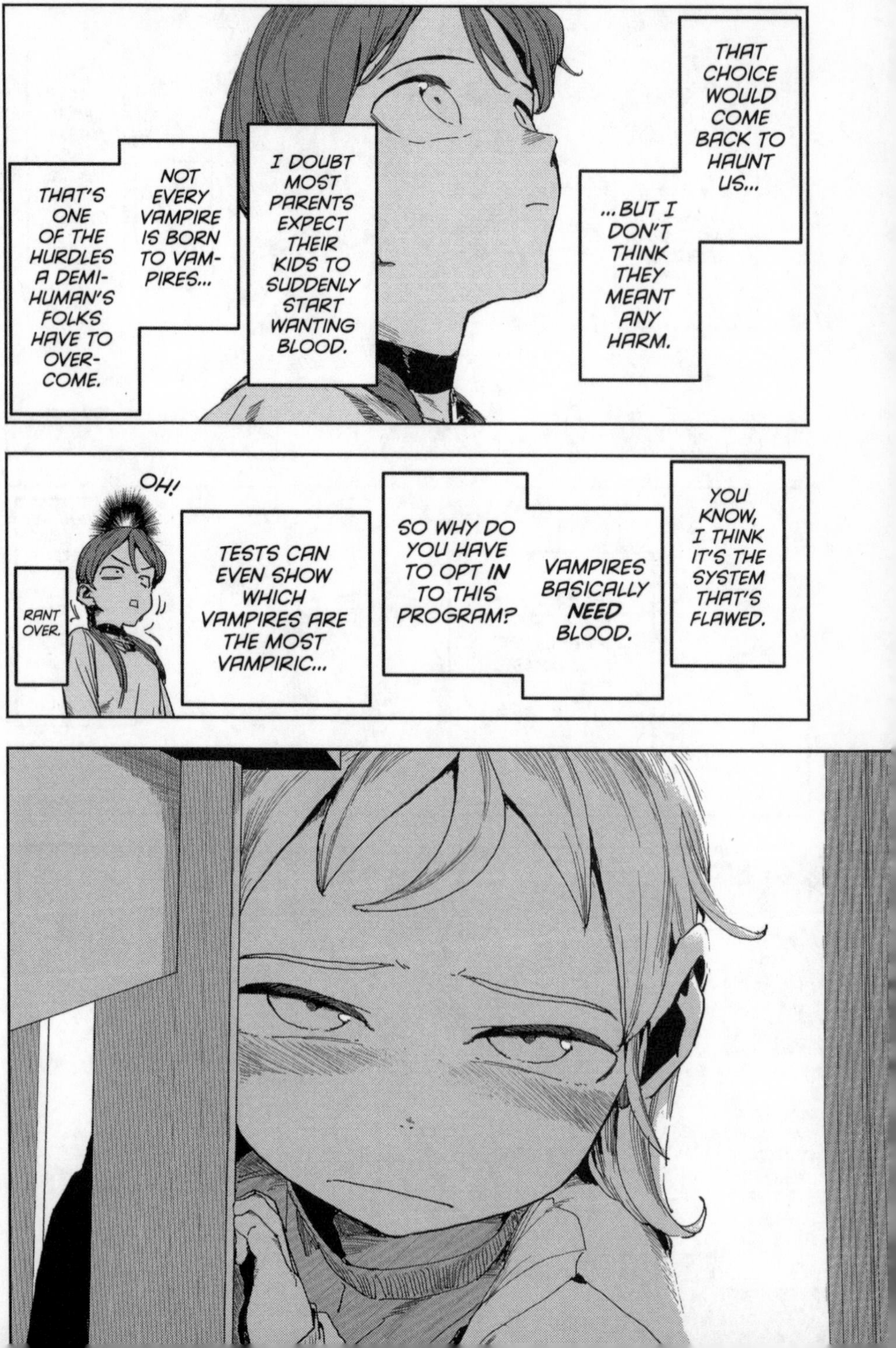
THAT CHOICE WOULD COME BACK TO HAUNT US...
...BUT I DON'T THINK THEY MEANT ANY HARM.
I DOUBT MOST PARENTS EXPECT THEIR KIDS TO SUDDENLY START WANTING BLOOD.
NOT EVERY VAMPIRE IS BORN TO VAM-PIRES...
THAT'S ONE OF THE HURDLES A DEMI-HUMAN'S FOLKS HAVE TO OVER-COME.
YOU KNOW, I THINK IT'S THE SYSTEM THAT'S FLAWED.
VAMPIRES BASICALLY **NEED** BLOOD.
SO WHY DO YOU HAVE TO OPT **IN** TO THIS PROGRAM?
TESTS CAN EVEN SHOW WHICH VAMPIRES ARE THE MOST VAMPIRIC...
OH!
RANT OVER.

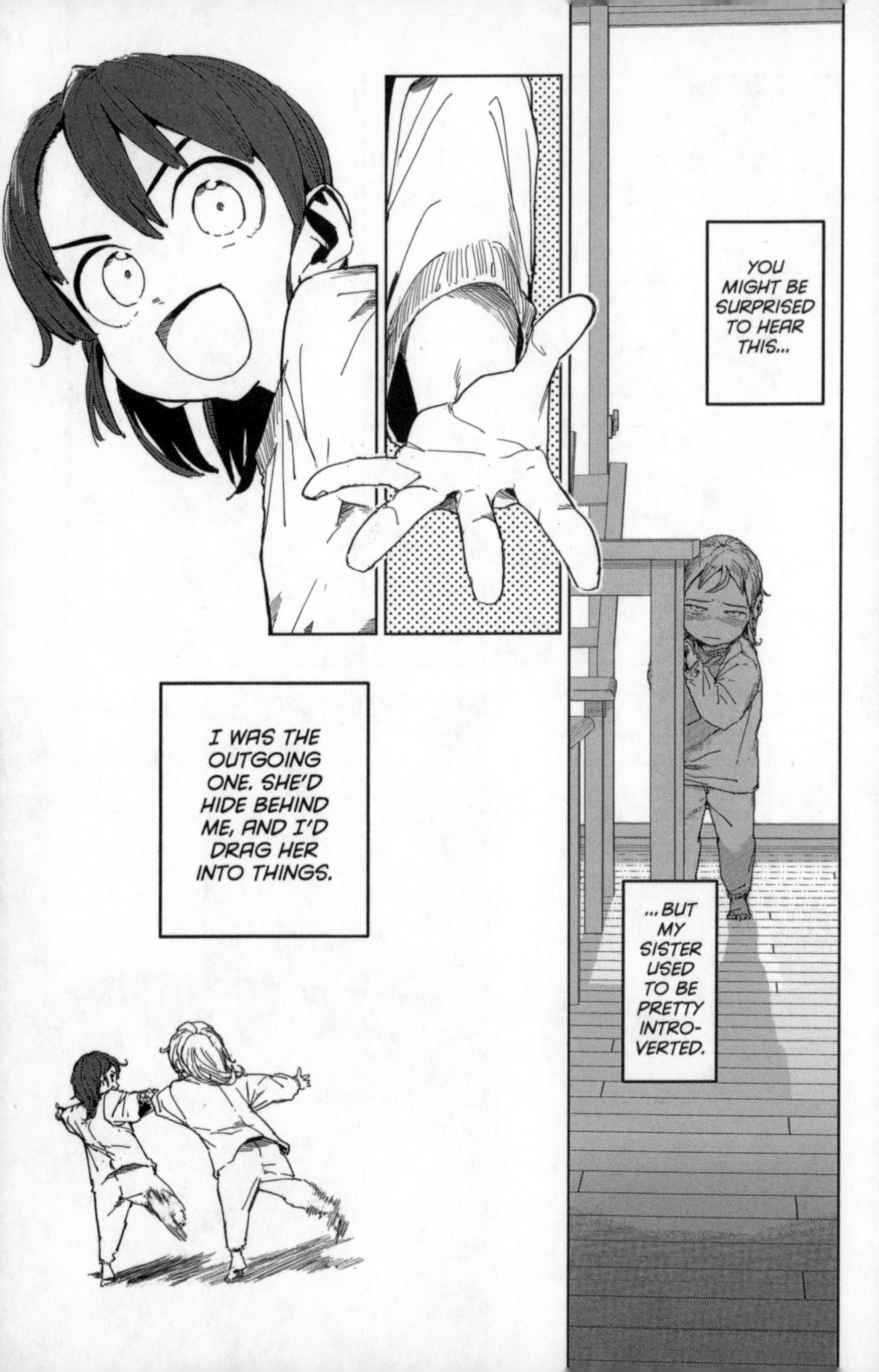
YOU MIGHT BE SURPRISED TO HEAR THIS...
...BUT MY SISTER USED TO BE PRETTY INTRO-VERTED.
I WAS THE OUTGOING ONE. SHE'D HIDE BEHIND ME, AND I'D DRAG HER INTO THINGS.

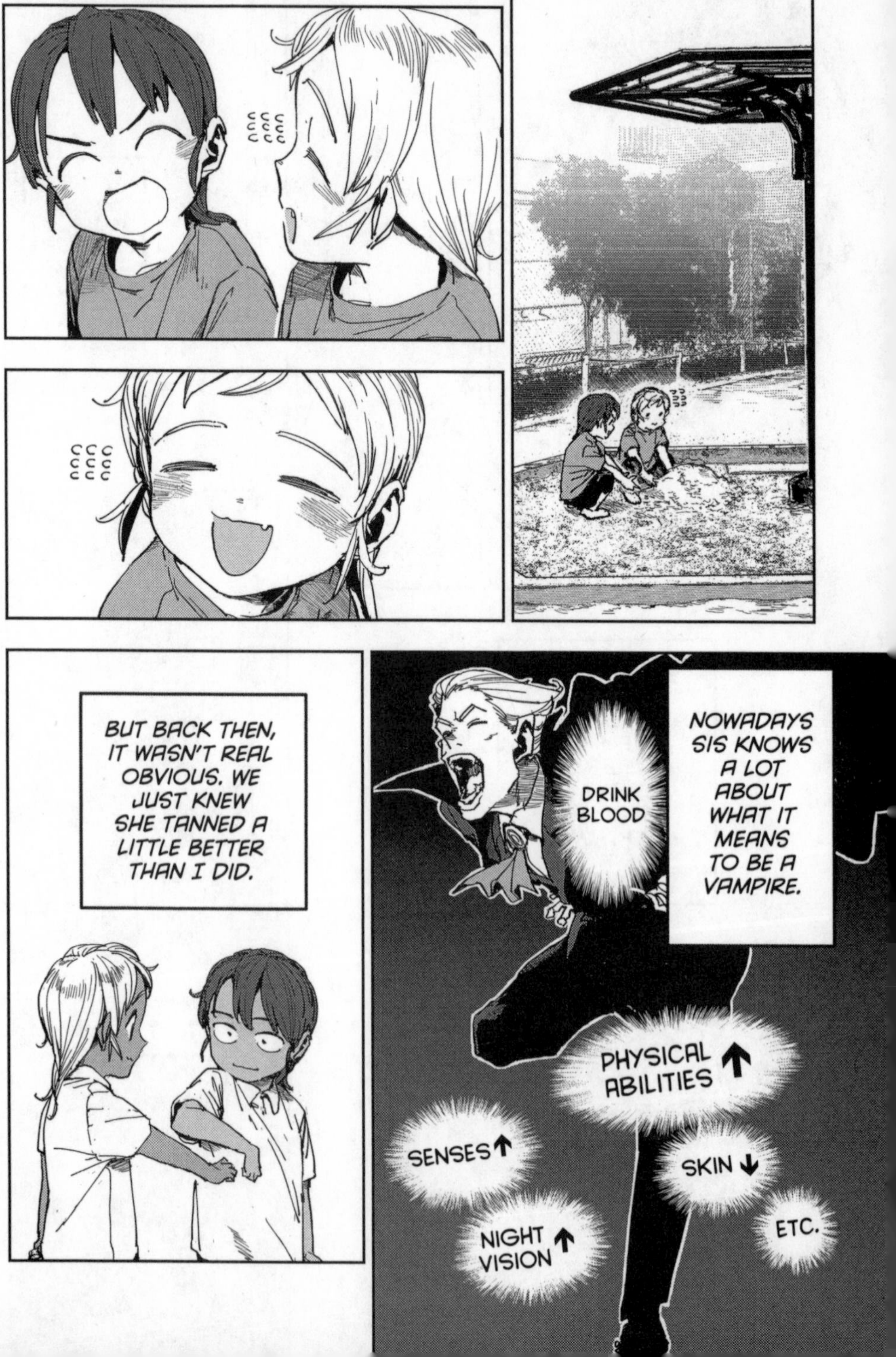
NOWADAYS SIS KNOWS A LOT ABOUT WHAT IT MEANS TO BE A VAMPIRE.
DRINK BLOOD
PHYSICAL ABILITIES ↑
SENSES ↑
SKIN ↓
NIGHT VISION ↑
ETC.
BUT BACK THEN, IT WASN'T REAL OBVIOUS. WE JUST KNEW SHE TANNED A LITTLE BETTER THAN I DID.

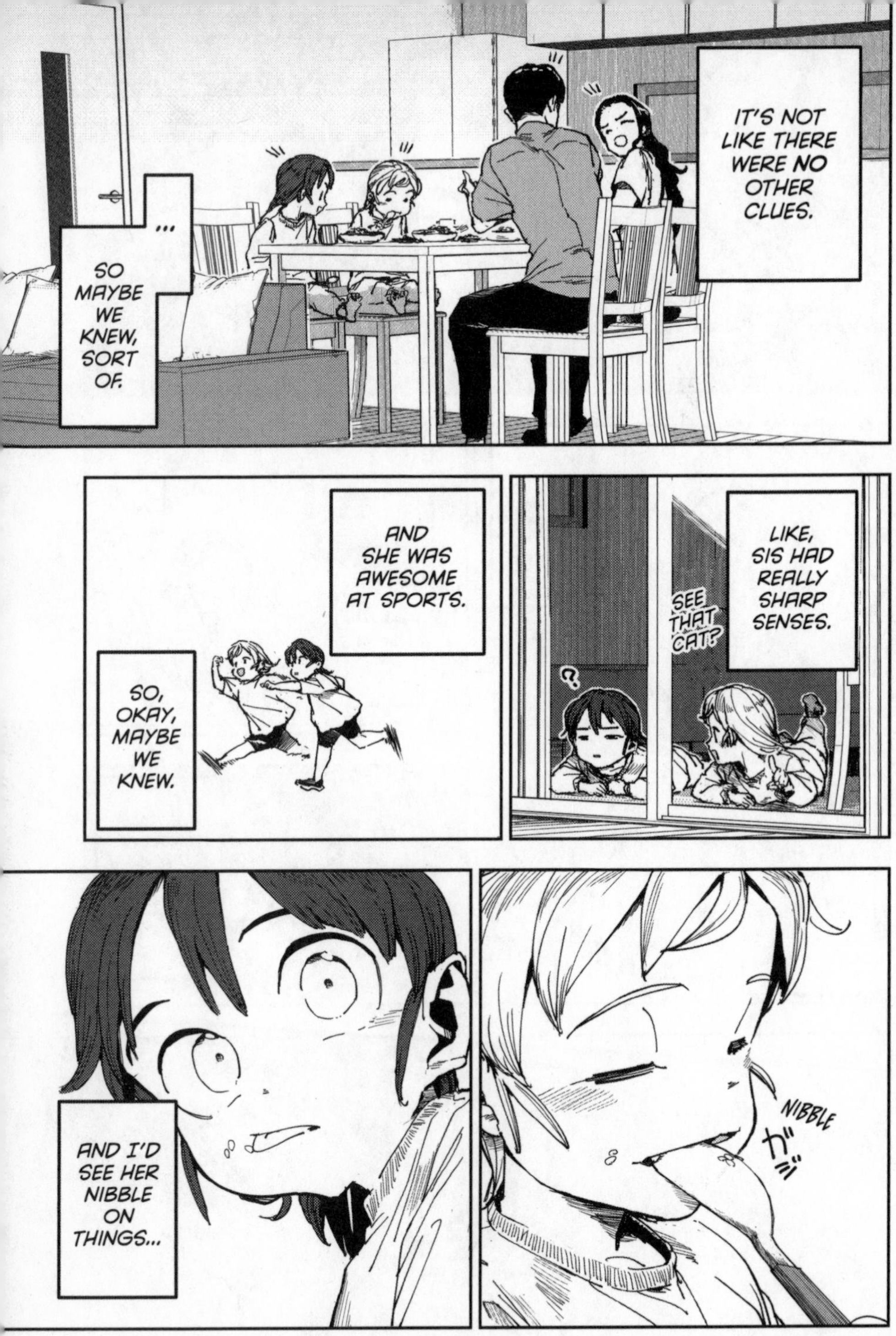
IT'S NOT LIKE THERE WERE **NO** OTHER CLUES.
...
SO MAYBE WE KNEW, SORT OF.
LIKE, SIS HAD REALLY SHARP SENSES.
SEE THAT CAT?
AND SHE WAS AWESOME AT SPORTS.
SO, OKAY, MAYBE WE KNEW.
NIBBLE
ガジ
AND I'D SEE HER NIBBLE ON THINGS...

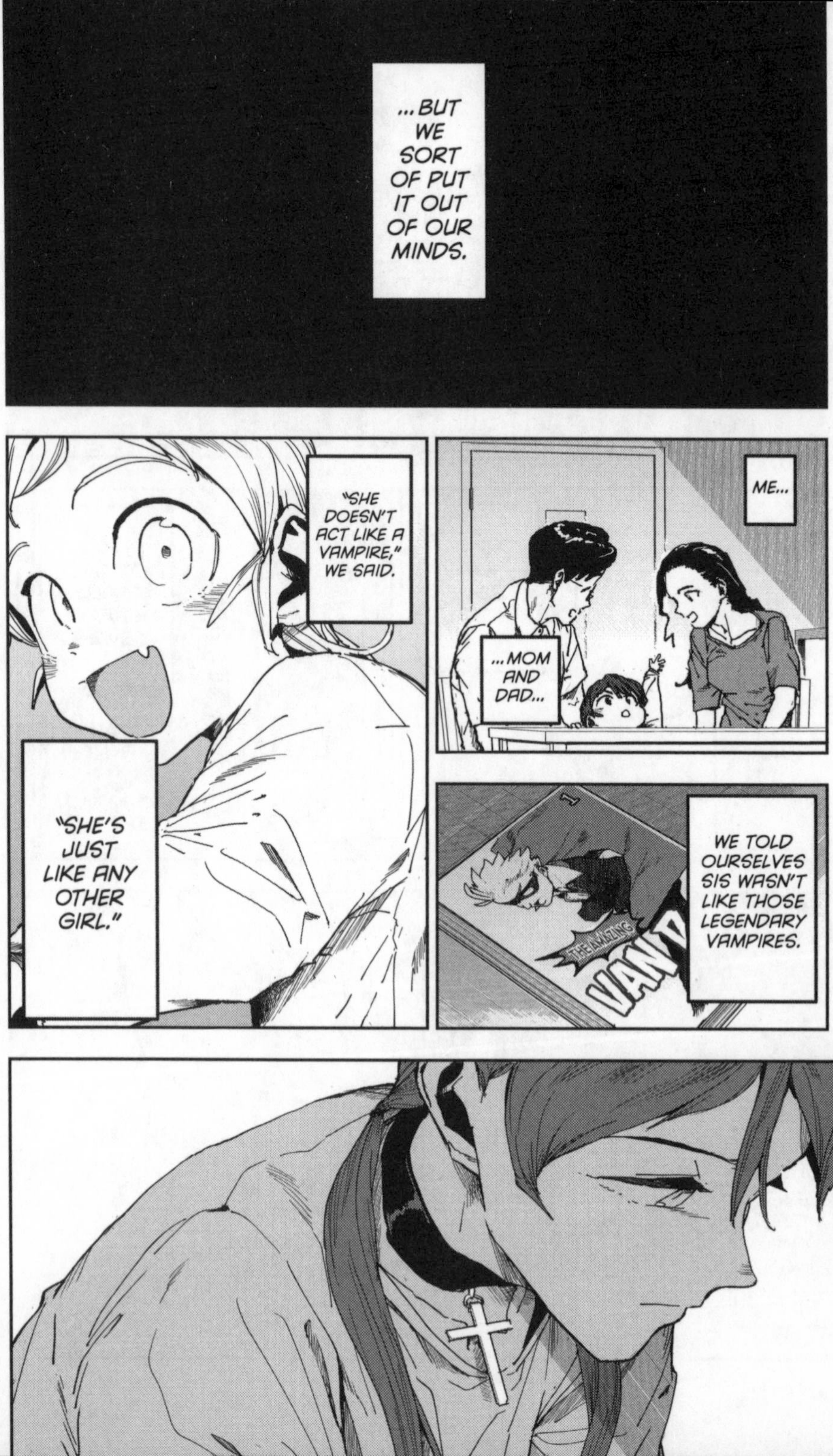
...BUT WE SORT OF PUT IT OUT OF OUR MINDS.
ME...
...MOM AND DAD...
WE TOLD OURSELVES SIS WASN'T LIKE THOSE LEGENDARY VAMPIRES.
THE AMAZING
"SHE DOESN'T ACT LIKE A VAMPIRE," WE SAID.
"SHE'S JUST LIKE ANY OTHER GIRL."

AND THEN
ONE DAY,
SHE BIT
ME.

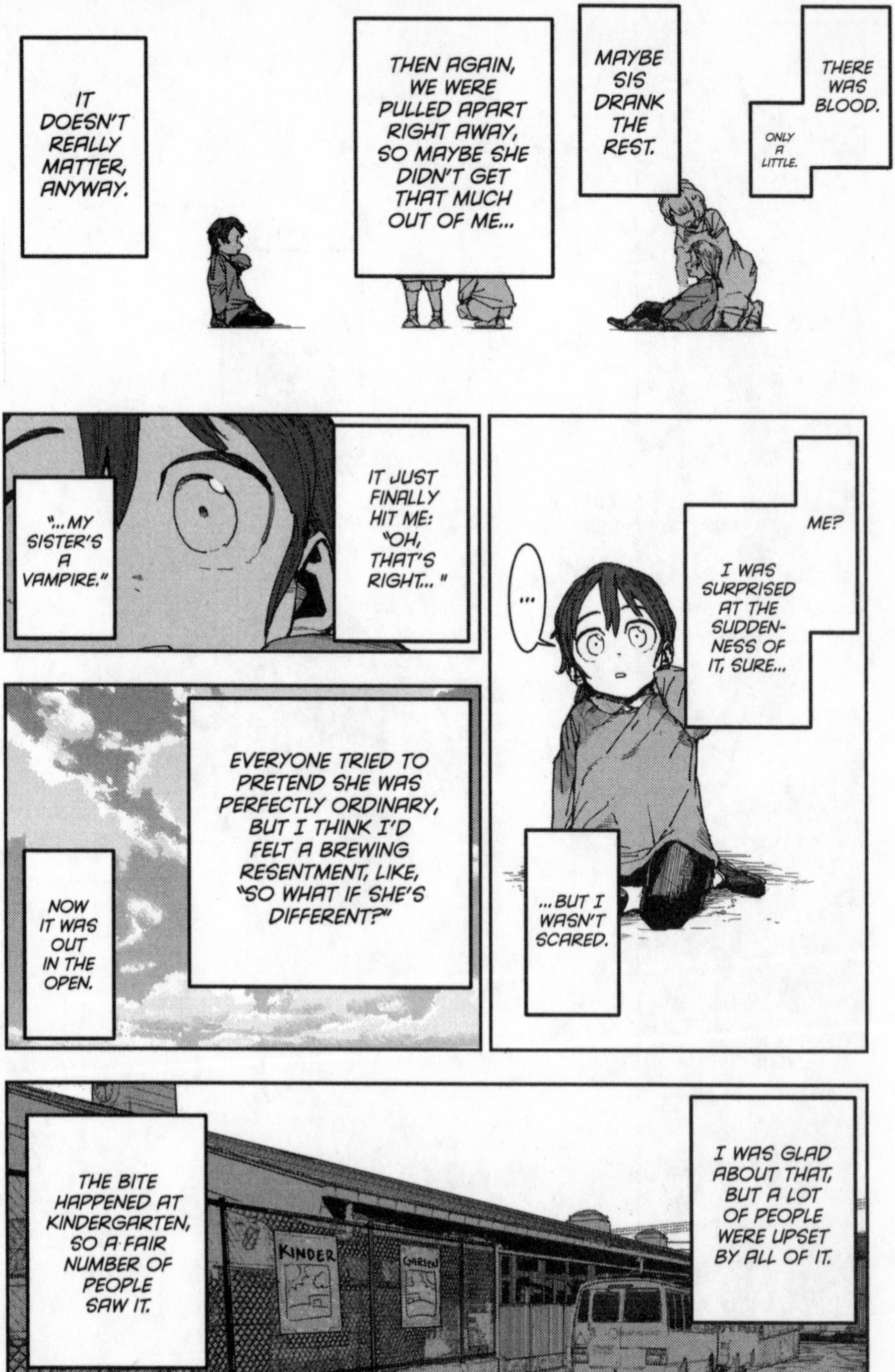
THERE WAS BLOOD.
ONLY A LITTLE.
MAYBE SIS DRANK THE REST.
THEN AGAIN, WE WERE PULLED APART RIGHT AWAY, SO MAYBE SHE DIDN'T GET THAT MUCH OUT OF ME...
IT DOESN'T REALLY MATTER, ANYWAY.
...
ME?
I WAS SURPRISED AT THE SUDDENNESS OF IT, SURE...
...BUT I WASN'T SCARED.
IT JUST FINALLY HIT ME: "OH, THAT'S RIGHT..."
"...MY SISTER'S A VAMPIRE."
EVERYONE TRIED TO PRETEND SHE WAS PERFECTLY ORDINARY, BUT I THINK I'D FELT A BREWING RESENTMENT, LIKE, "SO WHAT IF SHE'S DIFFERENT?"
NOW IT WAS OUT IN THE OPEN.
I WAS GLAD ABOUT THAT, BUT A LOT OF PEOPLE WERE UPSET BY ALL OF IT.
THE BITE HAPPENED AT KINDERGARTEN, SO A FAIR NUMBER OF PEOPLE SAW IT.
KINDER
GARTEN

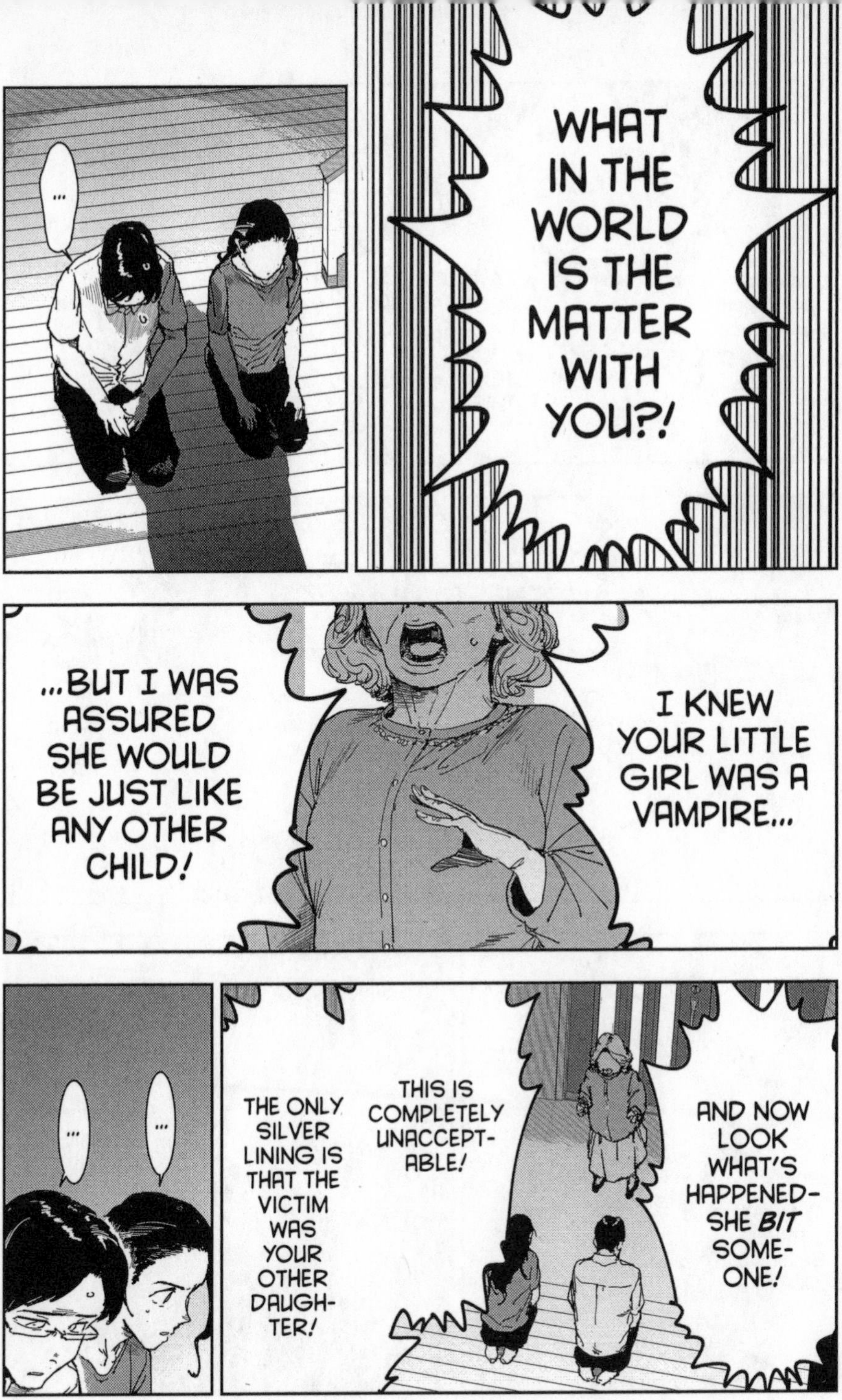
WHAT IN THE WORLD IS THE MATTER WITH YOU?!
...
I KNEW YOUR LITTLE GIRL WAS A VAMPIRE...
...BUT I WAS ASSURED SHE WOULD BE JUST LIKE ANY OTHER CHILD!
AND NOW LOOK WHAT'S HAPPENED–SHE *BIT* SOME-ONE!
THIS IS COMPLETELY UNACCEPT-ABLE!
THE ONLY SILVER LINING IS THAT THE VICTIM WAS YOUR OTHER DAUGH-TER!
...
...

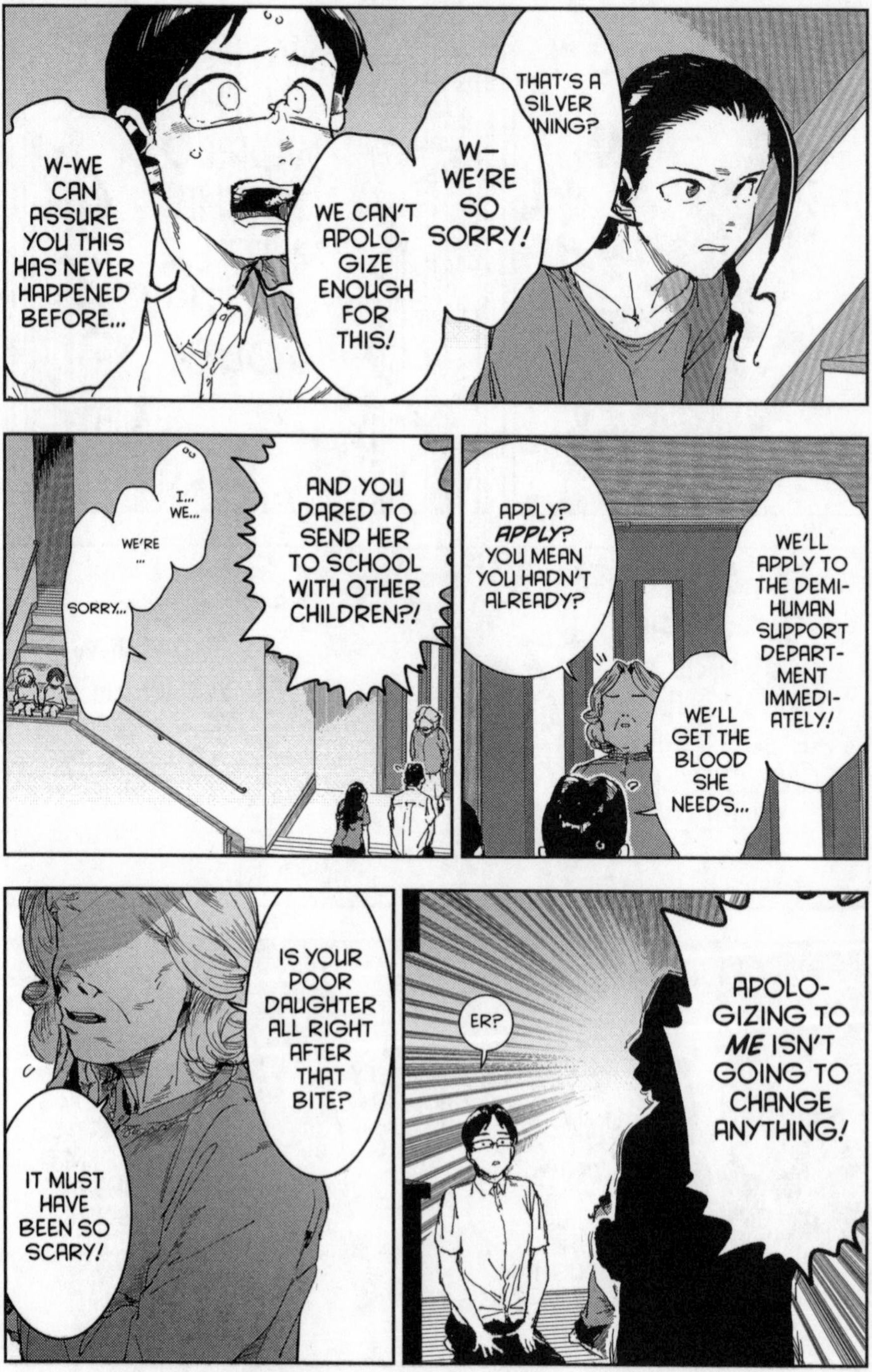
THAT'S A SILVER NING?
W— WE'RE SO SORRY!
WE CAN'T APOLO-GIZE ENOUGH FOR THIS!
W-WE CAN ASSURE YOU THIS HAS NEVER HAPPENED BEFORE...
WE'LL APPLY TO THE DEMI-HUMAN SUPPORT DEPART-MENT IMMEDI-ATELY!
APPLY? *APPLY*? YOU MEAN YOU HADN'T ALREADY?
WE'LL GET THE BLOOD SHE NEEDS...
AND YOU DARED TO SEND HER TO SCHOOL WITH OTHER CHILDREN?!
I... WE...
WE'RE ...
SORRY...
APOLO-GIZING TO *ME* ISN'T GOING TO CHANGE ANYTHING!
ER?
IS YOUR POOR DAUGHTER ALL RIGHT AFTER THAT BITE?
IT MUST HAVE BEEN SO SCARY!

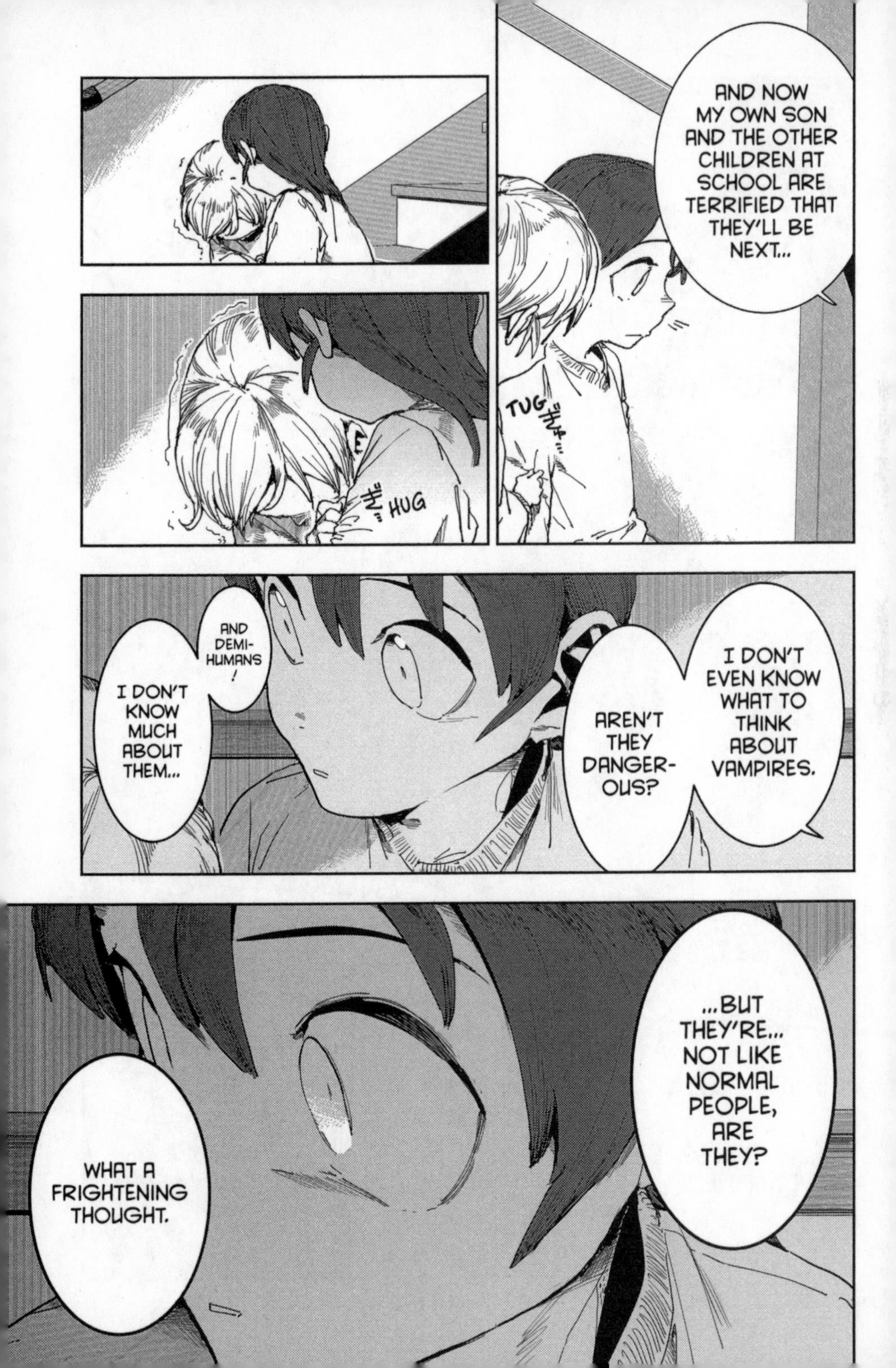
AND NOW MY OWN SON AND THE OTHER CHILDREN AT SCHOOL ARE TERRIFIED THAT THEY'LL BE NEXT...
TUG
HUG
I DON'T EVEN KNOW WHAT TO THINK ABOUT VAMPIRES.
AREN'T THEY DANGER-OUS?
AND DEMI-HUMANS!
I DON'T KNOW MUCH ABOUT THEM...
...BUT THEY'RE... NOT LIKE NORMAL PEOPLE, ARE THEY?
WHAT A FRIGHTENING THOUGHT.

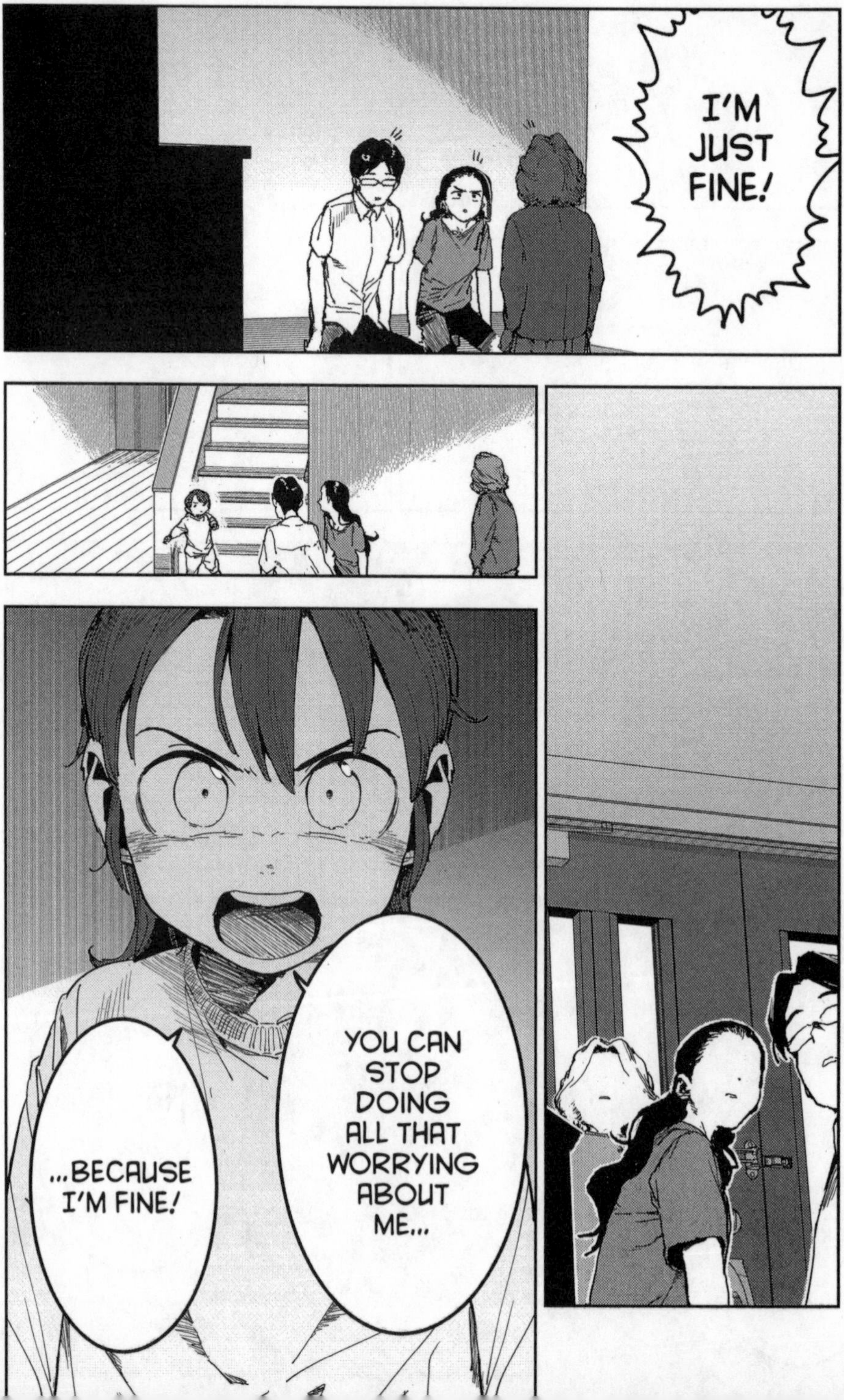
I'M JUST FINE!
YOU CAN STOP DOING ALL THAT WORRYING ABOUT ME...
...BECAUSE I'M FINE!

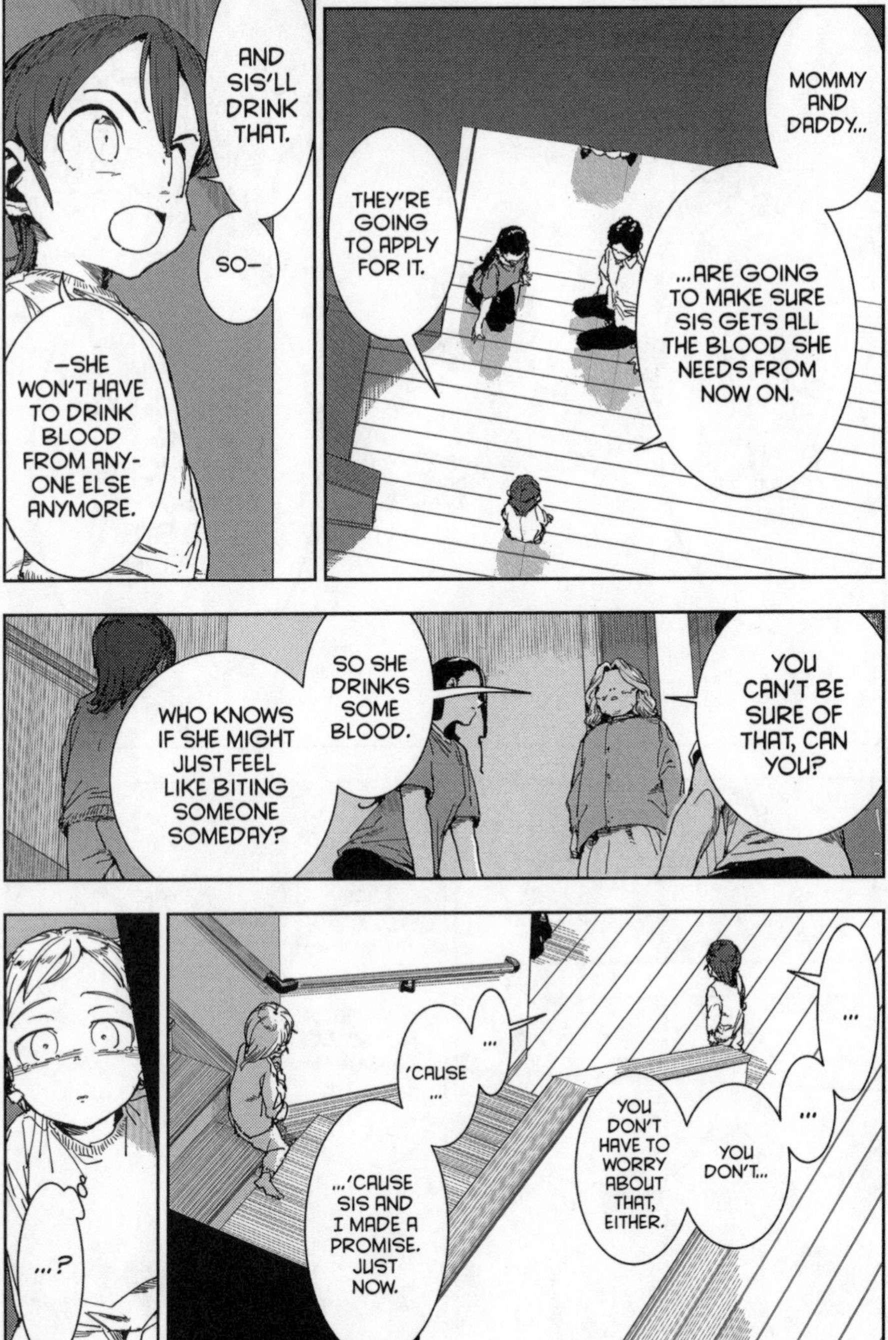
MOMMY AND DADDY...
...ARE GOING TO MAKE SURE SIS GETS ALL THE BLOOD SHE NEEDS FROM NOW ON.
THEY'RE GOING TO APPLY FOR IT.
AND SIS'LL DRINK THAT.
SO—
—SHE WON'T HAVE TO DRINK BLOOD FROM ANY-ONE ELSE ANYMORE.
YOU CAN'T BE SURE OF THAT, CAN YOU?
SO SHE DRINKS SOME BLOOD.
WHO KNOWS IF SHE MIGHT JUST FEEL LIKE BITING SOMEONE SOMEDAY?
...
...
YOU DON'T...
YOU DON'T HAVE TO WORRY ABOUT THAT, EITHER.
...
'CAUSE ...
...'CAUSE SIS AND I MADE A PROMISE. JUST NOW.
...?

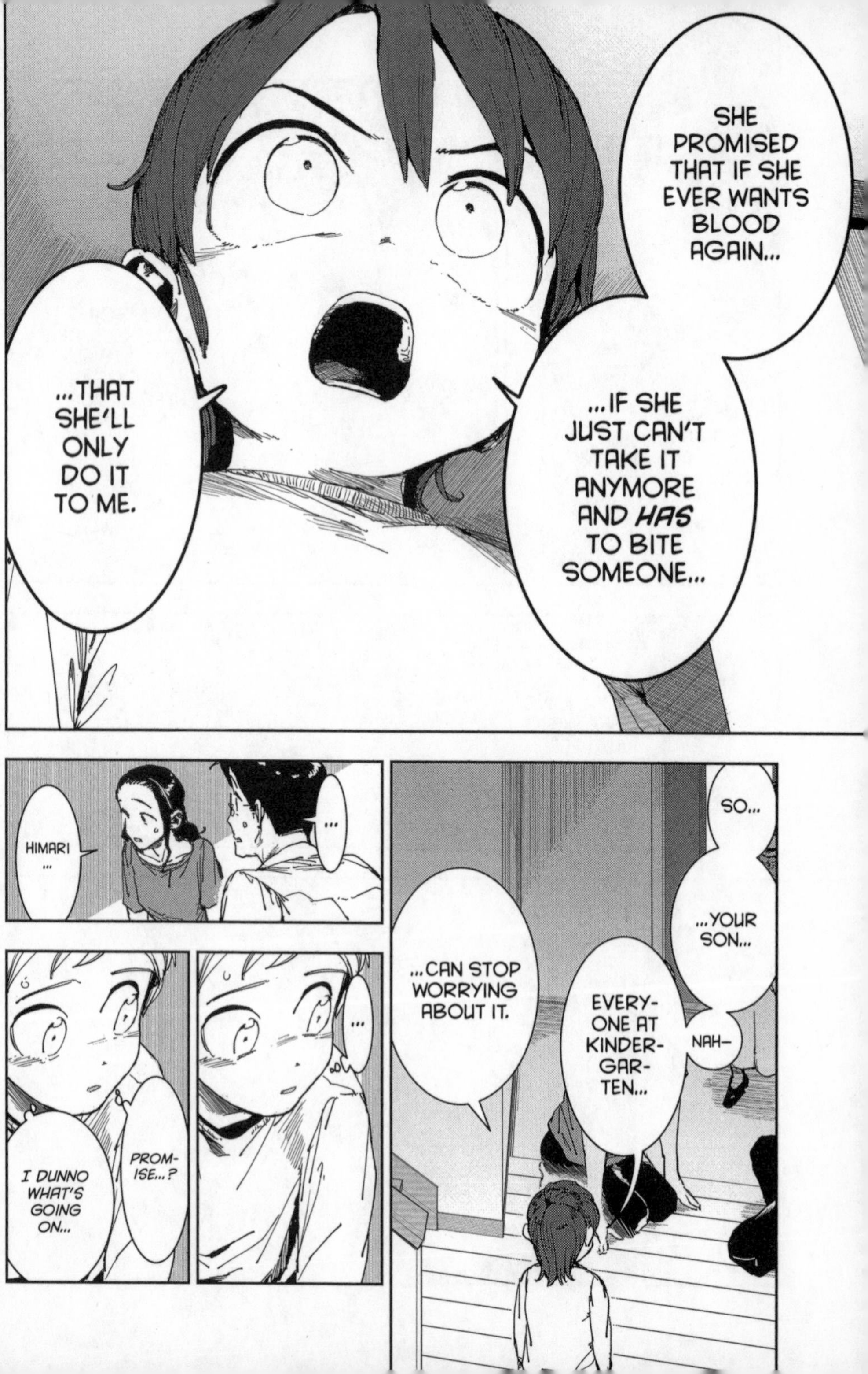
SHE PROMISED THAT IF SHE EVER WANTS BLOOD AGAIN...
...IF SHE JUST CAN'T TAKE IT ANYMORE AND *HAS* TO BITE SOMEONE...
...THAT SHE'LL ONLY DO IT TO ME.
SO...
...YOUR SON...
EVERY-ONE AT KINDER-GAR-TEN...
NAH—
...CAN STOP WORRYING ABOUT IT.
...
HIMARI ...
...
PROM-ISE...?
I DUNNO WHAT'S GOING ON...

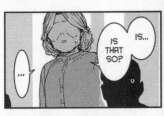

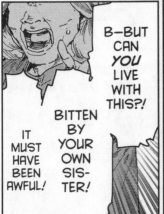

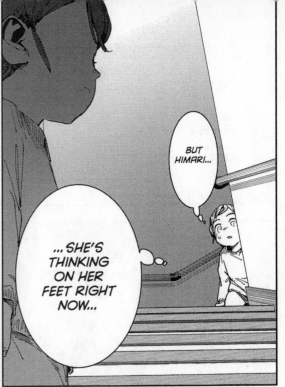

BUT HIMARI...
...SHE'S THINKING ON HER FEET RIGHT NOW...
IS...
IS THAT SO?
...
B-BUT CAN *YOU* LIVE WITH THIS?!
BITTEN BY YOUR OWN SIS-TER!
IT MUST HAVE BEEN AWFUL!
AND IT MIGHT... IT MIGHT HAPPEN AGAIN!
S-SOME-ONE MIGHT GET HURT...
THESE VAM-PIRES...
THEY AREN'T LIKE NORMAL PEOPLE, YOU KNOW...

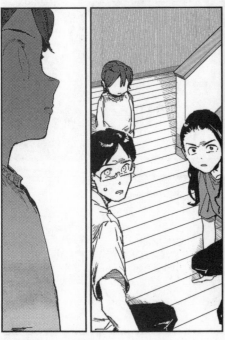

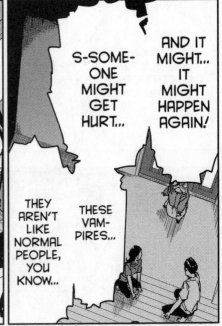

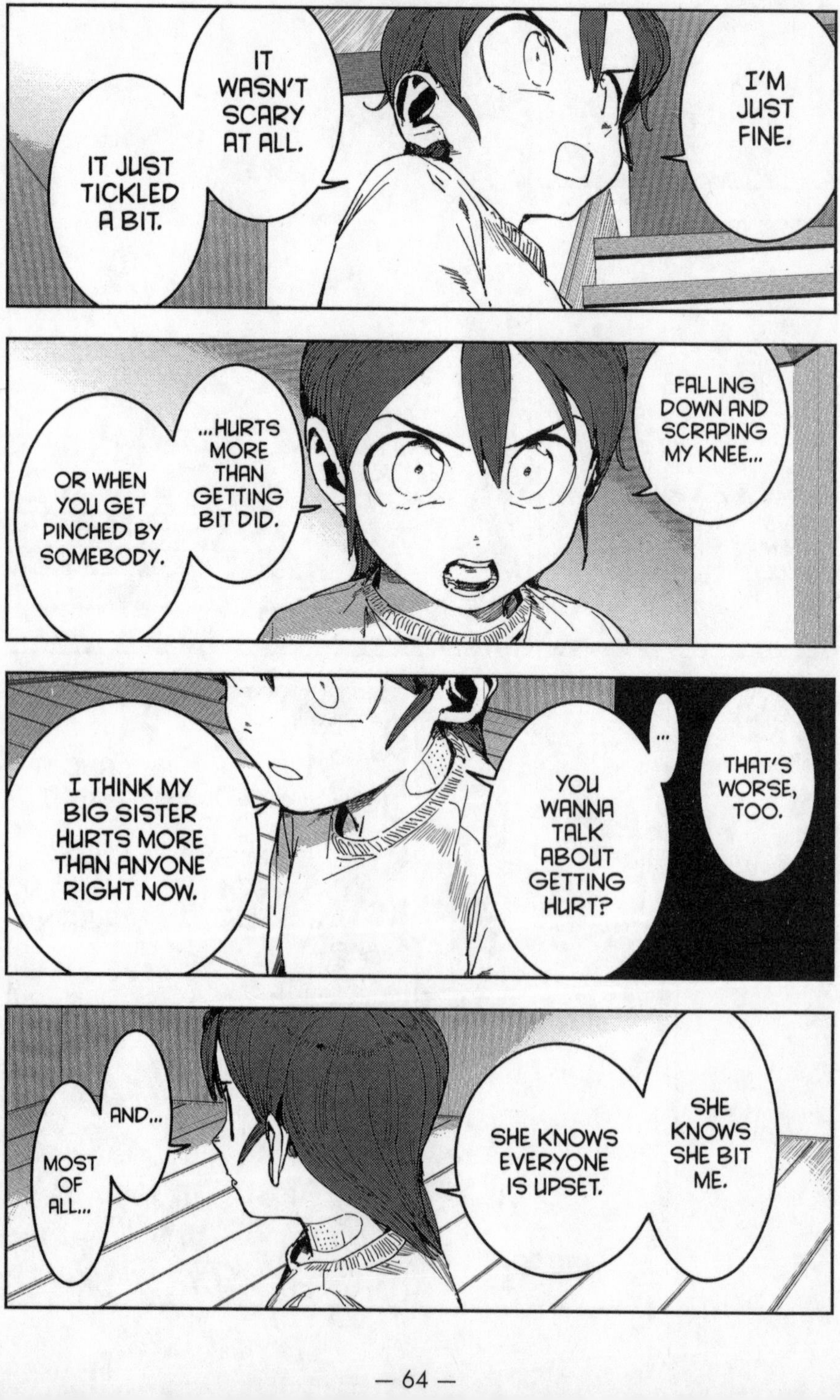
I'M JUST FINE.
IT WASN'T SCARY AT ALL.
IT JUST TICKLED A BIT.
FALLING DOWN AND SCRAPING MY KNEE...
...HURTS MORE THAN GETTING BIT DID.
OR WHEN YOU GET PINCHED BY SOMEBODY.
THAT'S WORSE, TOO.
...
YOU WANNA TALK ABOUT GETTING HURT?
I THINK MY BIG SISTER HURTS MORE THAN ANYONE RIGHT NOW.
SHE KNOWS SHE BIT ME.
SHE KNOWS EVERYONE IS UPSET.
AND...
MOST OF ALL...

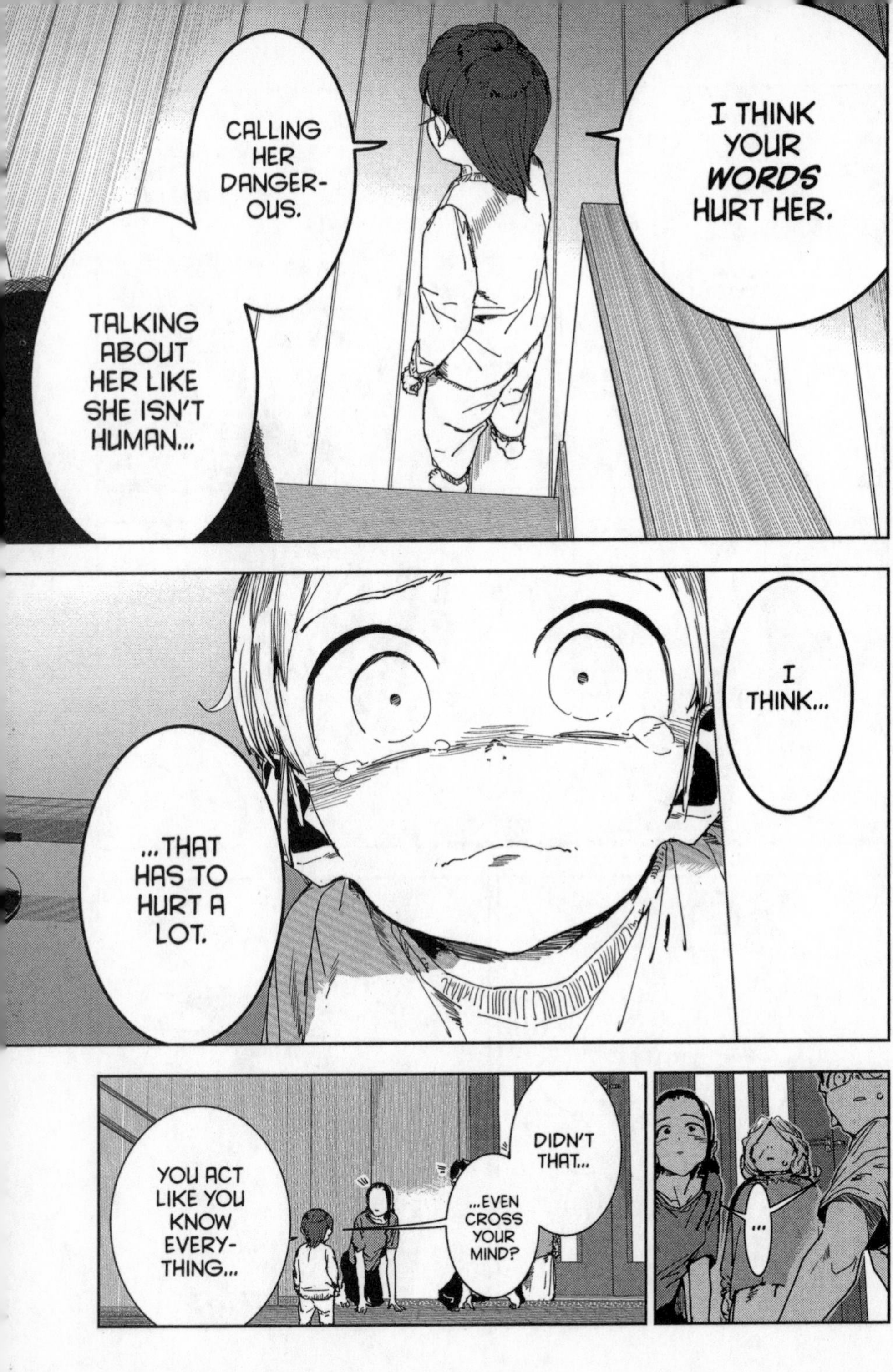
I THINK YOUR WORDS HURT HER.
CALLING HER DANGER-OUS.
TALKING ABOUT HER LIKE SHE ISN'T HUMAN...
I THINK...
...THAT HAS TO HURT A LOT.
...
DIDN'T THAT...
...EVEN CROSS YOUR MIND?
YOU ACT LIKE YOU KNOW EVERY-THING...

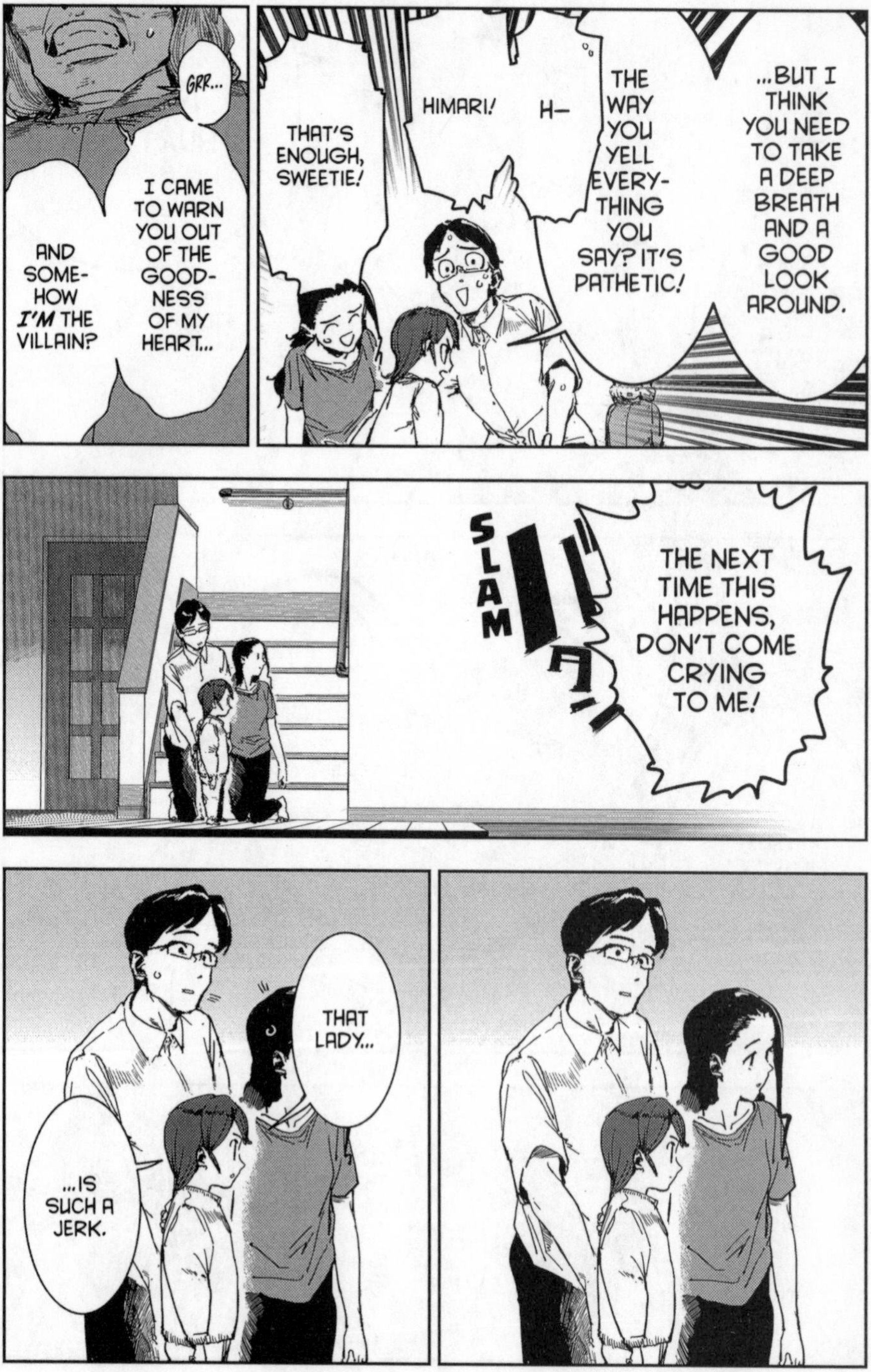
...BUT I THINK YOU NEED TO TAKE A DEEP BREATH AND A GOOD LOOK AROUND.
THE WAY YOU YELL EVERYTHING YOU SAY? IT'S PATHETIC!
H—
HIMARI!
THAT'S ENOUGH, SWEETIE!
GRR...
I CAME TO WARN YOU OUT OF THE GOODNESS OF MY HEART...
AND SOMEHOW *I'M* THE VILLAIN?
THE NEXT TIME THIS HAPPENS, DON'T COME CRYING TO ME!
SLAM
THAT LADY...
...IS SUCH A JERK.

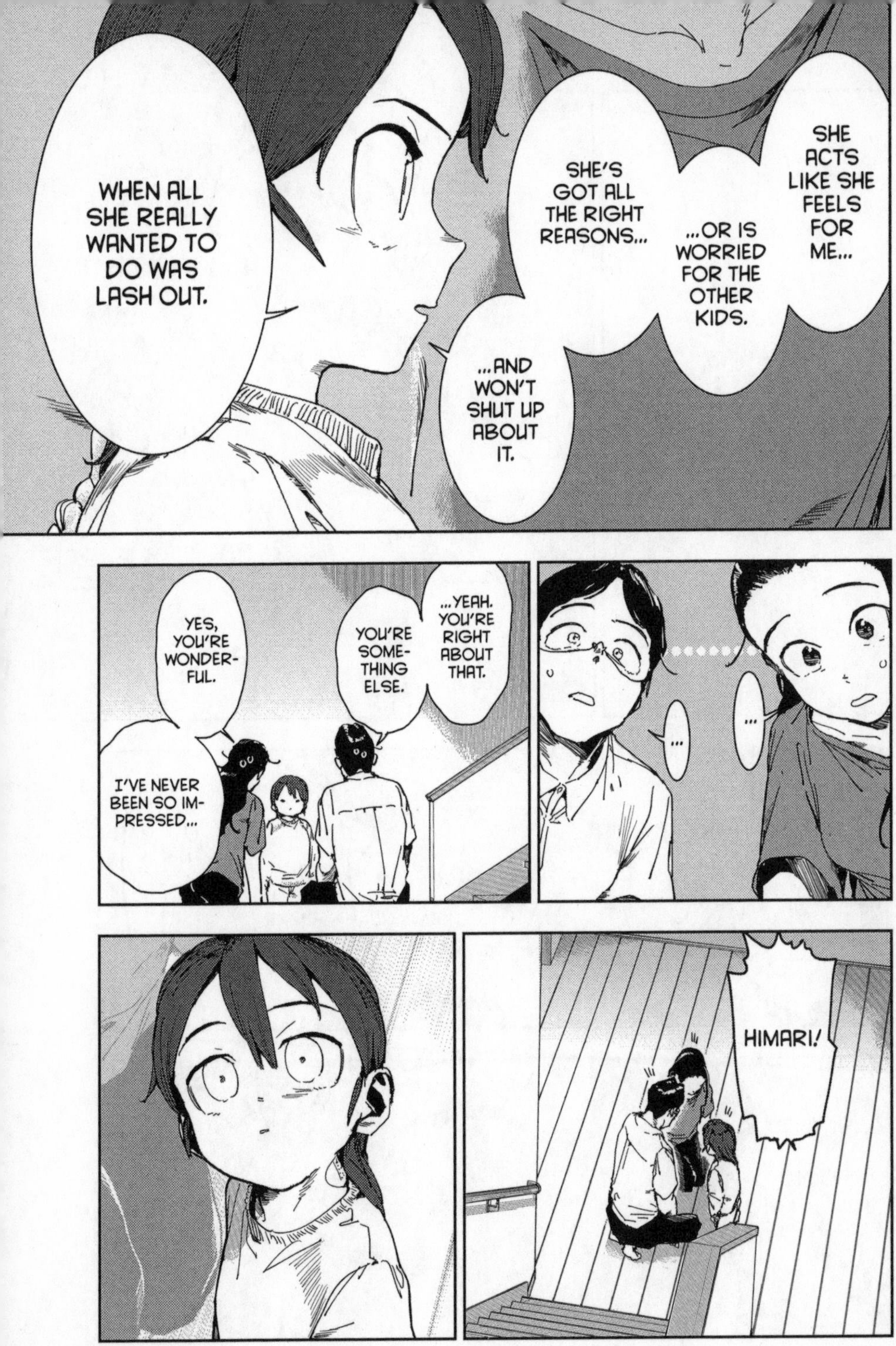
SHE ACTS LIKE SHE FEELS FOR ME...
...OR IS WORRIED FOR THE OTHER KIDS.
SHE'S GOT ALL THE RIGHT REASONS...
...AND WON'T SHUT UP ABOUT IT.
WHEN ALL SHE REALLY WANTED TO DO WAS LASH OUT.
...
...
...YEAH. YOU'RE RIGHT ABOUT THAT.
YOU'RE SOMETHING ELSE.
YES, YOU'RE WONDERFUL.
I'VE NEVER BEEN SO IMPRESSED...
HIMARI!

YOU WERE...

...AWESOME.

THANK YOU, HIMARI...

THANK YOU!

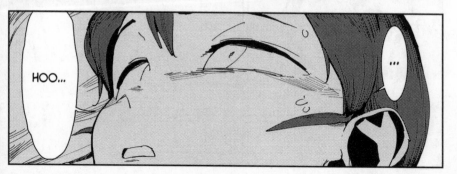

HOO...

...

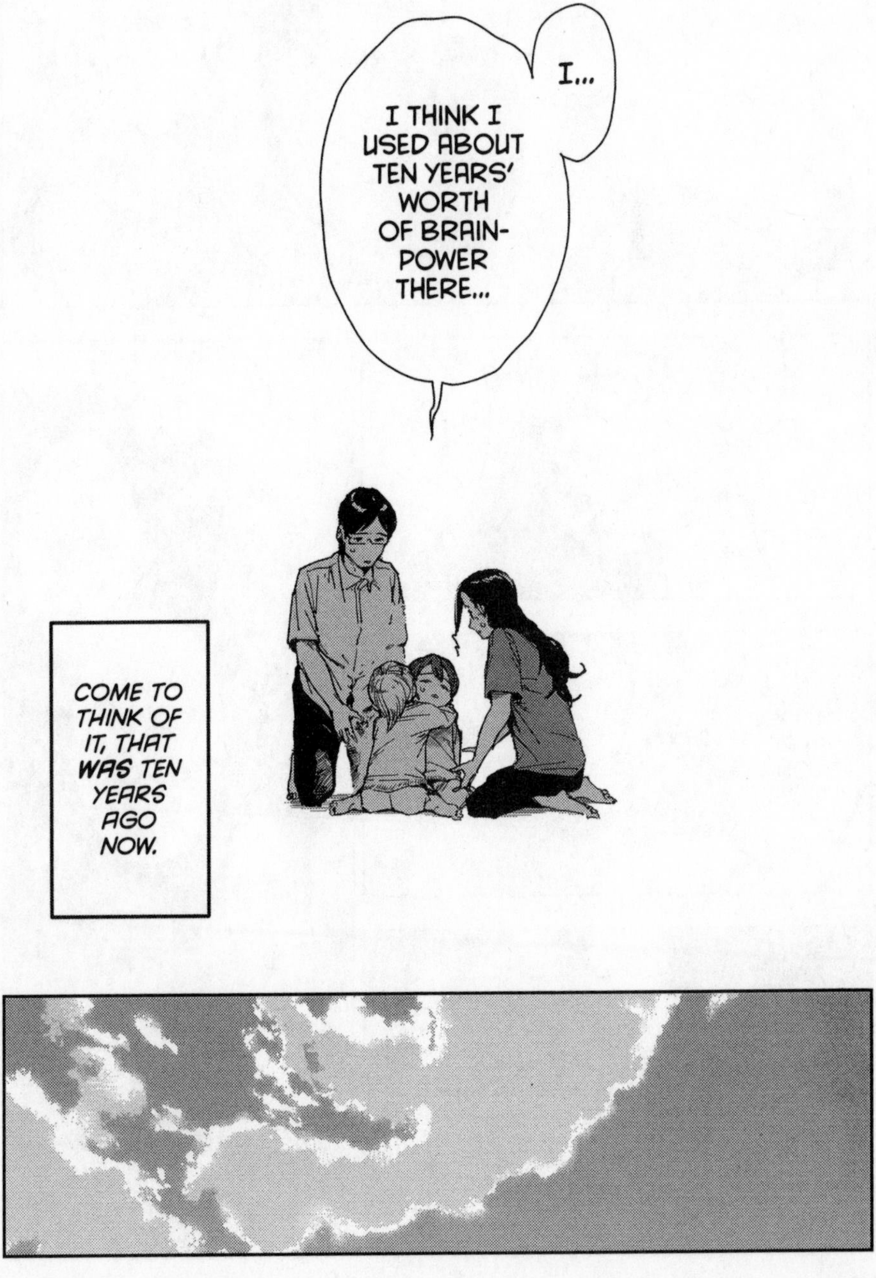
I...
I THINK I USED ABOUT TEN YEARS' WORTH OF BRAIN-POWER THERE...
COME TO THINK OF IT, THAT *WAS* TEN YEARS AGO NOW.

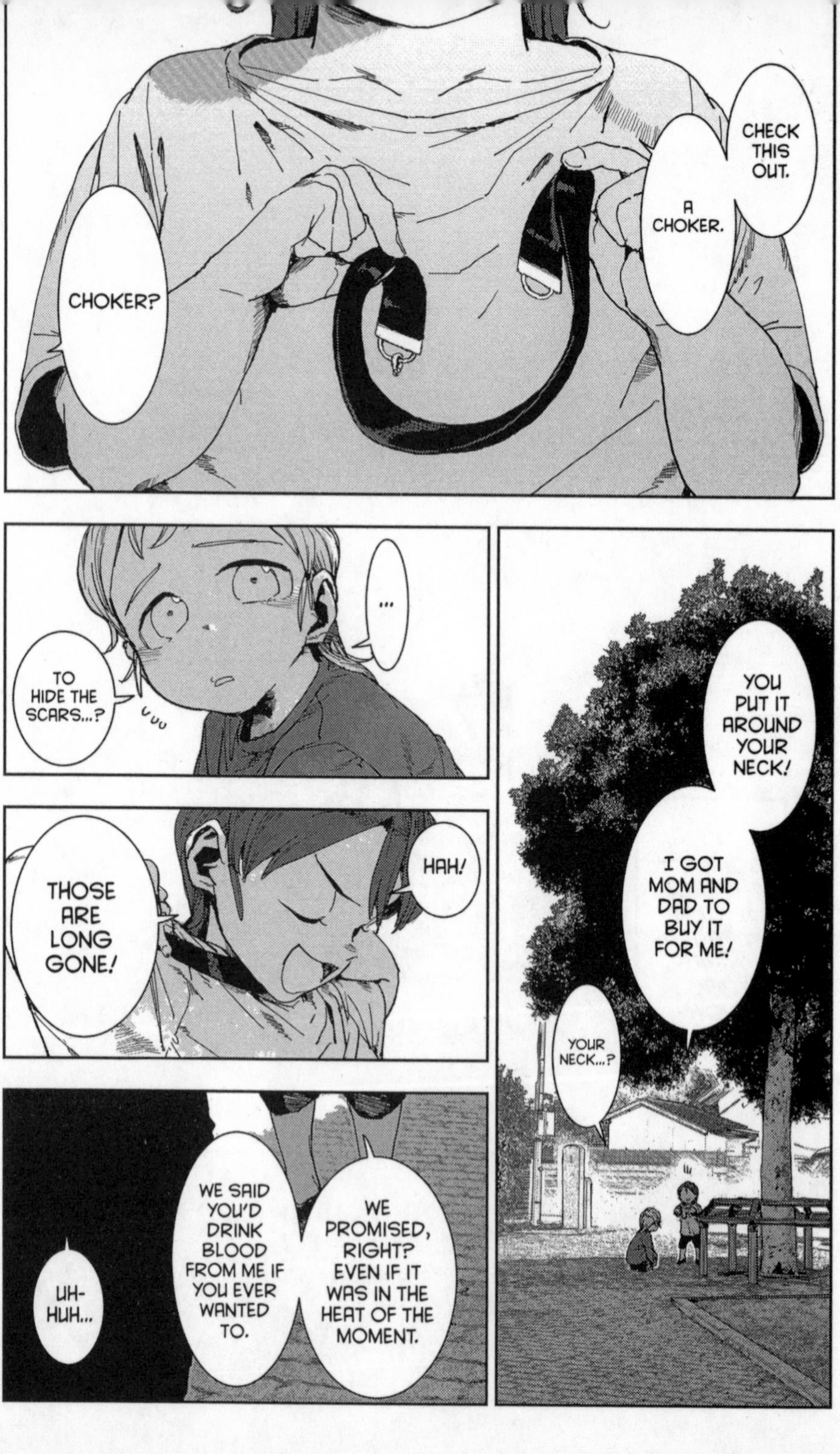
CHECK THIS OUT.
A CHOKER.
CHOKER?
YOU PUT IT AROUND YOUR NECK!
I GOT MOM AND DAD TO BUY IT FOR ME!
YOUR NECK...?
...
TO HIDE THE SCARS...?
HAH!
THOSE ARE LONG GONE!
WE PROMISED, RIGHT? EVEN IF IT WAS IN THE HEAT OF THE MOMENT.
WE SAID YOU'D DRINK BLOOD FROM ME IF YOU EVER WANTED TO.
UH-HUH...

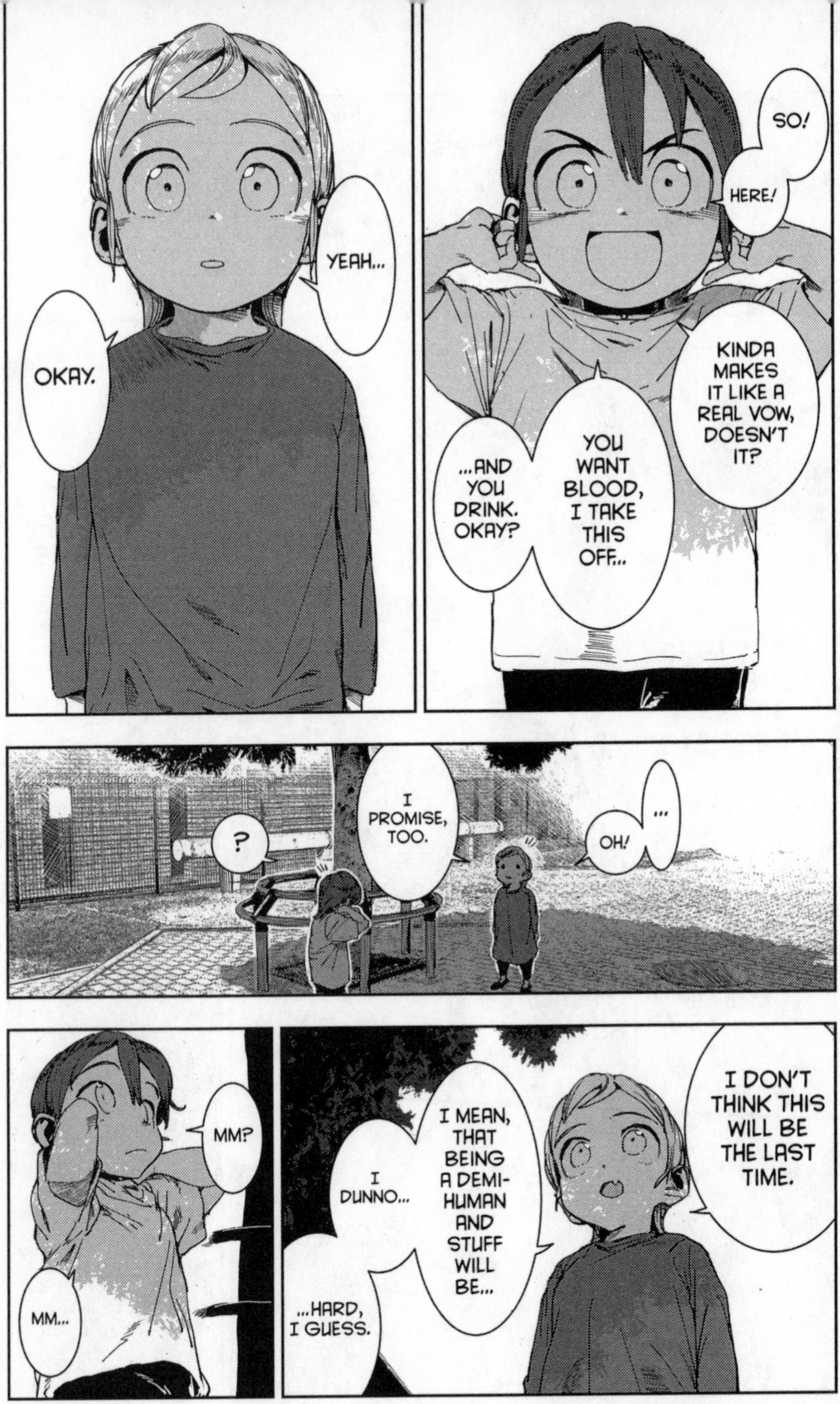
SO!
HERE!
KINDA MAKES IT LIKE A REAL VOW, DOESN'T IT?
YOU WANT BLOOD, I TAKE THIS OFF...
...AND YOU DRINK. OKAY?
YEAH...
OKAY.
...
OH!
I PROMISE, TOO.
?
I DON'T THINK THIS WILL BE THE LAST TIME.
I MEAN, THAT BEING A DEMI-HUMAN AND STUFF WILL BE...
I DUNNO...
...HARD, I GUESS.
MM?
MM...

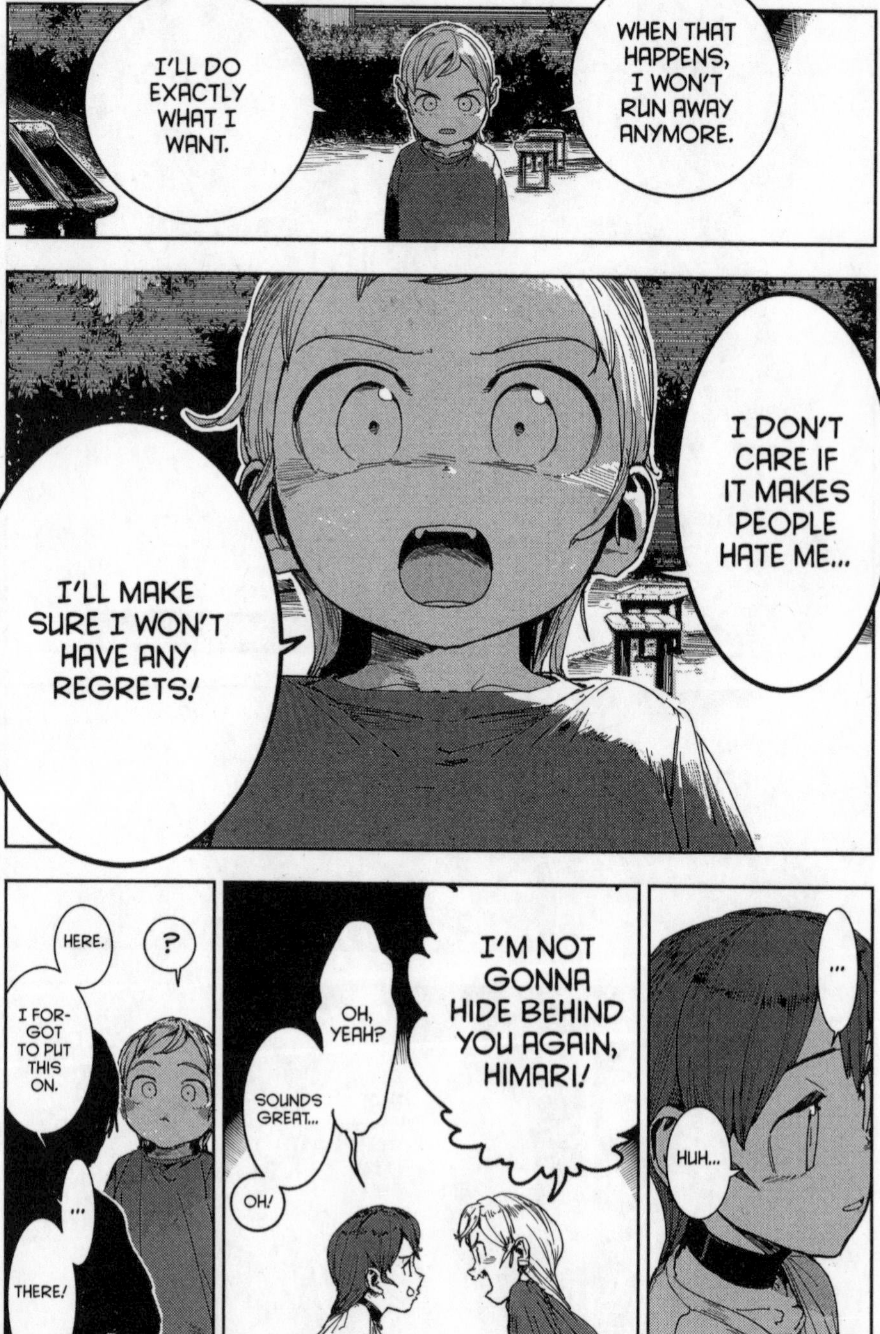

WHEN THAT HAPPENS, I WON'T RUN AWAY ANYMORE.
I'LL DO EXACTLY WHAT I WANT.
I DON'T CARE IF IT MAKES PEOPLE HATE ME...
I'LL MAKE SURE I WON'T HAVE ANY REGRETS!
...
HUH...
I'M NOT GONNA HIDE BEHIND YOU AGAIN, HIMARI!
OH, YEAH?
SOUNDS GREAT...
OH!
?
HERE.
I FOR-GOT TO PUT THIS ON.
...
THERE!

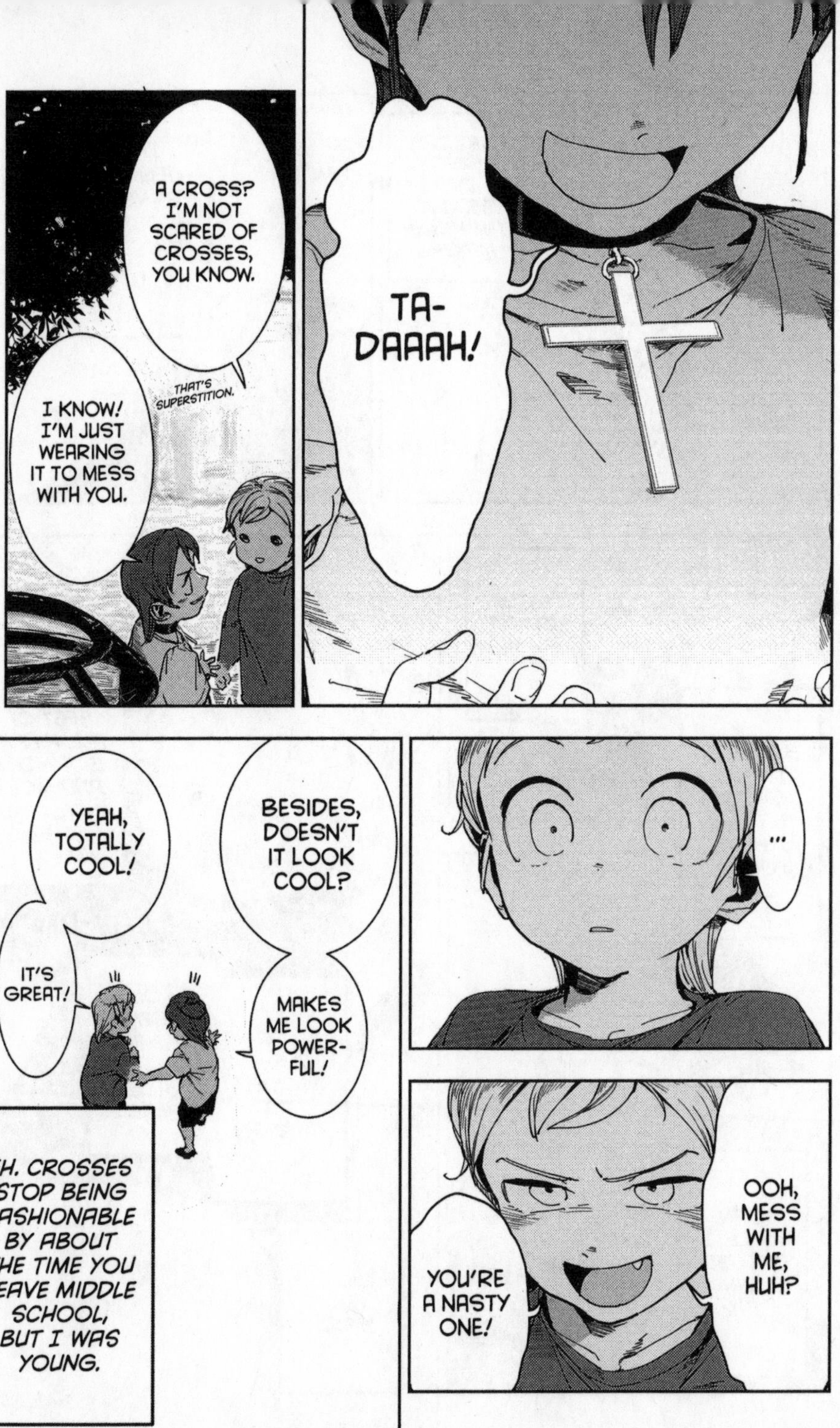
TA-DAAAH!
A CROSS? I'M NOT SCARED OF CROSSES, YOU KNOW.
THAT'S SUPERSTITION.
I KNOW! I'M JUST WEARING IT TO MESS WITH YOU.
...
OOH, MESS WITH ME, HUH?
YOU'RE A NASTY ONE!
BESIDES, DOESN'T IT LOOK COOL?
MAKES ME LOOK POWER-FUL!
YEAH, TOTALLY COOL!
IT'S GREAT!
EH. CROSSES STOP BEING FASHIONABLE BY ABOUT THE TIME YOU LEAVE MIDDLE SCHOOL, BUT I WAS YOUNG.

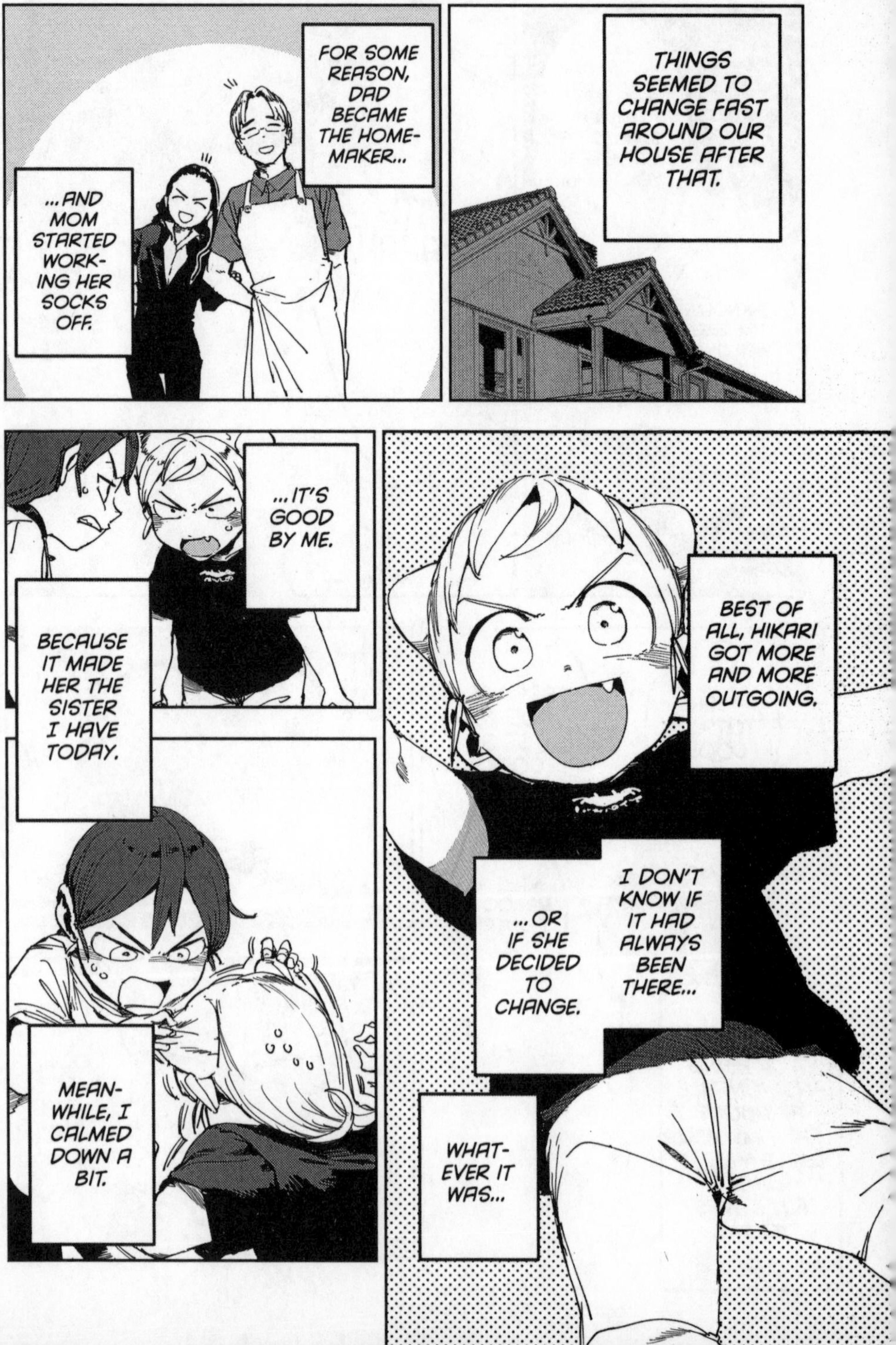
THINGS SEEMED TO CHANGE FAST AROUND OUR HOUSE AFTER THAT.
FOR SOME REASON, DAD BECAME THE HOME-MAKER...
...AND MOM STARTED WORK-ING HER SOCKS OFF.
BEST OF ALL, HIKARI GOT MORE AND MORE OUTGOING.
I DON'T KNOW IF IT HAD ALWAYS BEEN THERE...
...OR IF SHE DECIDED TO CHANGE.
WHAT-EVER IT WAS...
...IT'S GOOD BY ME.
BECAUSE IT MADE HER THE SISTER I HAVE TODAY.
MEAN-WHILE, I CALMED DOWN A BIT.

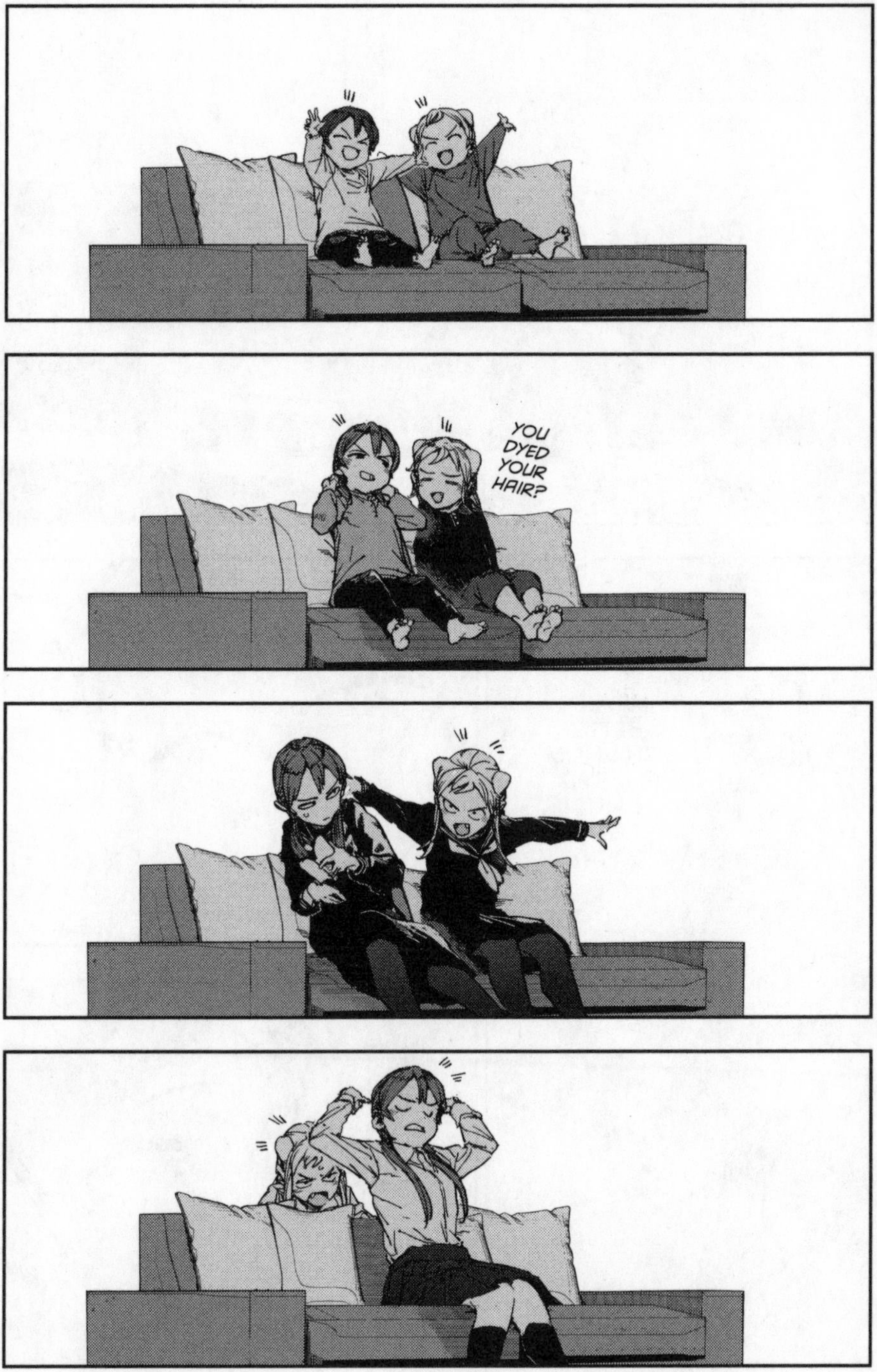
YOU DYED YOUR HAIR?

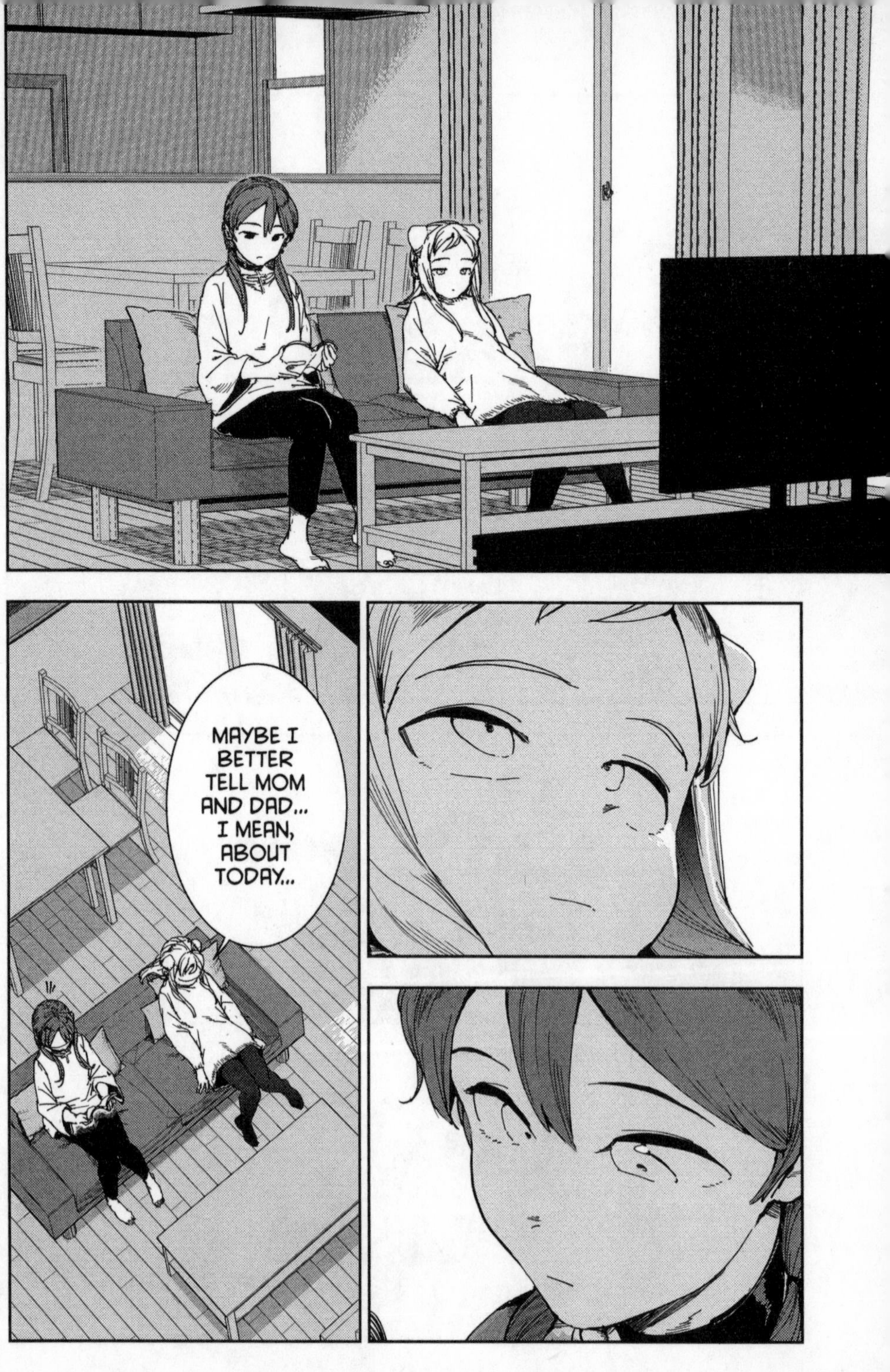
MAYBE I BETTER TELL MOM AND DAD... I MEAN, ABOUT TODAY...

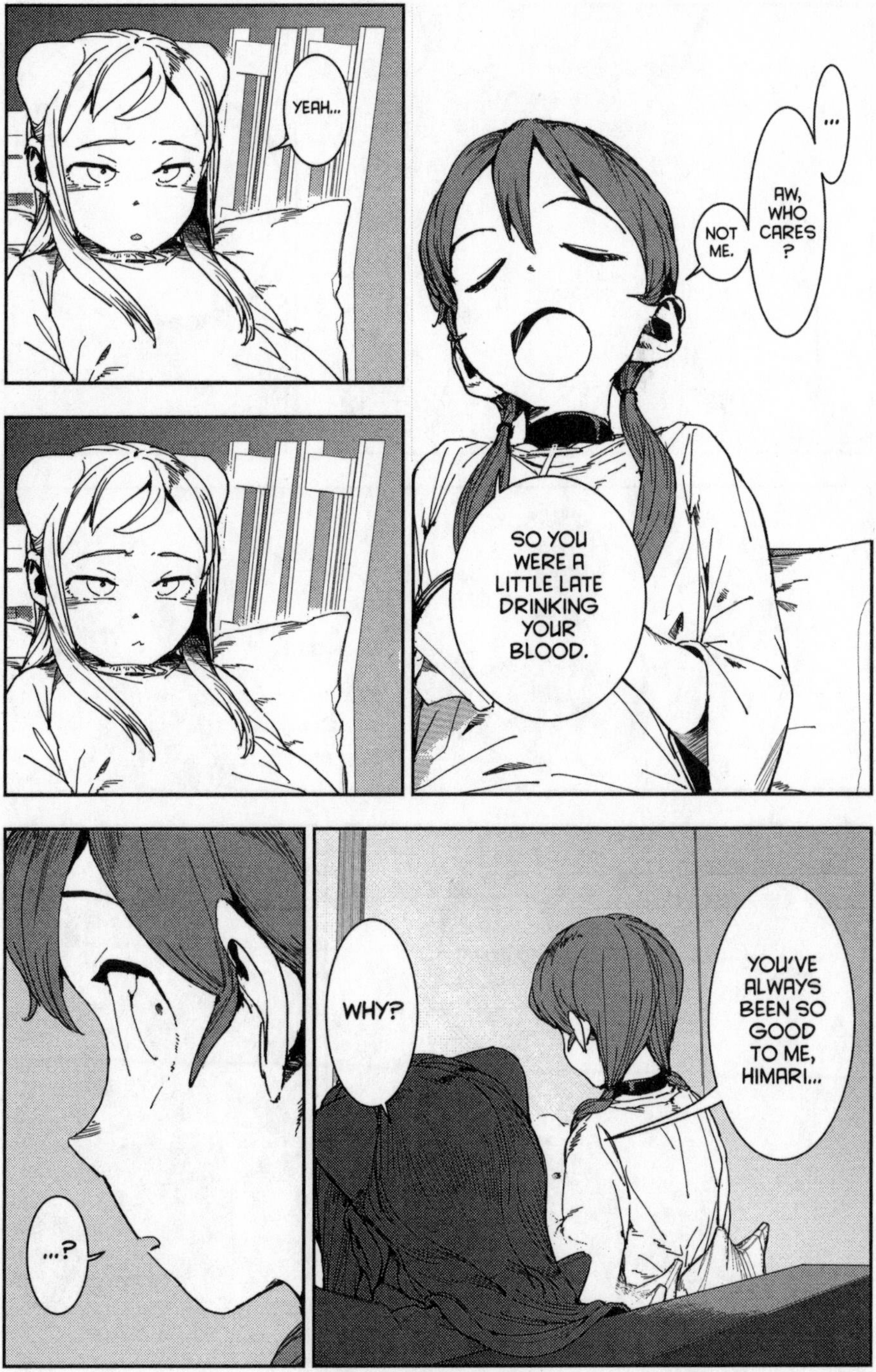
...
AW, WHO CARES?
NOT ME.
SO YOU WERE A LITTLE LATE DRINKING YOUR BLOOD.
YEAH...
YOU'VE ALWAYS BEEN SO GOOD TO ME, HIMARI...
WHY?
...?

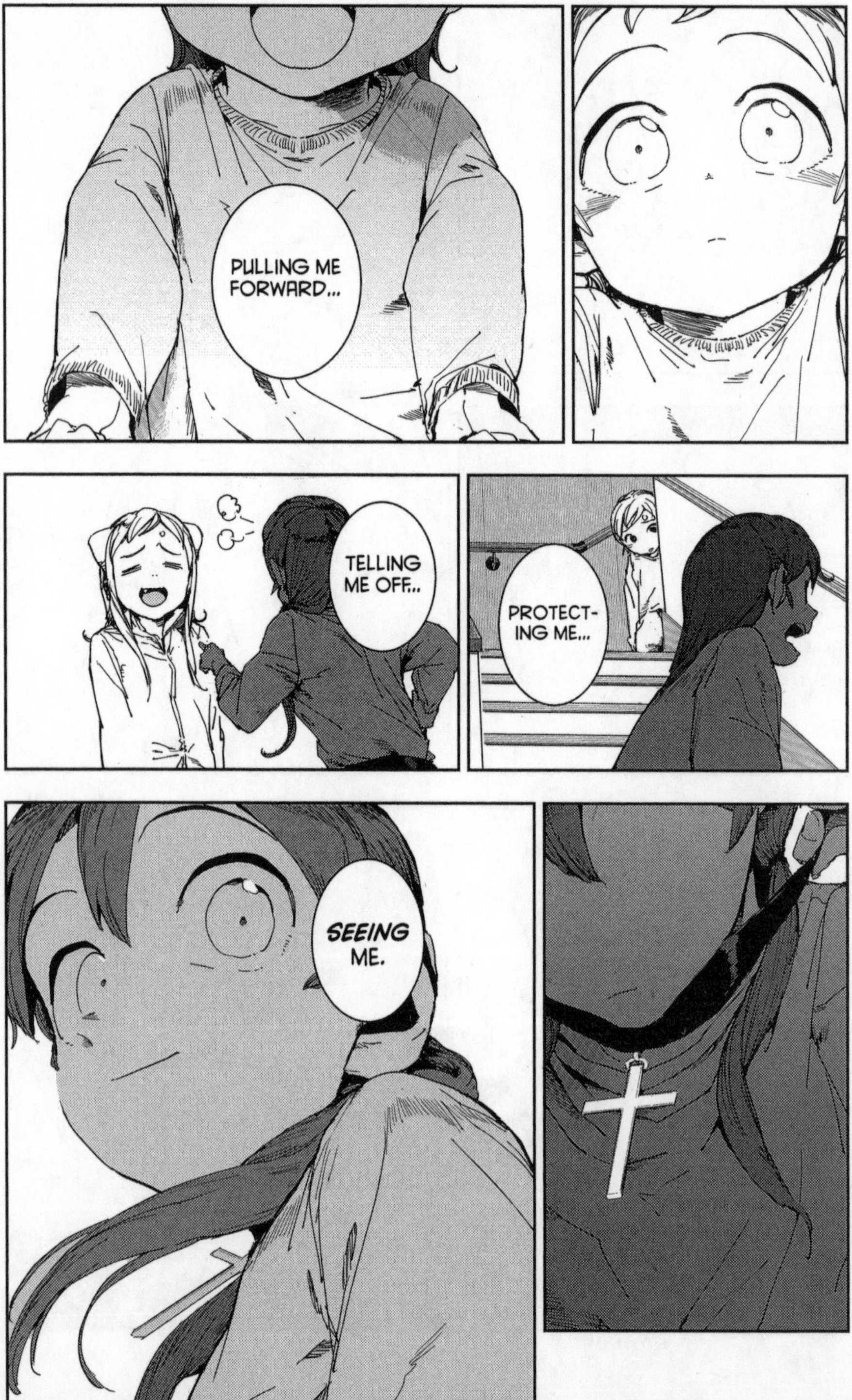
PULLING ME FORWARD...
PROTECTING ME...
TELLING ME OFF...
SEEING ME.

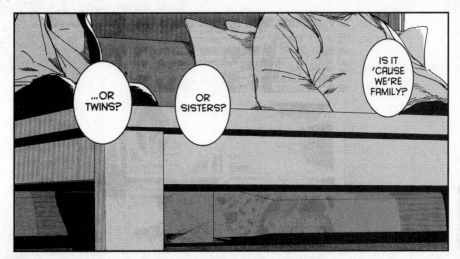

...OR TWINS?

OR SISTERS?

IS IT 'CAUSE WE'RE FAMILY?

OR BE-CAUSE...

...

...I'M A DEMI?

...

THE QUES-TION...

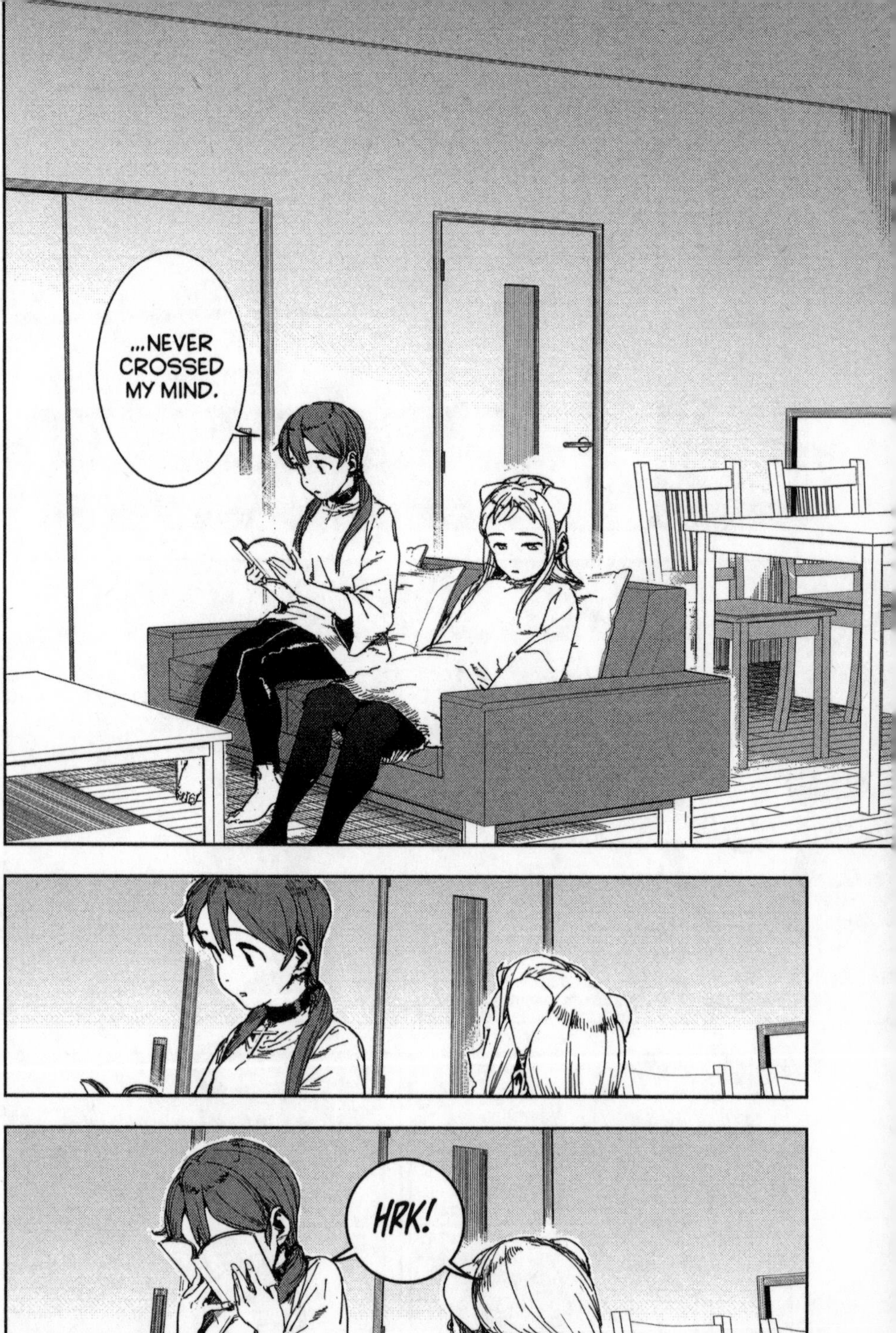
...NEVER CROSSED MY MIND.
HRK!

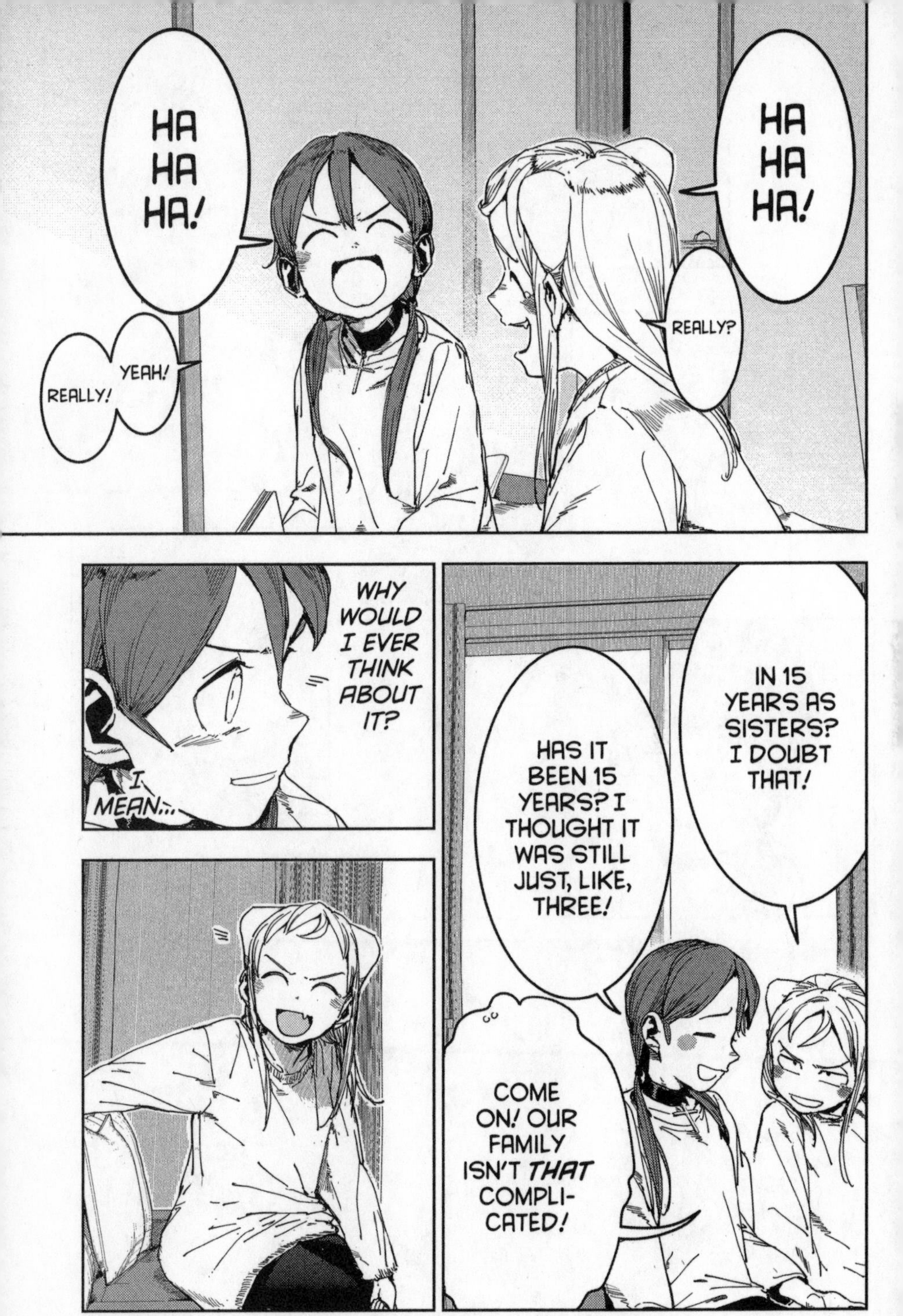
HA HA HA!
REALLY?
HA HA HA!
YEAH! REALLY!
IN 15 YEARS AS SISTERS? I DOUBT THAT!
HAS IT BEEN 15 YEARS? I THOUGHT IT WAS STILL JUST, LIKE, THREE!
COME ON! OUR FAMILY ISN'T *THAT* COMPLICATED!
WHY WOULD I EVER THINK ABOUT IT?
I MEAN...

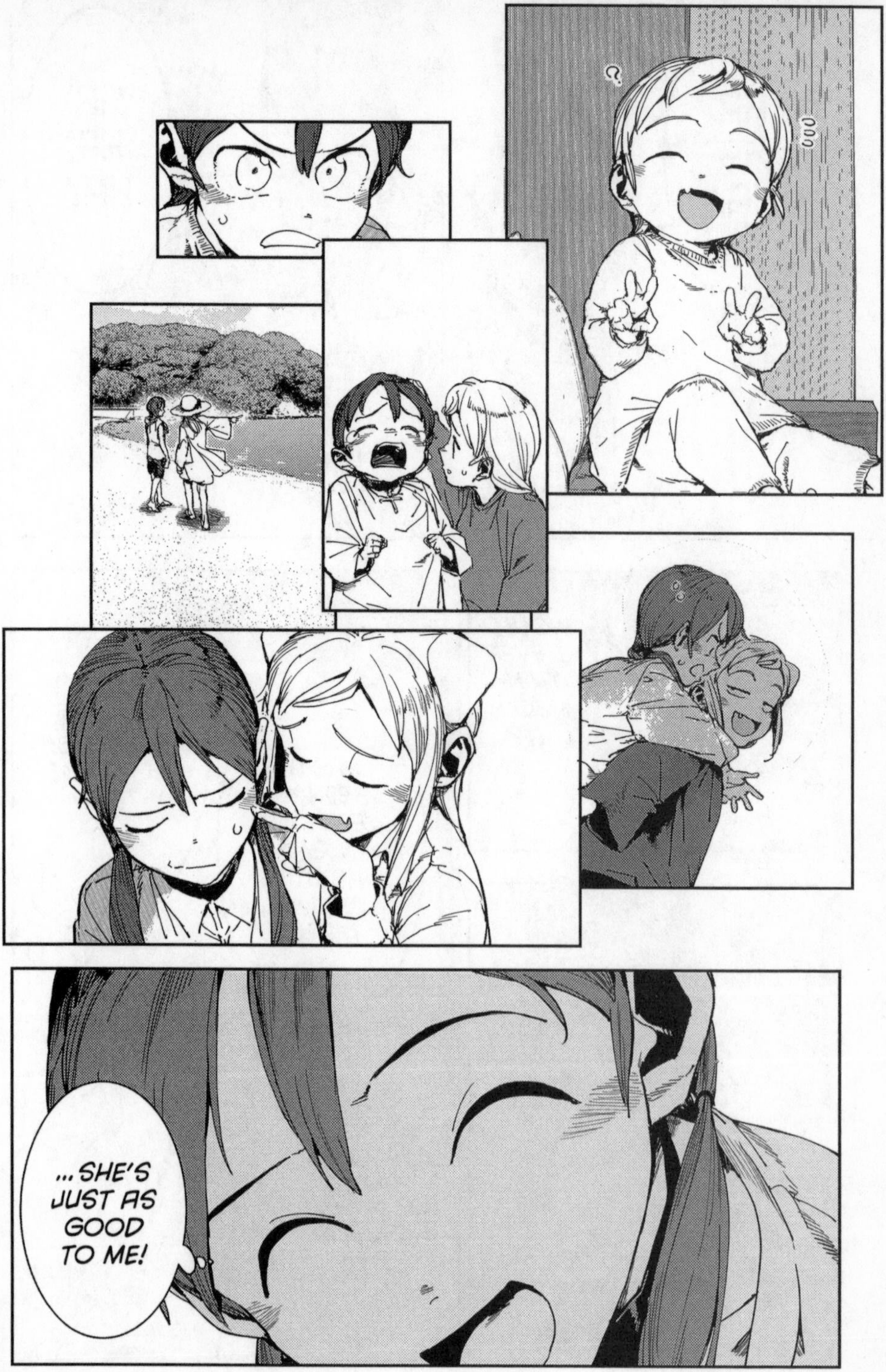
...SHE'S JUST AS GOOD TO ME!

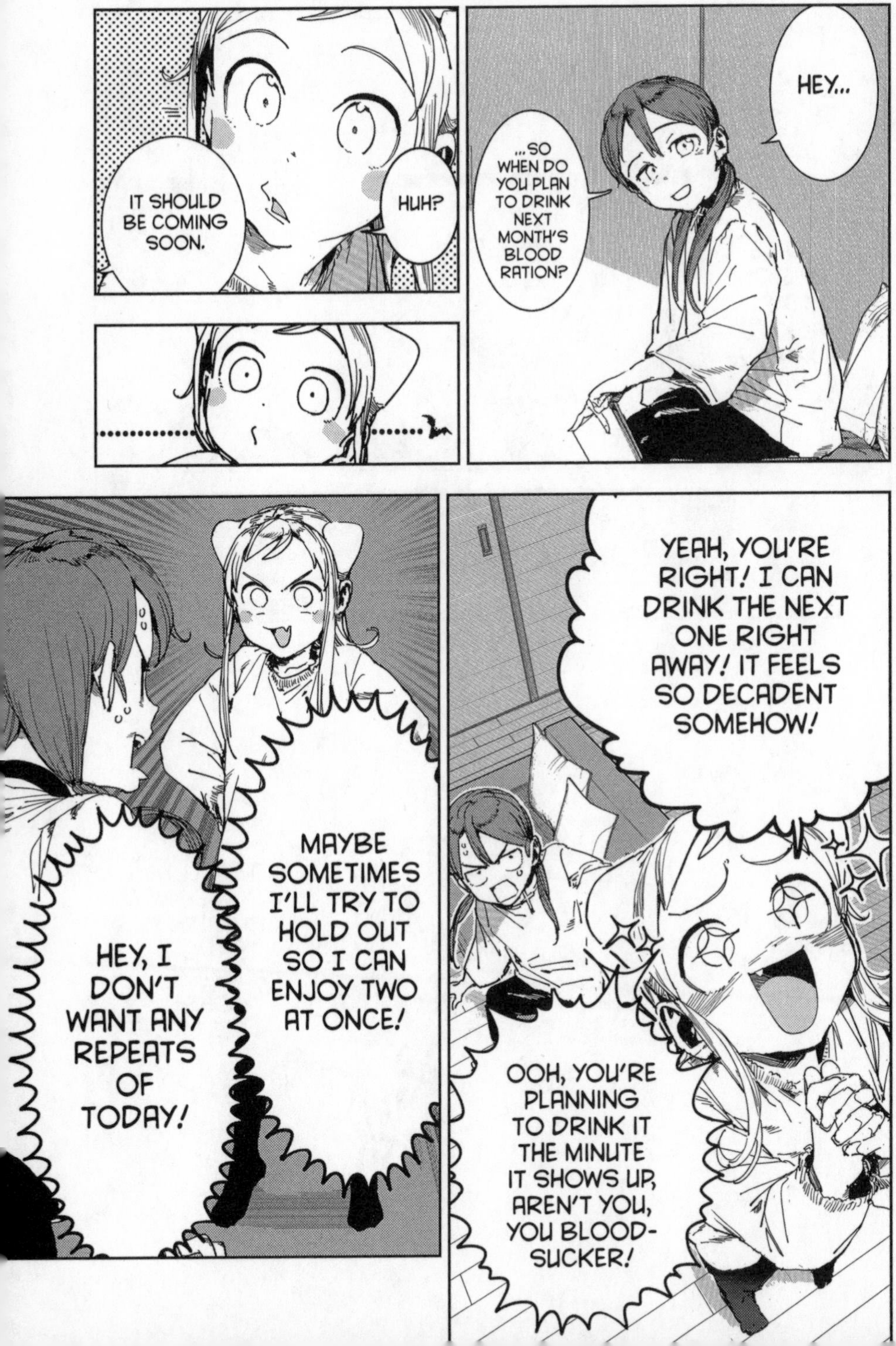
HEY...
...SO WHEN DO YOU PLAN TO DRINK NEXT MONTH'S BLOOD RATION?
HUH?
IT SHOULD BE COMING SOON.
YEAH, YOU'RE RIGHT! I CAN DRINK THE NEXT ONE RIGHT AWAY! IT FEELS SO DECADENT SOMEHOW!
OOH, YOU'RE PLANNING TO DRINK IT THE MINUTE IT SHOWS UP, AREN'T YOU, YOU BLOOD-SUCKER!
MAYBE SOMETIMES I'LL TRY TO HOLD OUT SO I CAN ENJOY TWO AT ONCE!
HEY, I DON'T WANT ANY REPEATS OF TODAY!

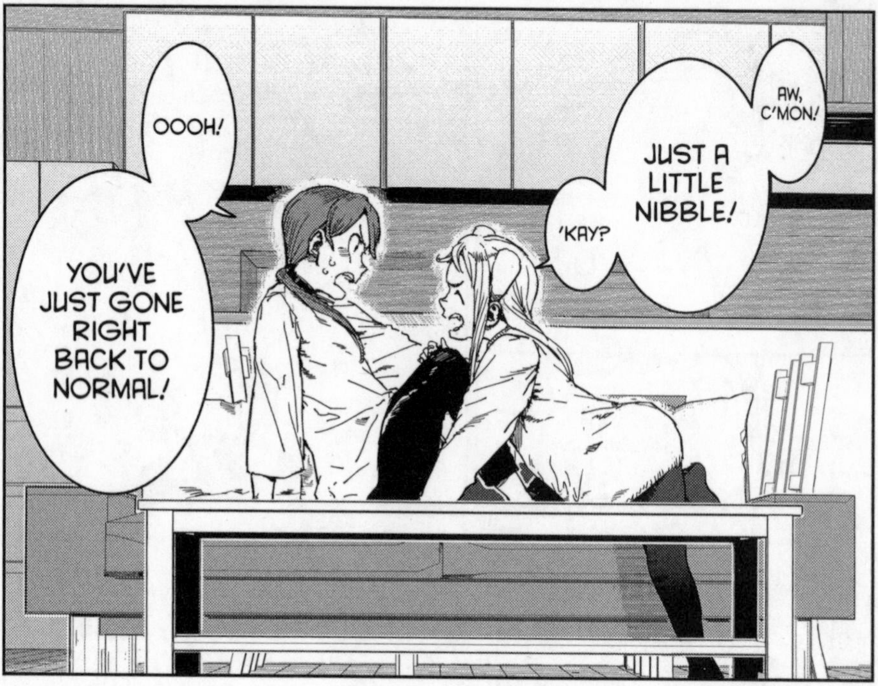
AW, C'MON!
JUST A LITTLE NIBBLE!
'KAY?
OOOH!
YOU'VE JUST GONE RIGHT BACK TO NORMAL!
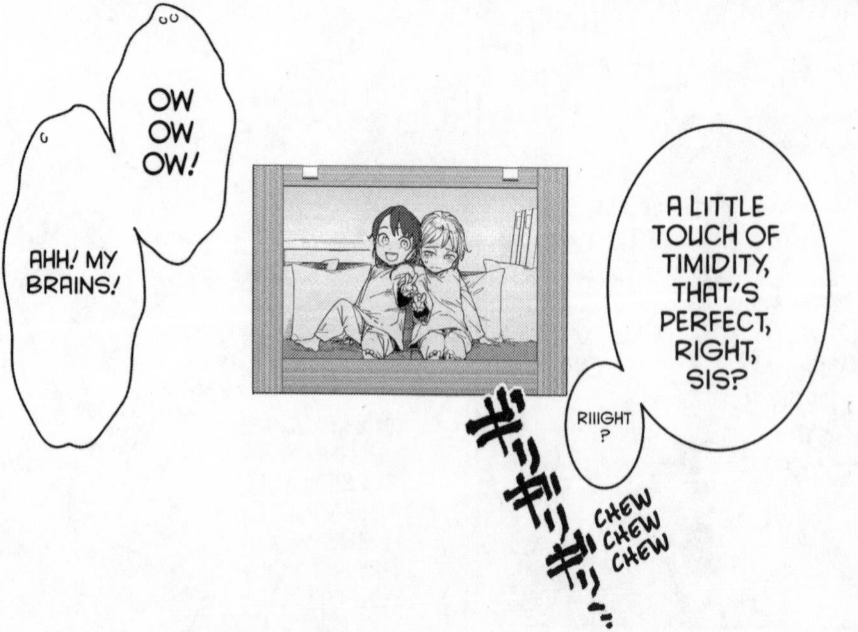
A LITTLE TOUCH OF TIMIDITY, THAT'S PERFECT, RIGHT, SIS?
RIIIGHT?
ギリギリ
CHEW CHEW CHEW
OW OW OW!
AHH! MY BRAINS!

...WHAT'S WITH THE HAIRDO?
I'M A PROUD DEMI NOW, AND I WANT TO STAND OUT! MY HAIR SEEMS LIKE A GREAT WAY!
...
UH... HUH.
UH.
SURE... WHY NOT?
SO! I THOUGHT YOU COULD LEARN HOW TO TIE IT...
WHY ...?
SO YOU CAN HELP ME DO IT UP EVERY MORN-ING!
AND I WOULD DO THAT WHY?!

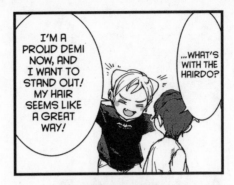

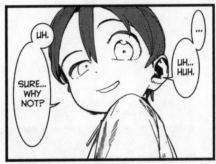

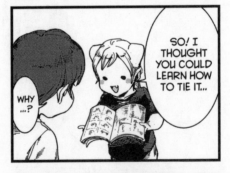

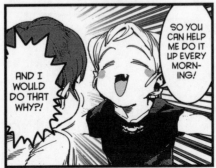

INTERVIEWS WITH MONSTER GIRLS

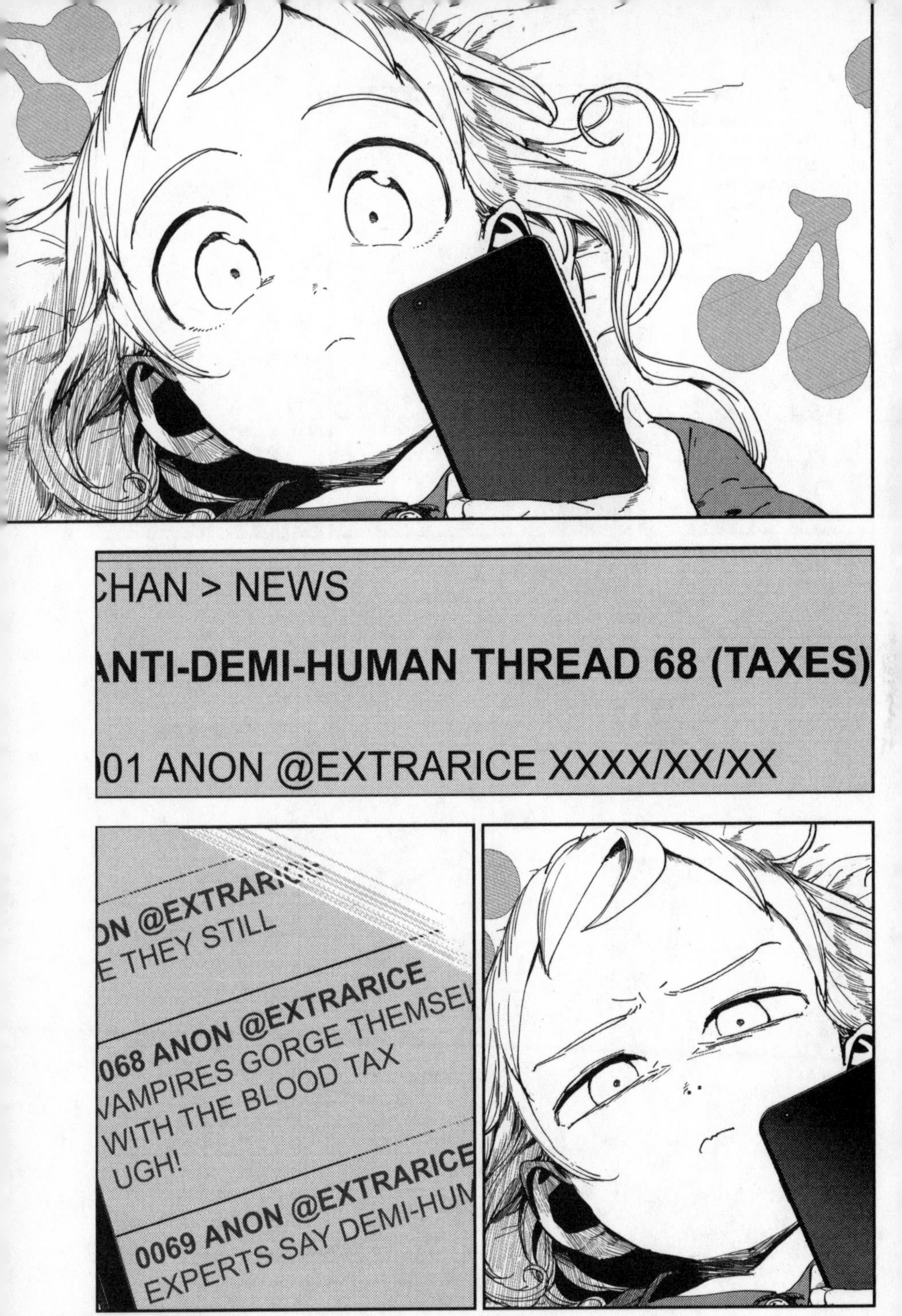
CHAN > NEWS
ANTI-DEMI-HUMAN THREAD 68 (TAXES)
001 ANON @EXTRARICE XXXX/XX/XX
ON @EXTRARICE
E THEY STILL
068 ANON @EXTRARICE
VAMPIRES GORGE THEMSEL
WITH THE BLOOD TAX
UGH!
0069 ANON @EXTRARICE
EXPERTS SAY DEMI-HUM

Chapter 62: I Adore Demi-Humans

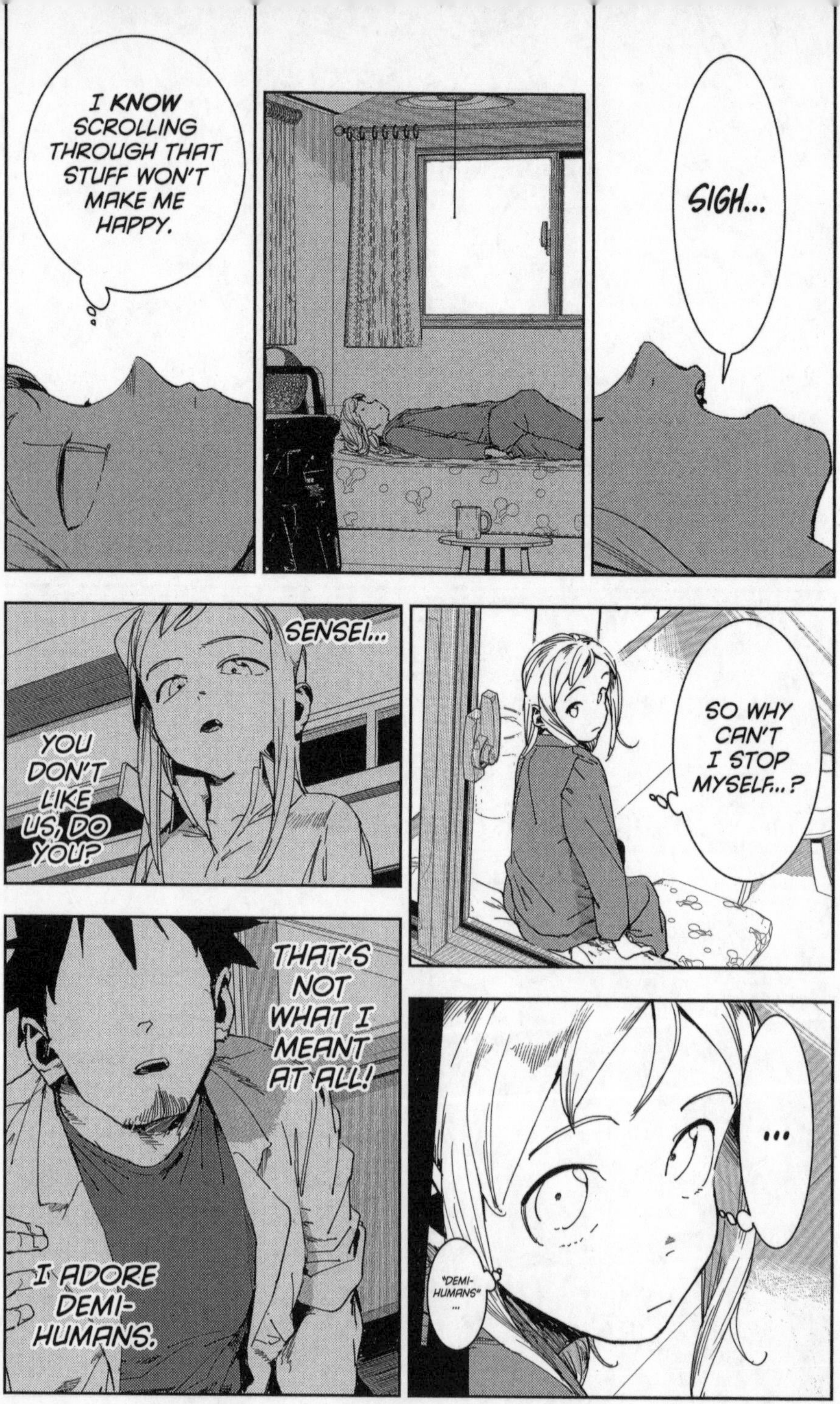
SIGH...
I KNOW SCROLLING THROUGH THAT STUFF WON'T MAKE ME HAPPY.
SO WHY CAN'T I STOP MYSELF...?
SENSEI...
YOU DON'T LIKE US, DO YOU?
...
"DEMI-HUMANS" ...
THAT'S NOT WHAT I MEANT AT ALL!
I ADORE DEMI-HUMANS.

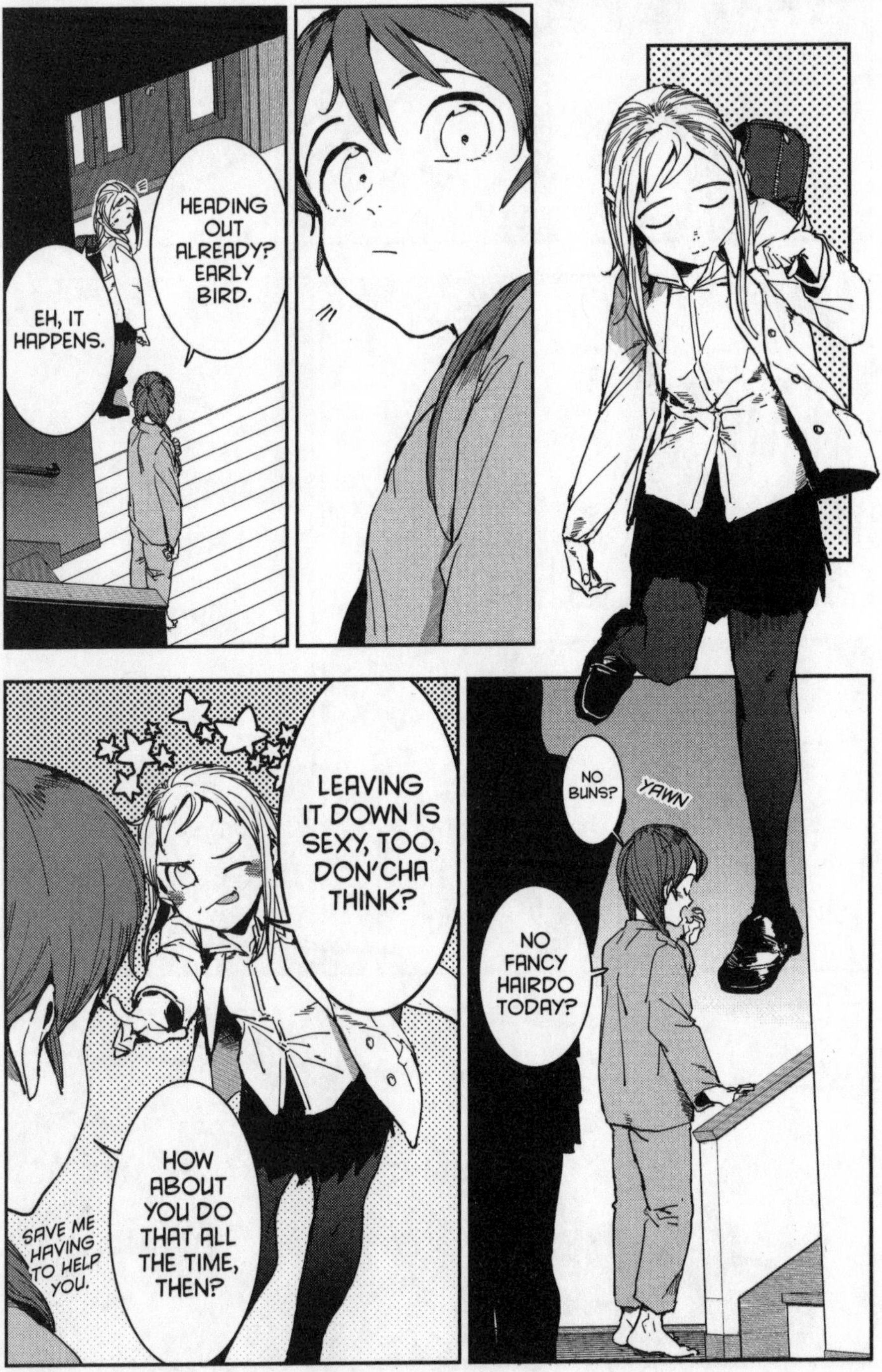
HEADING OUT ALREADY? EARLY BIRD.
EH, IT HAPPENS.
NO BUNS?
YAWN
NO FANCY HAIRDO TODAY?
LEAVING IT DOWN IS SEXY, TOO, DON'CHA THINK?
HOW ABOUT YOU DO THAT ALL THE TIME, THEN?
SAVE ME HAVING TO HELP YOU.

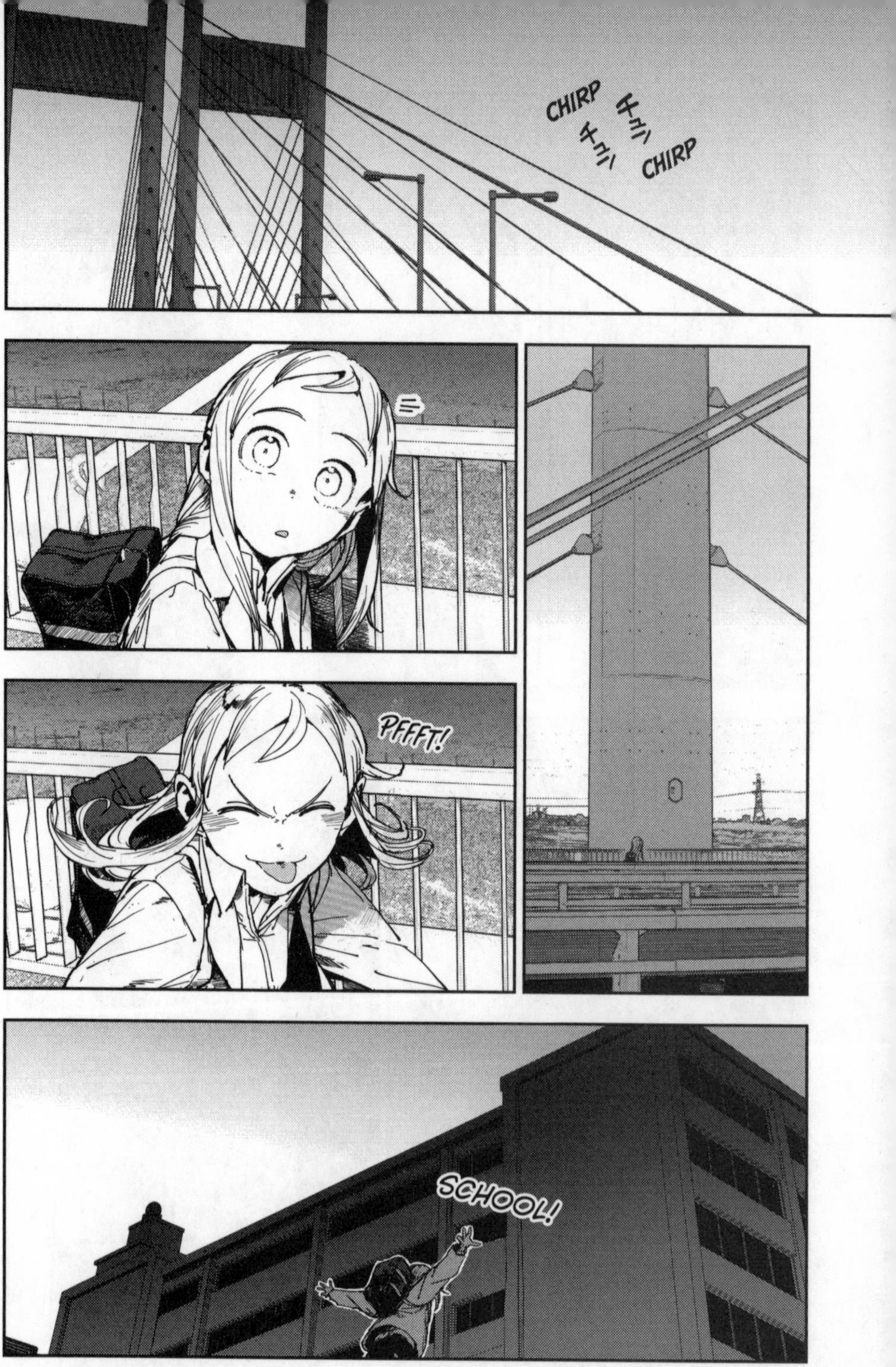
CHIRP
チュン
チュン
CHIRP
PFFFT!
SCHOOL!

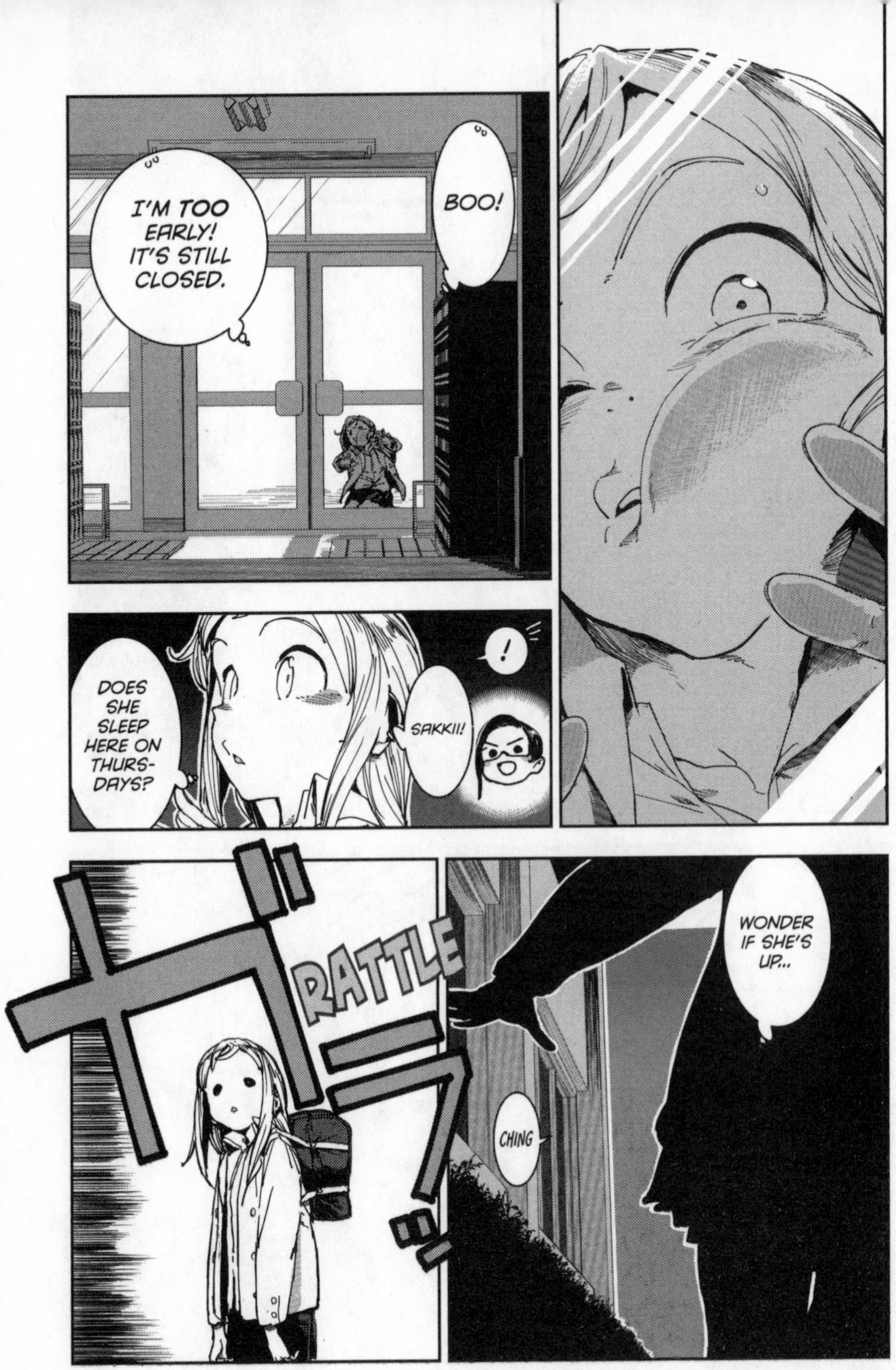
BOO!
I'M TOO EARLY! IT'S STILL CLOSED.
!
SAKKII!
DOES SHE SLEEP HERE ON THURS-DAYS?
WONDER IF SHE'S UP...
CHING
RATTLE

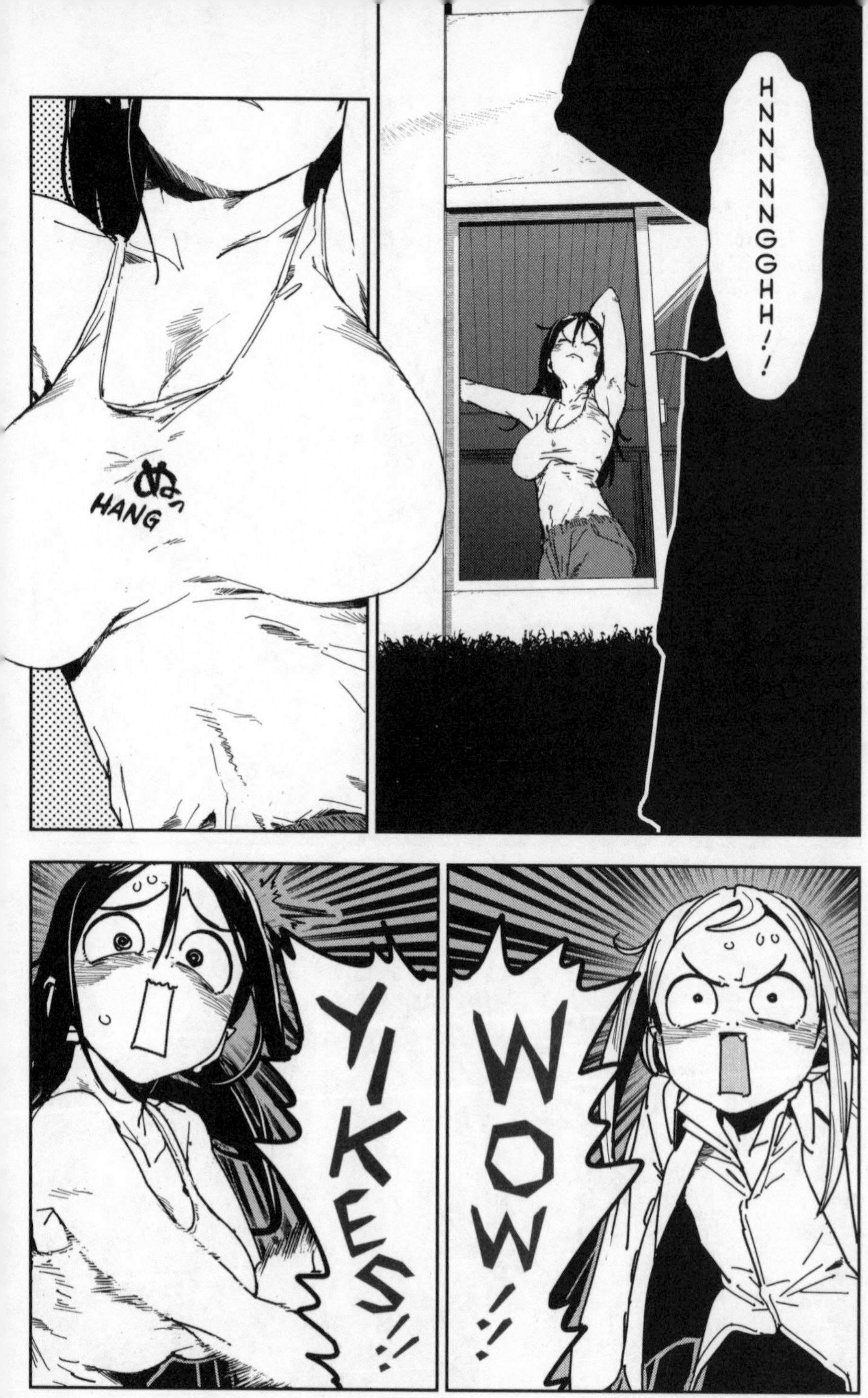
HNNNNNGGHH!!
HANG
WOW!!
YIKES!!

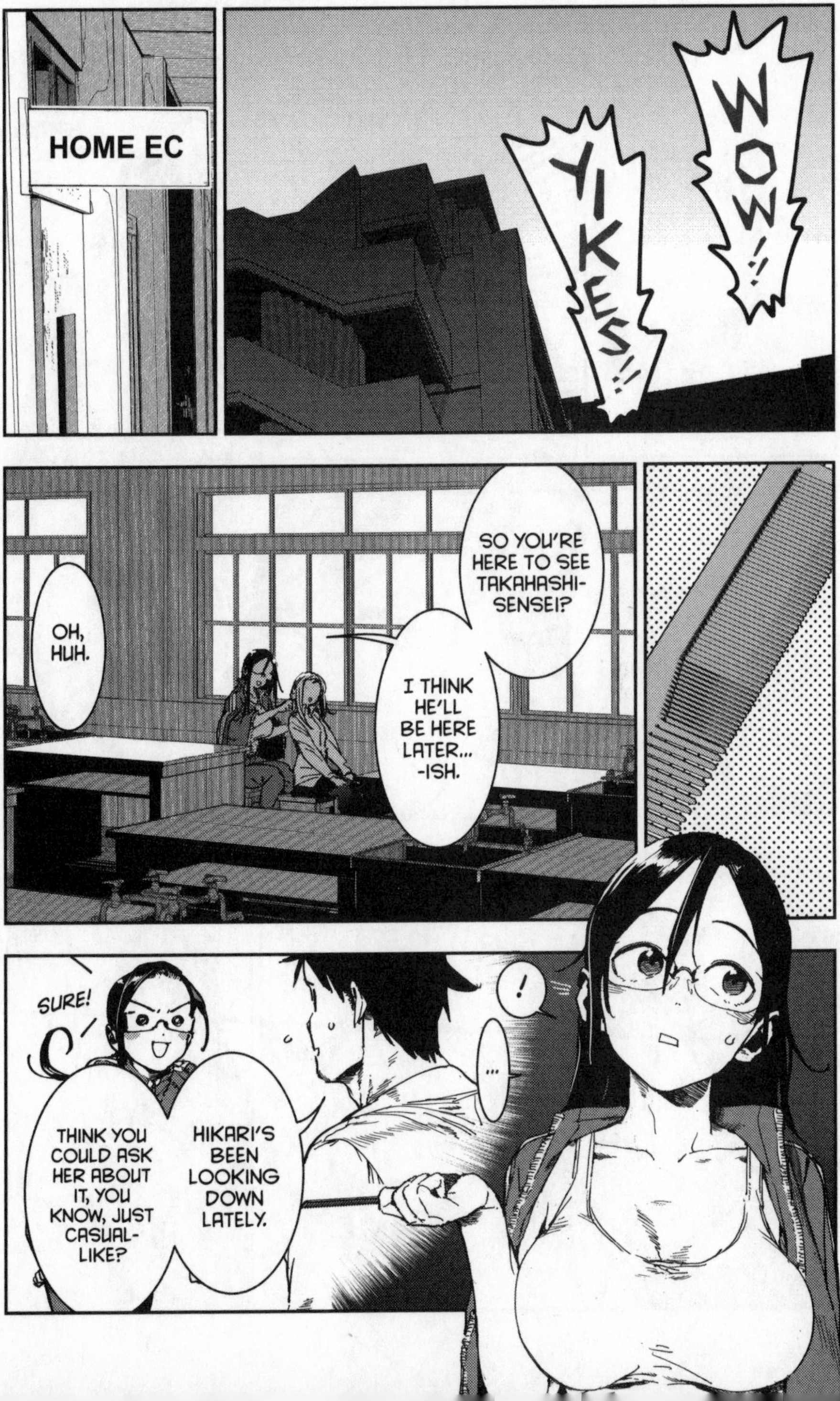
WOW!!
YIKES!!
HOME EC
SO YOU'RE HERE TO SEE TAKAHASHI-SENSEI?
I THINK HE'LL BE HERE LATER... -ISH.
OH, HUH.
!
...
HIKARI'S BEEN LOOKING DOWN LATELY.
THINK YOU COULD ASK HER ABOUT IT, YOU KNOW, JUST CASUAL-LIKE?
SURE!

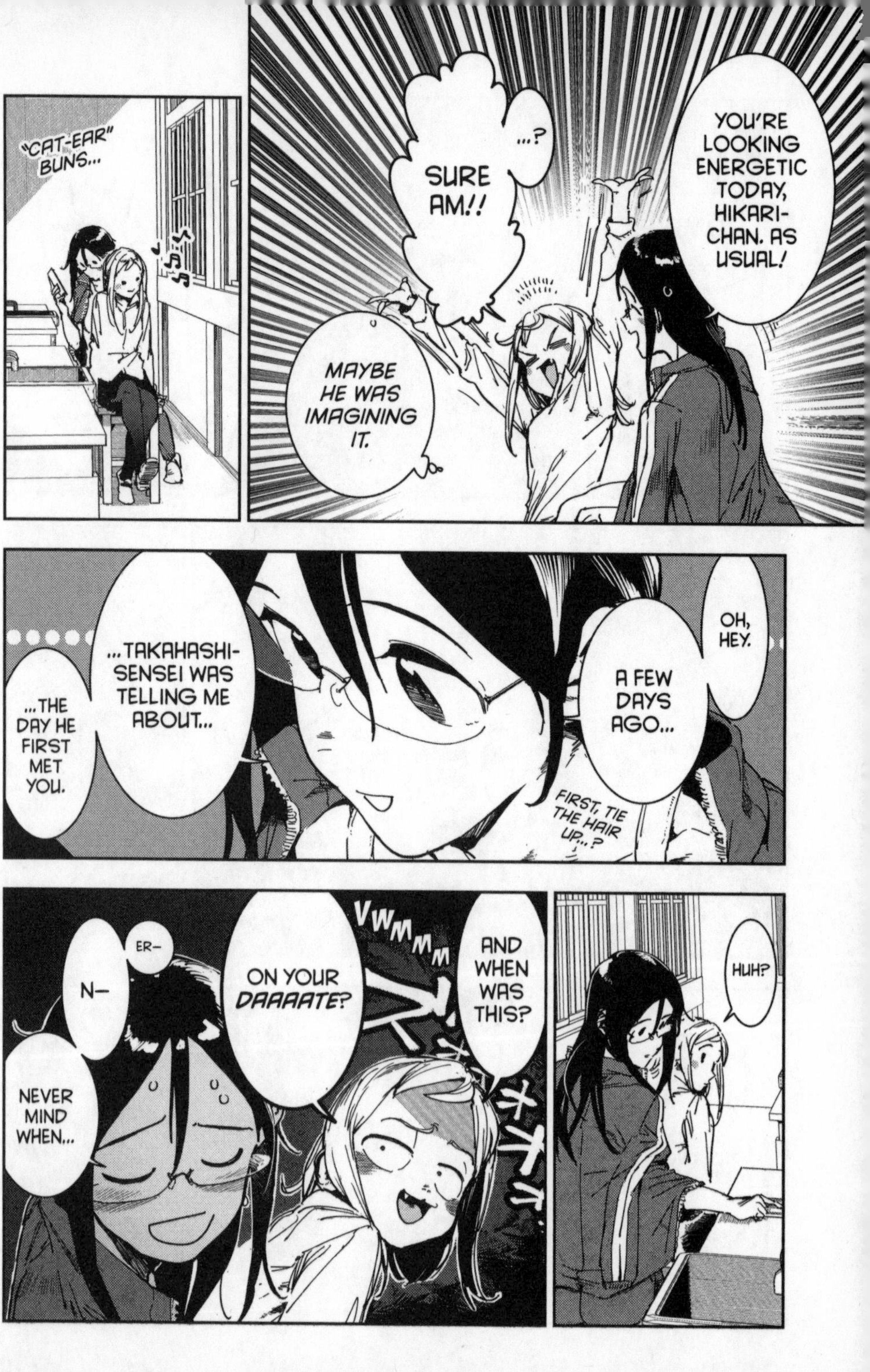
YOU'RE LOOKING ENERGETIC TODAY, HIKARI-CHAN. AS USUAL!
SURE AM!!
...?
MAYBE HE WAS IMAGINING IT.
"CAT-EAR" BUNS...
OH, HEY.
A FEW DAYS AGO...
FIRST, TIE THE HAIR UP...?
...TAKAHASHI-SENSEI WAS TELLING ME ABOUT...
...THE DAY HE FIRST MET YOU.
HUH?
AND WHEN WAS THIS?
VWMMM
ON YOUR DAAAATE?
ER-
N-
NEVER MIND WHEN...

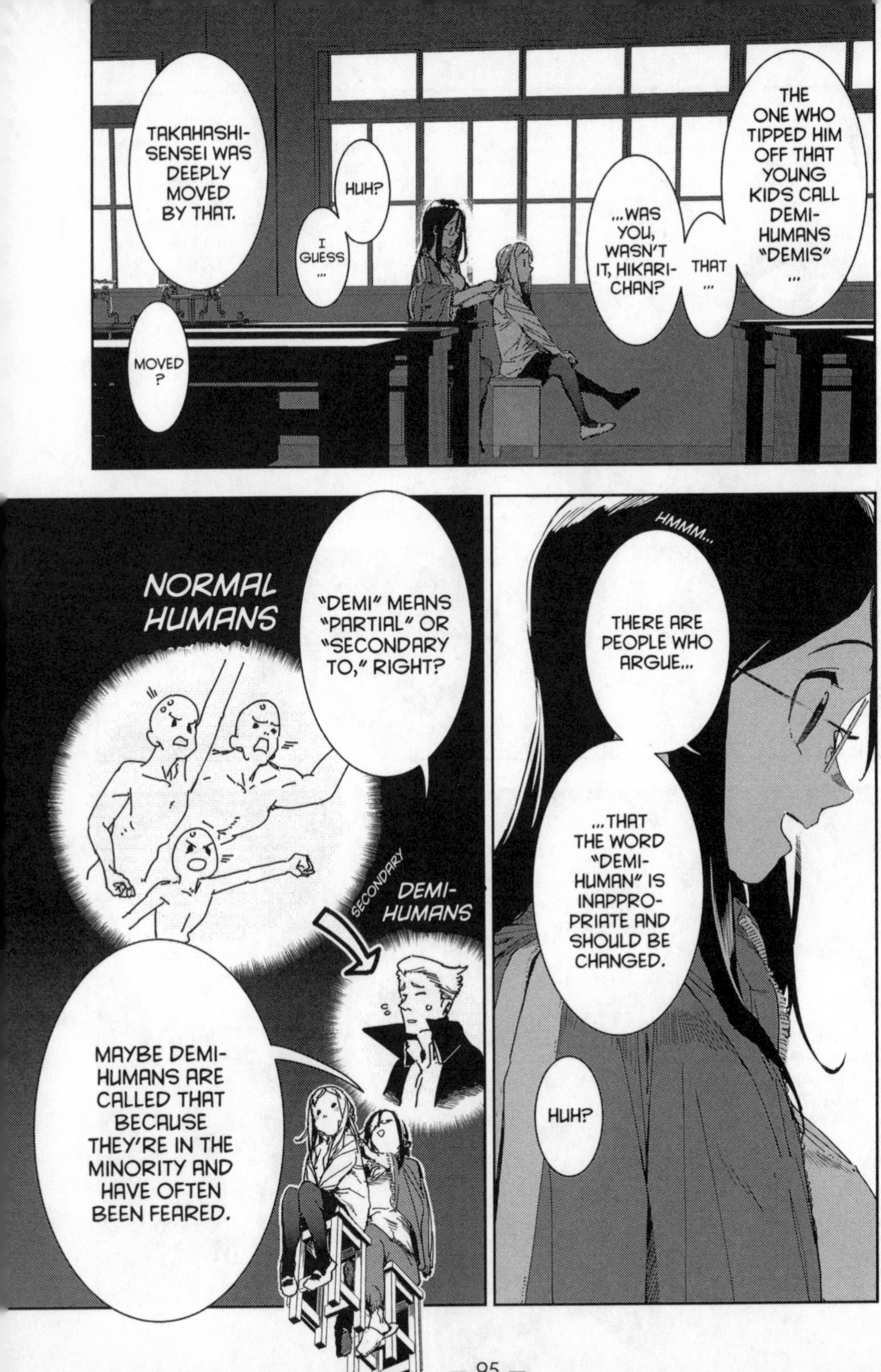
THE ONE WHO TIPPED HIM OFF THAT YOUNG KIDS CALL DEMI-HUMANS "DEMIS"...
THAT...
...WAS YOU, WASN'T IT, HIKARI-CHAN?
HUH?
I GUESS...
TAKAHASHI-SENSEI WAS DEEPLY MOVED BY THAT.
MOVED?
HMMM...
THERE ARE PEOPLE WHO ARGUE...
...THAT THE WORD "DEMI-HUMAN" IS INAPPROPRIATE AND SHOULD BE CHANGED.
HUH?
"DEMI" MEANS "PARTIAL" OR "SECONDARY TO," RIGHT?
NORMAL HUMANS
SECONDARY
DEMI-HUMANS
MAYBE DEMI-HUMANS ARE CALLED THAT BECAUSE THEY'RE IN THE MINORITY AND HAVE OFTEN BEEN FEARED.

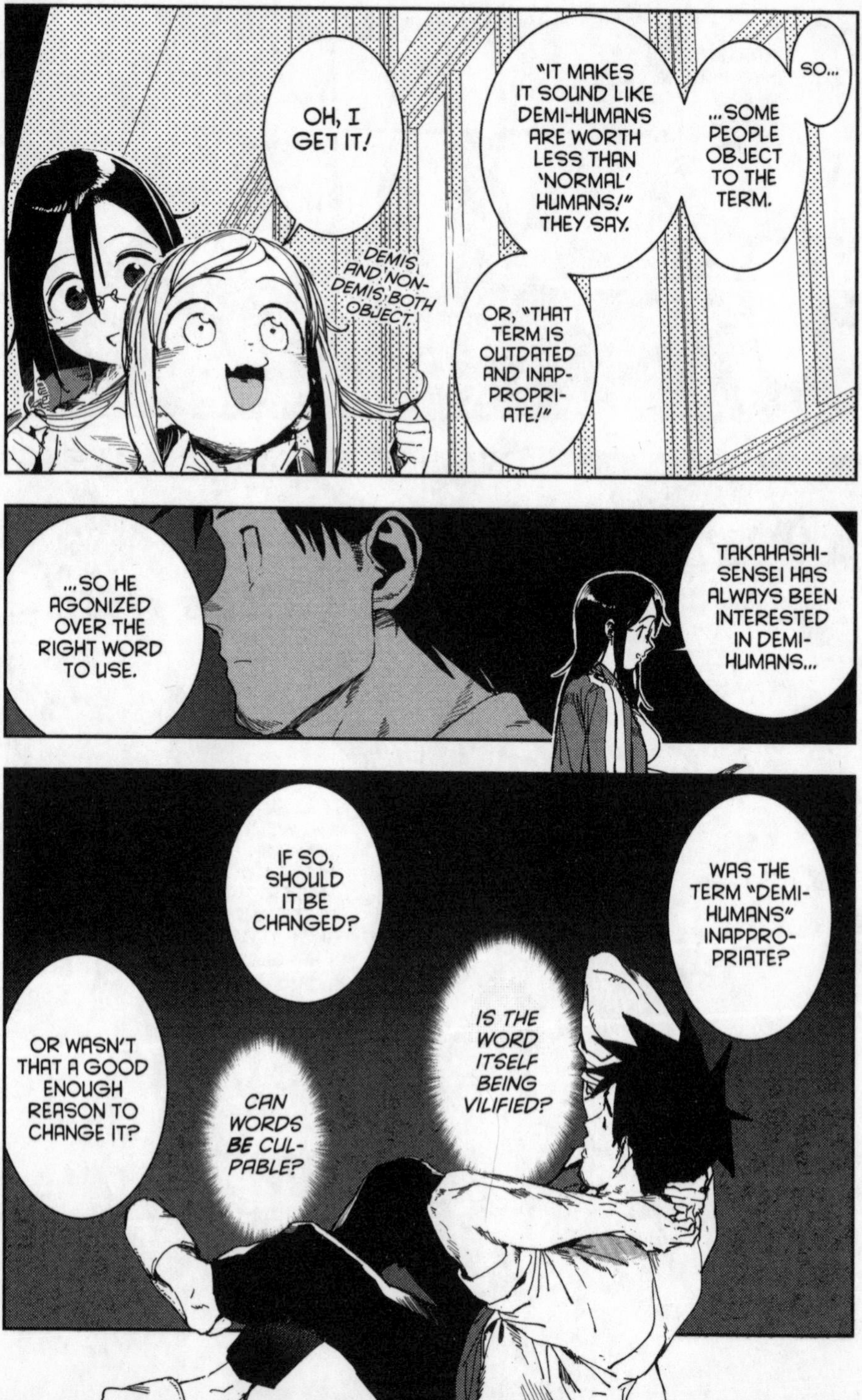

SO...
...SOME PEOPLE OBJECT TO THE TERM.
“IT MAKES IT SOUND LIKE DEMI-HUMANS ARE WORTH LESS THAN ‘NORMAL’ HUMANS!” THEY SAY.
OR, “THAT TERM IS OUTDATED AND INAPPROPRIATE!”
OH, I GET IT!
DEMIS AND NON-DEMIS BOTH OBJECT.
TAKAHASHI-SENSEI HAS ALWAYS BEEN INTERESTED IN DEMI-HUMANS...
...SO HE AGONIZED OVER THE RIGHT WORD TO USE.
WAS THE TERM “DEMI-HUMANS” INAPPROPRIATE?
IF SO, SHOULD IT BE CHANGED?
IS THE WORD ITSELF BEING VILIFIED?
CAN WORDS BE CULPABLE?
OR WASN'T THAT A GOOD ENOUGH REASON TO CHANGE IT?

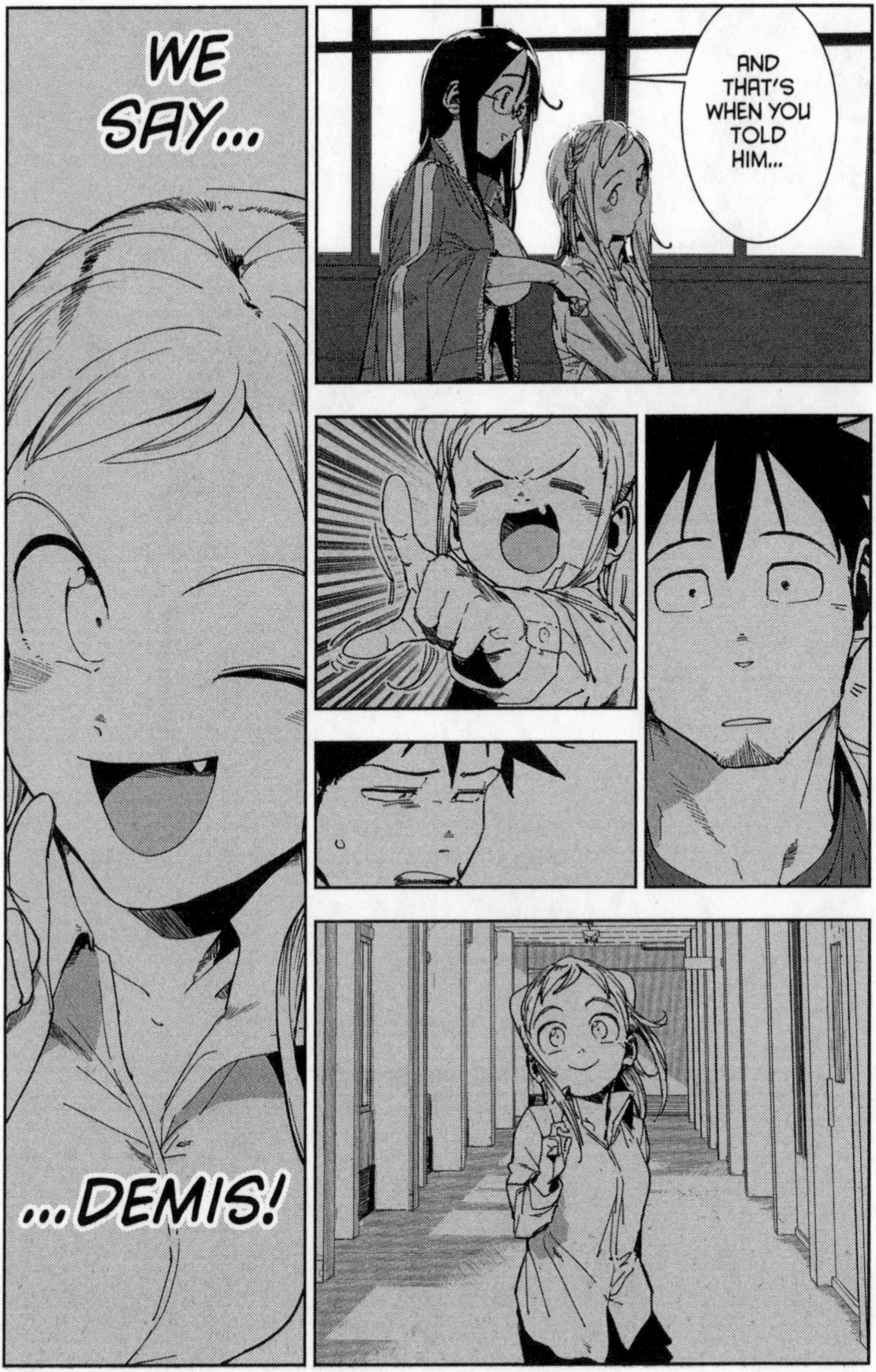
AND THAT'S WHEN YOU TOLD HIM...
WE SAY...
...DEMIS!

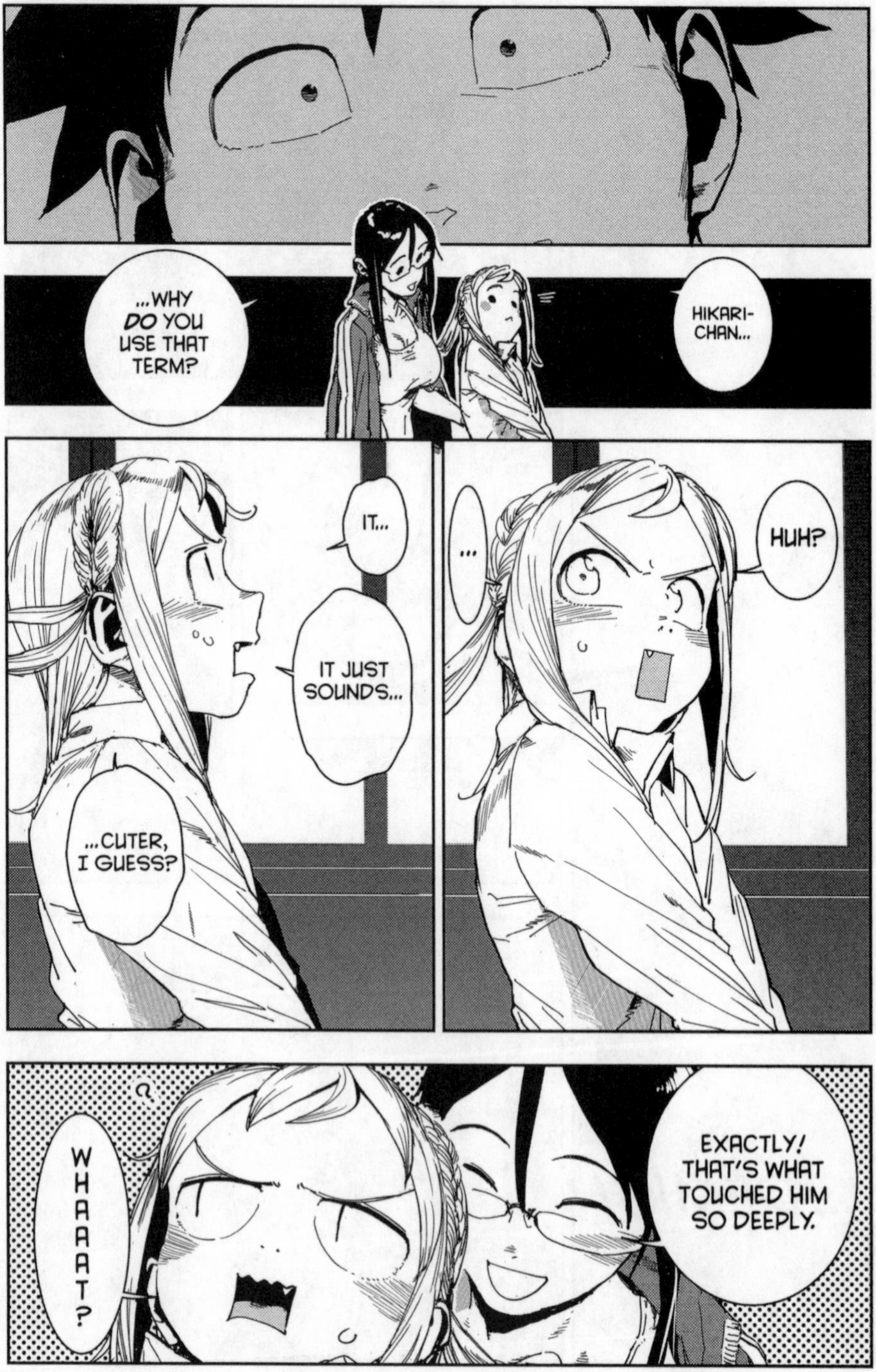
HIKARI-CHAN...
...WHY DO YOU USE THAT TERM?
HUH?
...
IT...
IT JUST SOUNDS...
...CUTER, I GUESS?
EXACTLY! THAT'S WHAT TOUCHED HIM SO DEEPLY.
WHAAAT?

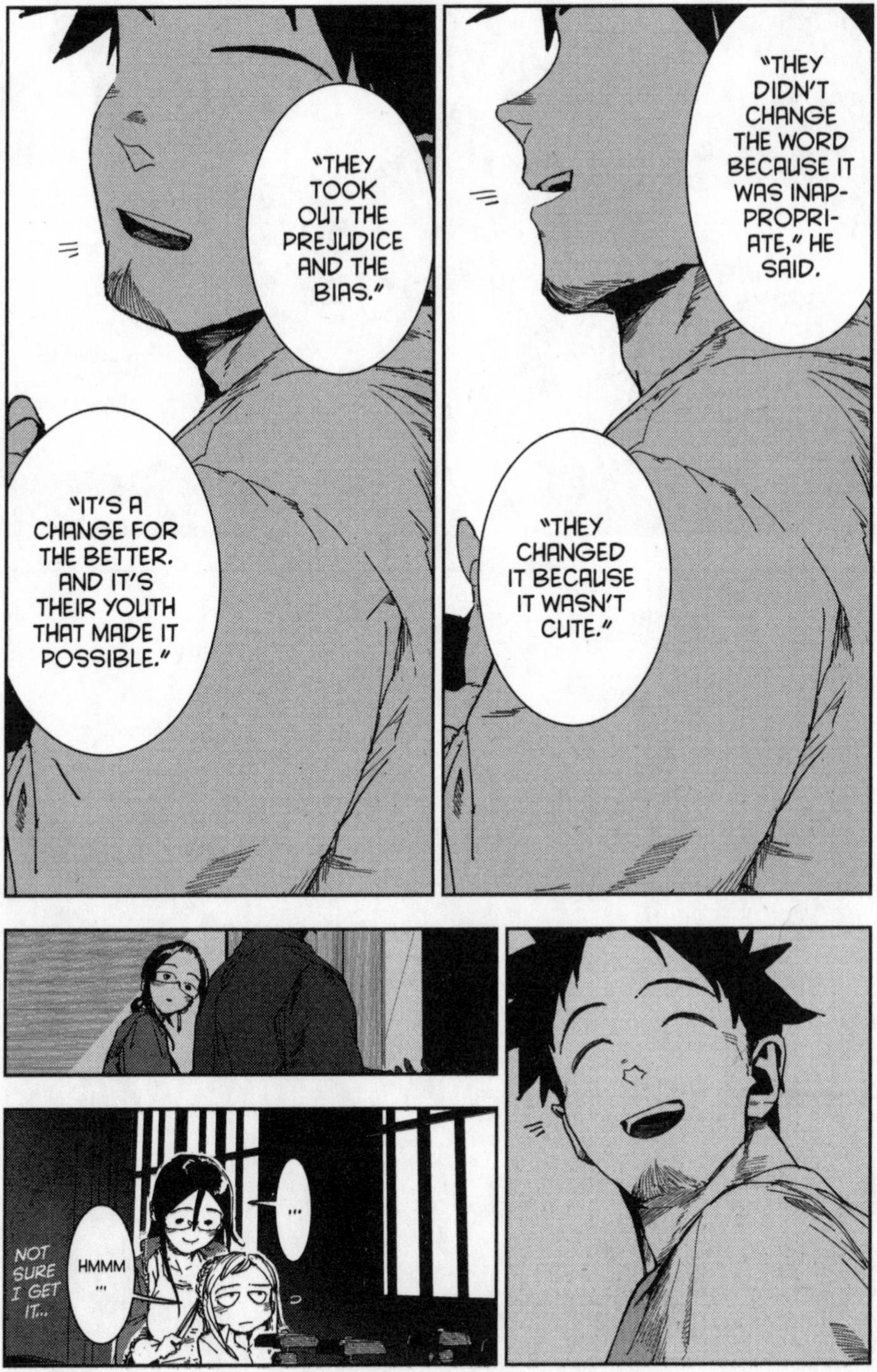
"THEY DIDN'T CHANGE THE WORD BECAUSE IT WAS INAP-PROPRI-ATE," HE SAID.
"THEY CHANGED IT BECAUSE IT WASN'T CUTE."
"THEY TOOK OUT THE PREJUDICE AND THE BIAS."
"IT'S A CHANGE FOR THE BETTER. AND IT'S THEIR YOUTH THAT MADE IT POSSIBLE."
...
HMMM ...
NOT SURE I GET IT...

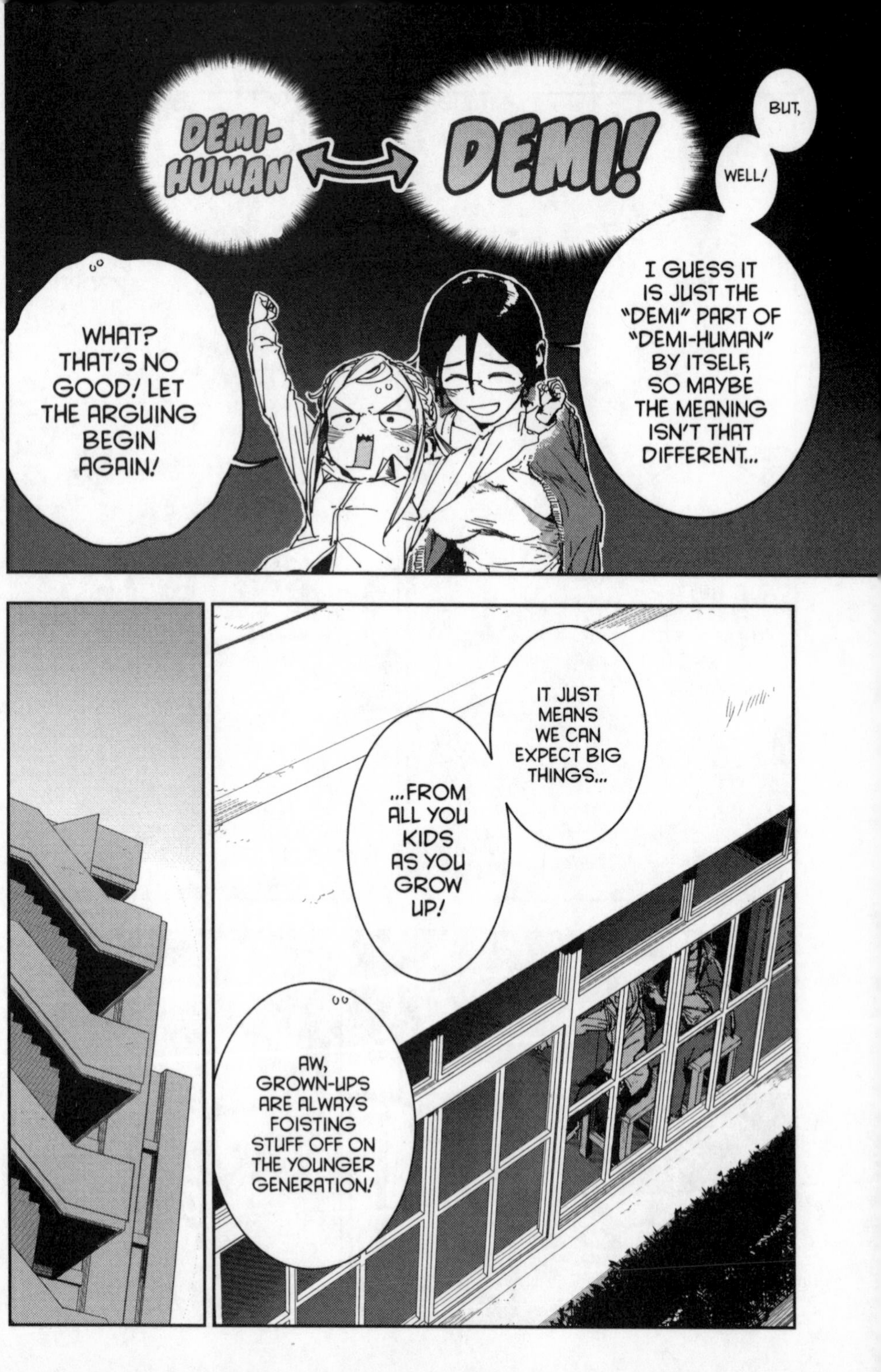
BUT,
WELL!
DEMI-HUMAN
DEMI!
I GUESS IT IS JUST THE "DEMI" PART OF "DEMI-HUMAN" BY ITSELF, SO MAYBE THE MEANING ISN'T THAT DIFFERENT...
WHAT? THAT'S NO GOOD! LET THE ARGUING BEGIN AGAIN!
IT JUST MEANS WE CAN EXPECT BIG THINGS...
...FROM ALL YOU KIDS AS YOU GROW UP!
AW, GROWN-UPS ARE ALWAYS FOISTING STUFF OFF ON THE YOUNGER GENERATION!

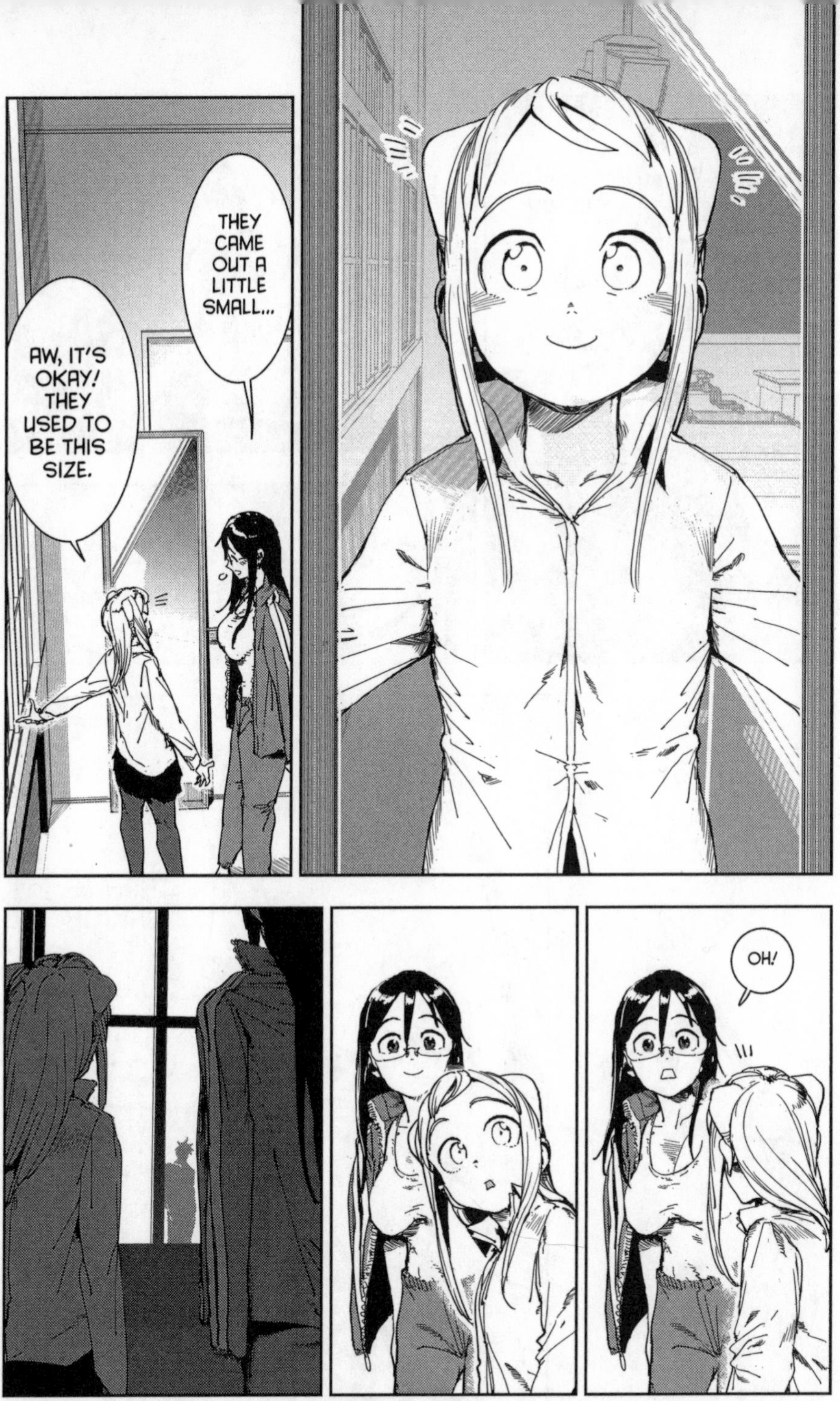
THEY CAME OUT A LITTLE SMALL...
AW, IT'S OKAY! THEY USED TO BE THIS SIZE.
OH!

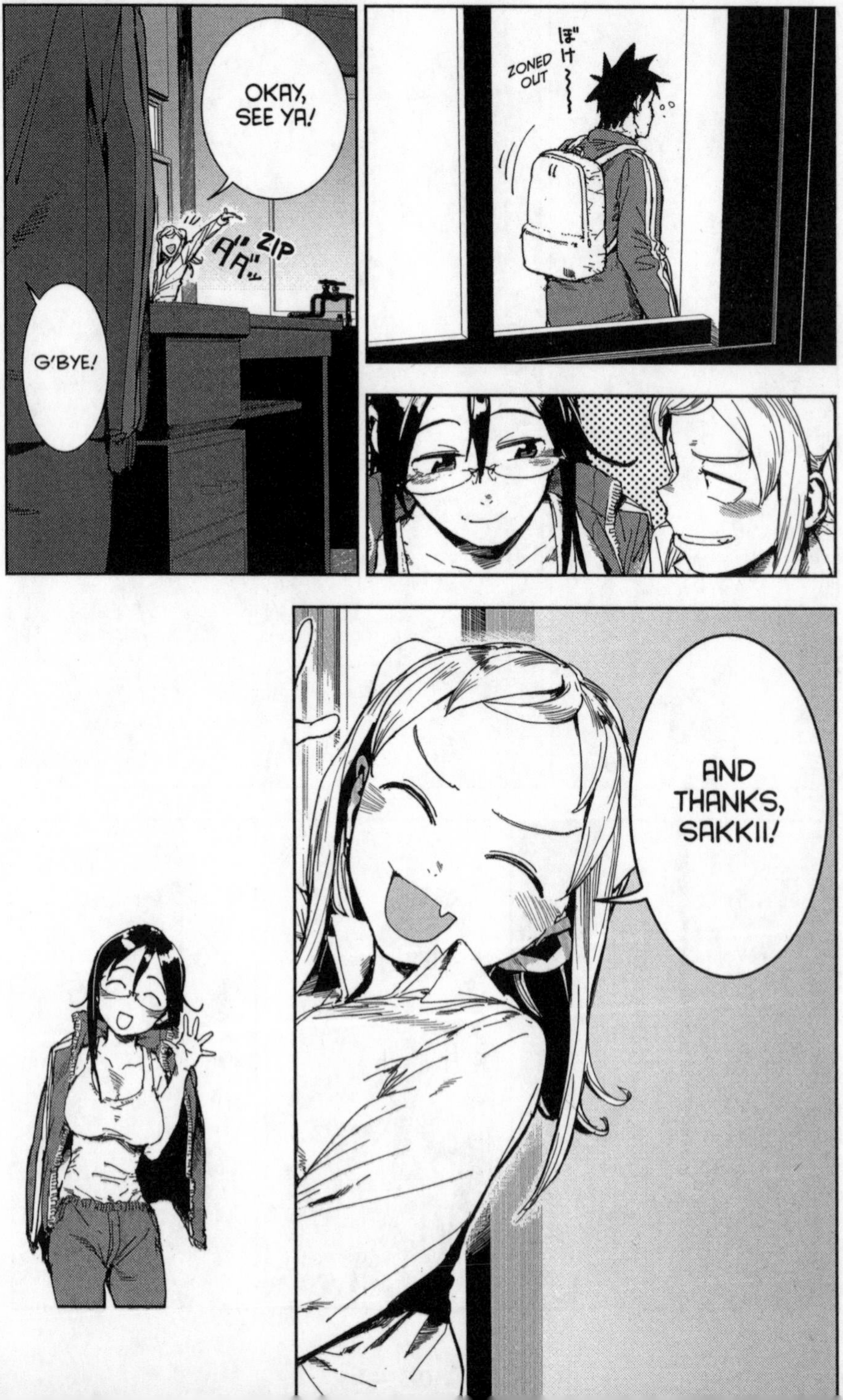
ぼけ〜〜
ZONED OUT
OKAY, SEE YA!
ダダッ
ZIP
G'BYE!
AND THANKS, SAKKII!

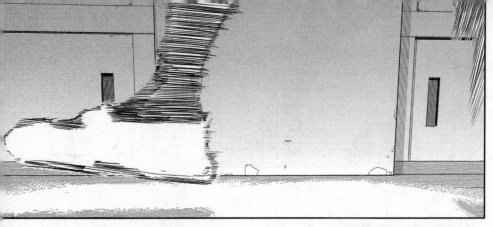

I KNOW SENSEI'S INTERESTED IN DEMIS.

THAT HE REALLY TRIES TO UNDERSTAND US.

BUT I CAN'T HELP WONDERING...

...WHY?

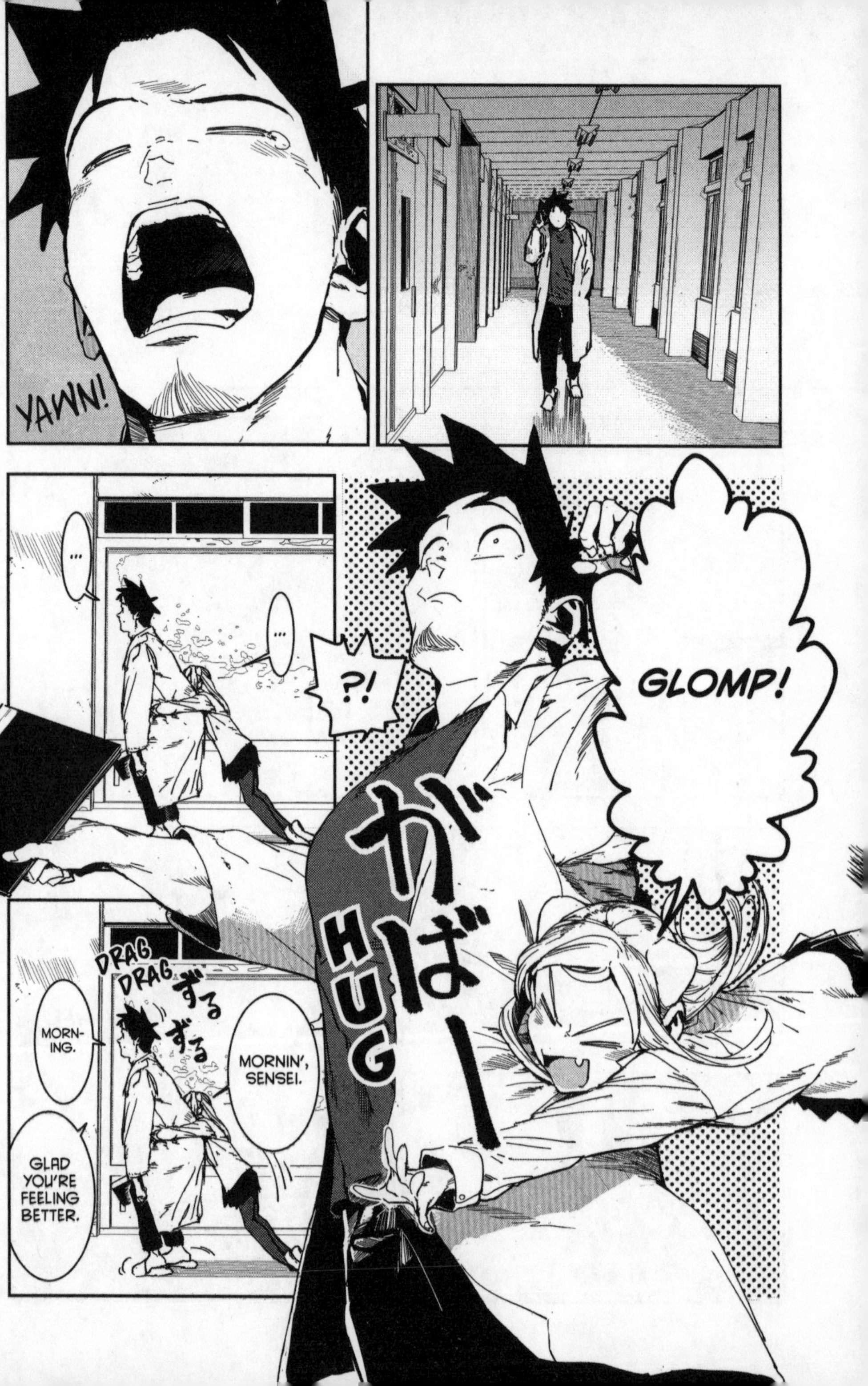
YAWN!
GLOMP!
?!
がばー
HUG
...
...
DRAG DRAG
ずる ずる
MORNIN', SENSEI.
MORN-ING.
GLAD YOU'RE FEELING BETTER.

HEY, SENSEI...

HM?

DRAG DRAG

...

BACK WHEN WE MET, YOU SAID...

...YOU ADORE DEMI-HUMANS, RIGHT?

HUH?

WHY?

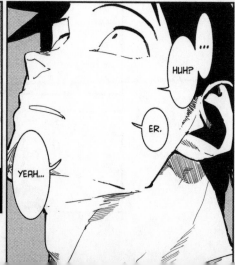

...

HUH?

ER.

YEAH...

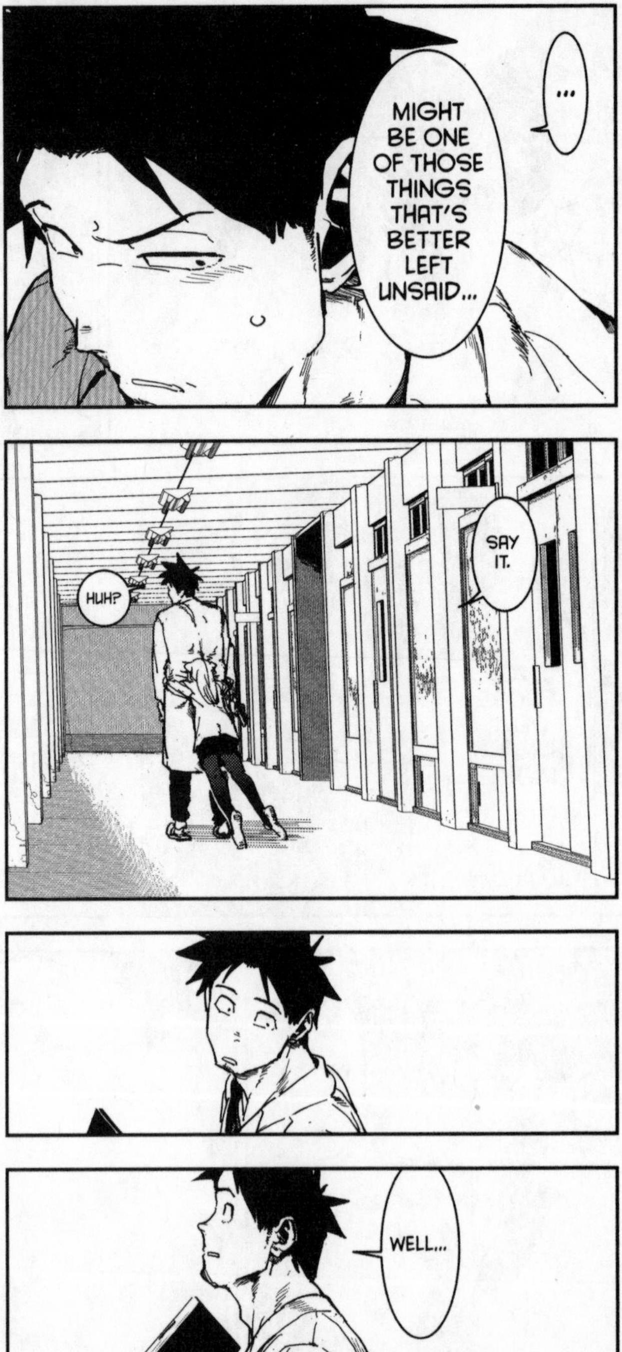
...
MIGHT BE ONE OF THOSE THINGS THAT'S BETTER LEFT UNSAID...
SAY IT.
HUH?
WELL...

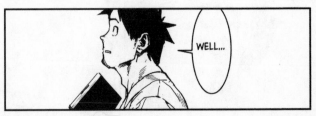

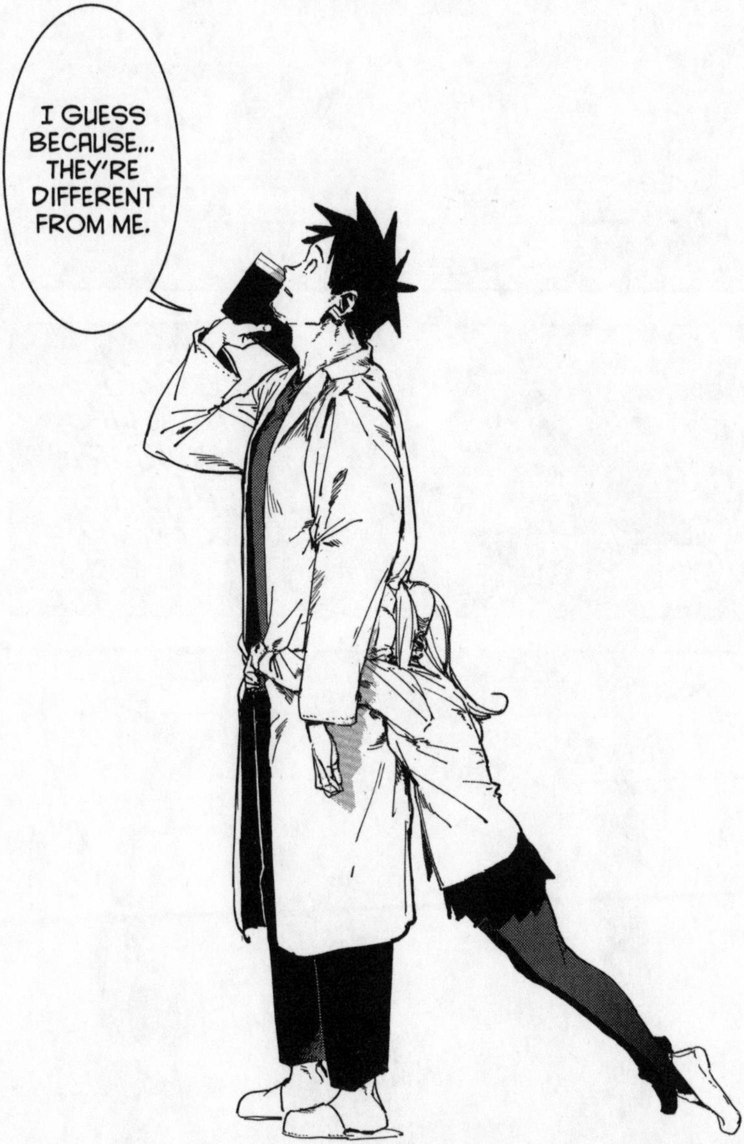
I GUESS BECAUSE... THEY'RE DIFFERENT FROM ME.

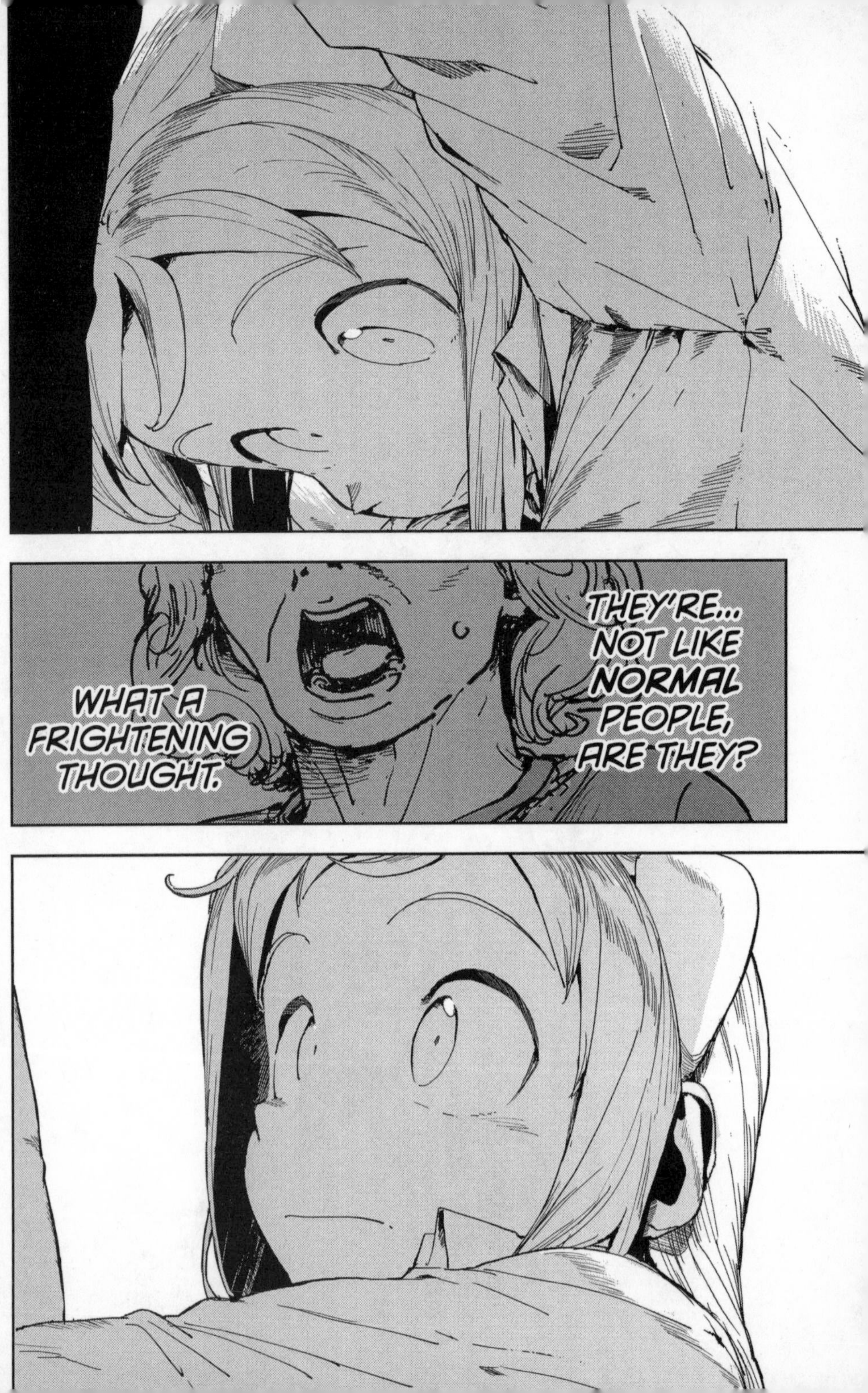
THEY'RE... NOT LIKE NORMAL PEOPLE, ARE THEY?
WHAT A FRIGHTENING THOUGHT.

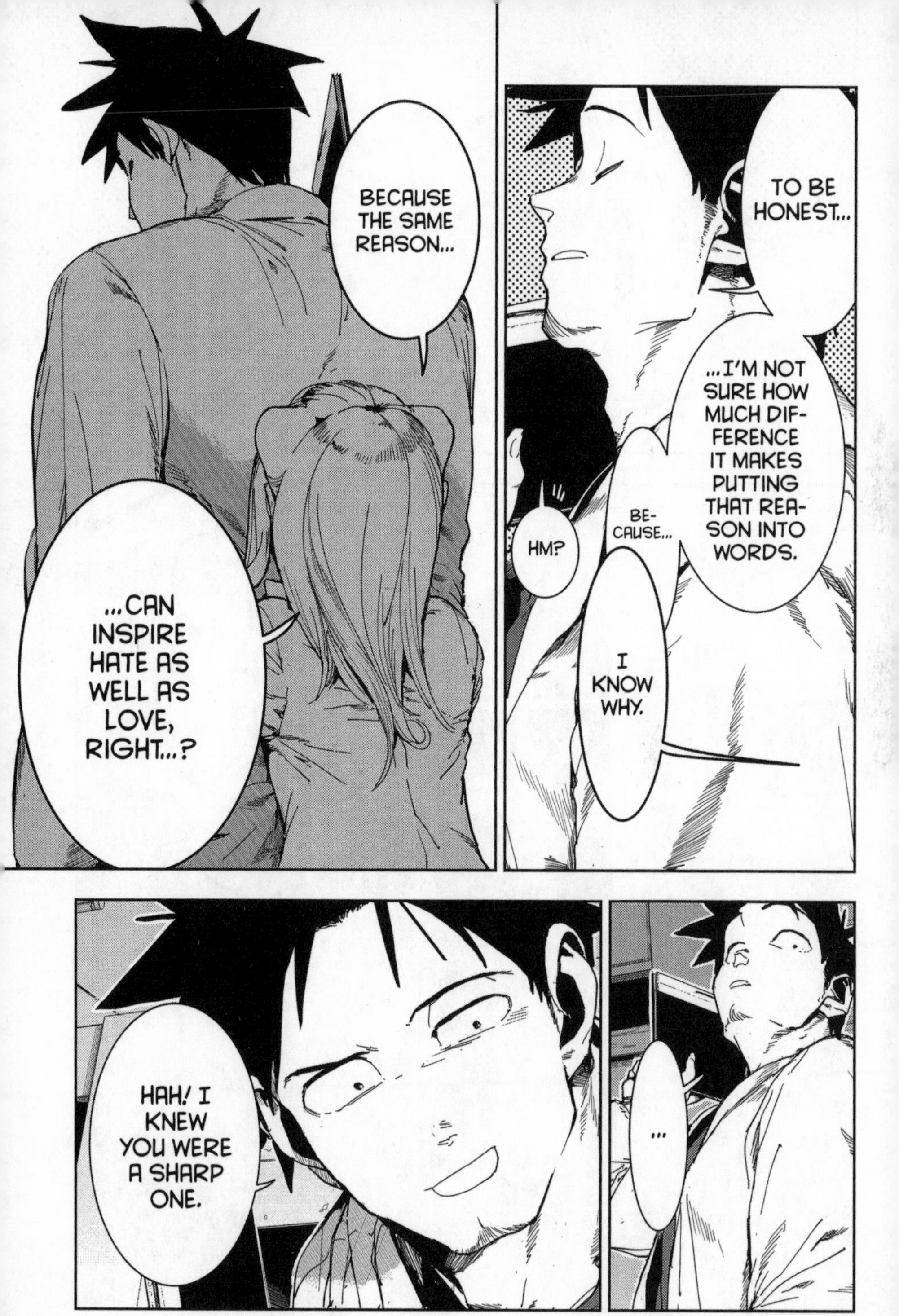
TO BE HONEST...
...I'M NOT SURE HOW MUCH DIF-FERENCE IT MAKES PUTTING THAT REA-SON INTO WORDS.
HM?
BE-CAUSE...
I KNOW WHY.
BECAUSE THE SAME REASON...
...CAN INSPIRE HATE AS WELL AS LOVE, RIGHT...?
...
HAH! I KNEW YOU WERE A SHARP ONE.

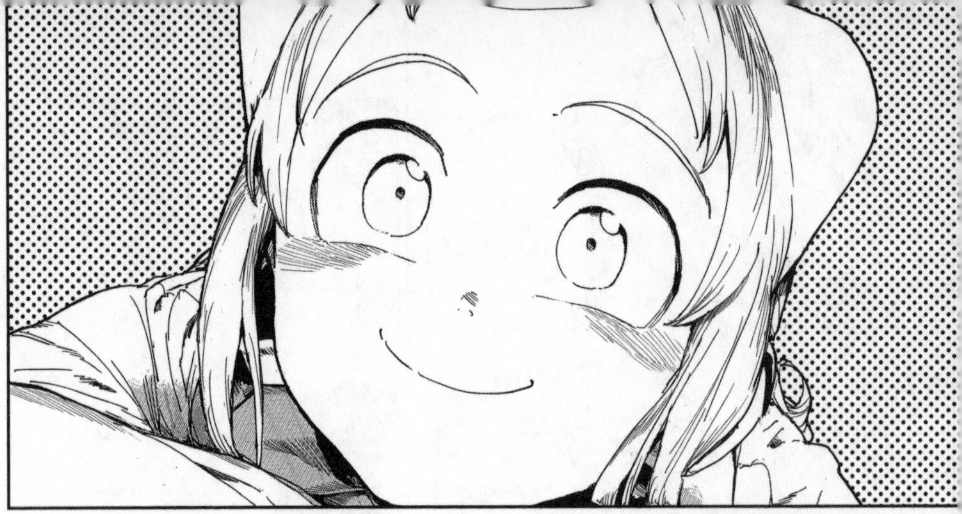

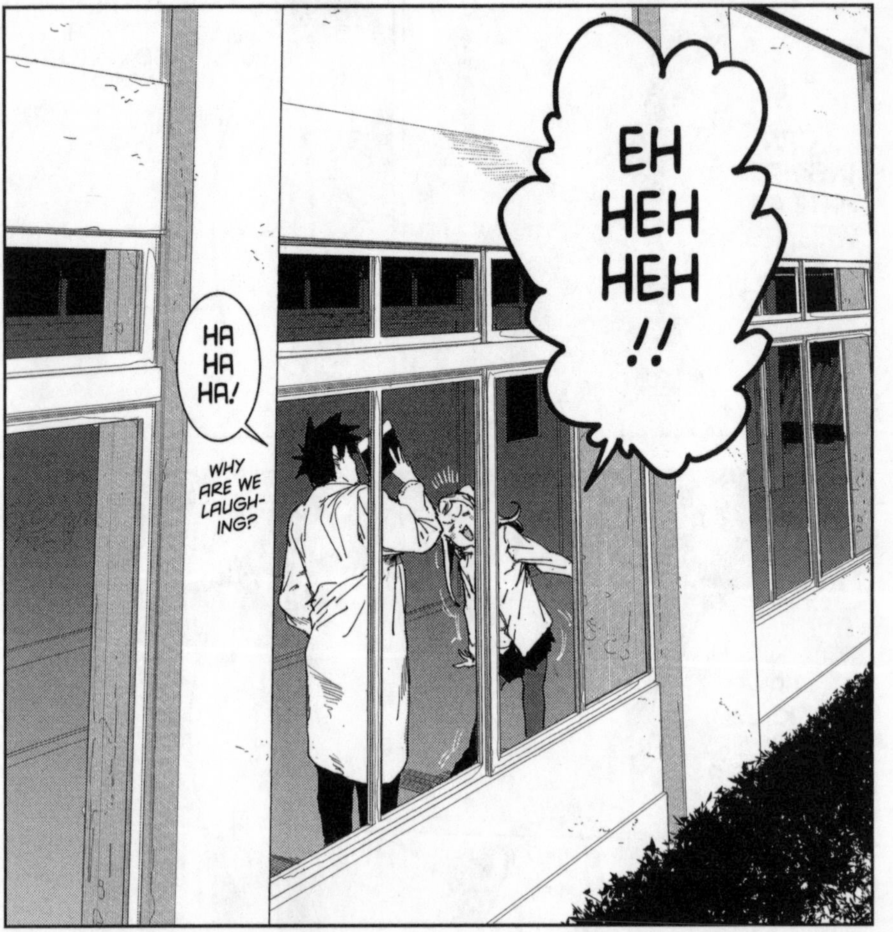
EH HEH HEH !!
HA HA HA!
WHY ARE WE LAUGHING?

HUH? I JUST REALIZED, I'M NOT FEELING ATTRACTED BY YOU.
NOT LIKE LAST TIME.
HEH!
REALLY?
WELL!
I'VE ACTUALLY BEEN WORKING HARD ON CONTROLLING MY POWERS LATELY!
REALLY?
ONE CAPABLE SUCCUBUS
WOW!
GEE, I NEVER IMAGINED IT WOULD HELP SO QUICKLY!
...
MAYBE IT'S JUST 'CAUSE I CAN'T SEE HER RIGHT NOW!!
BUT SHE WAS NICE ENOUGH NOT TO SAY SO OUT LOUD.

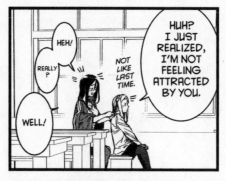

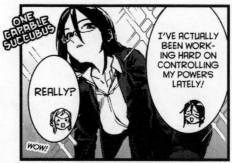

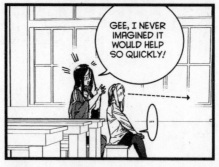

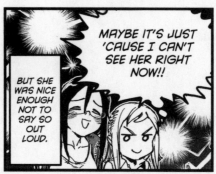

INTERVIEWS WITH MONSTER GIRLS

Chapter 63: In Autumn, The Twilight

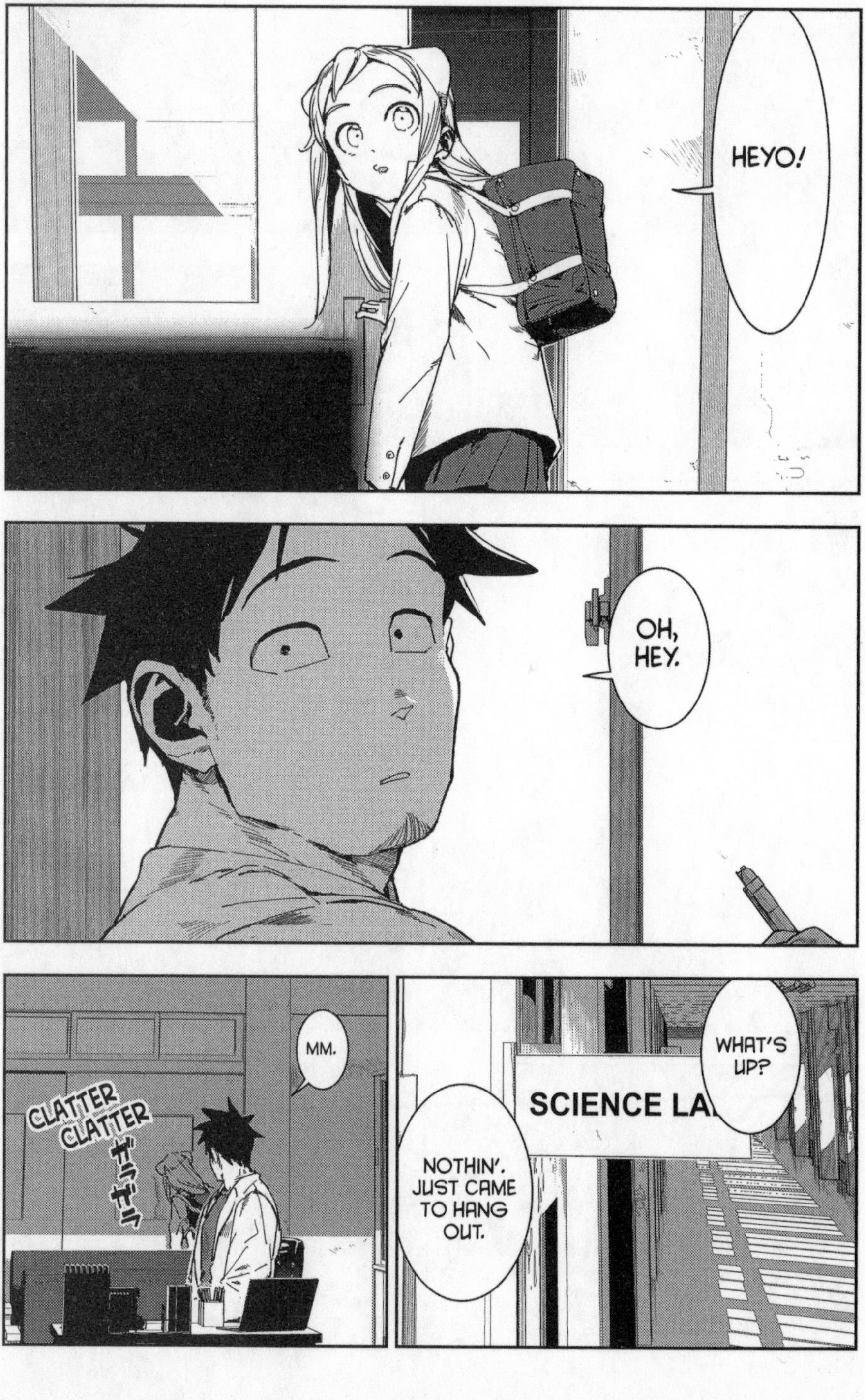
HEYO!
OH, HEY.
WHAT'S UP?
SCIENCE LA
NOTHIN'. JUST CAME TO HANG OUT.
MM.
CLATTER CLATTER
ガラガラ

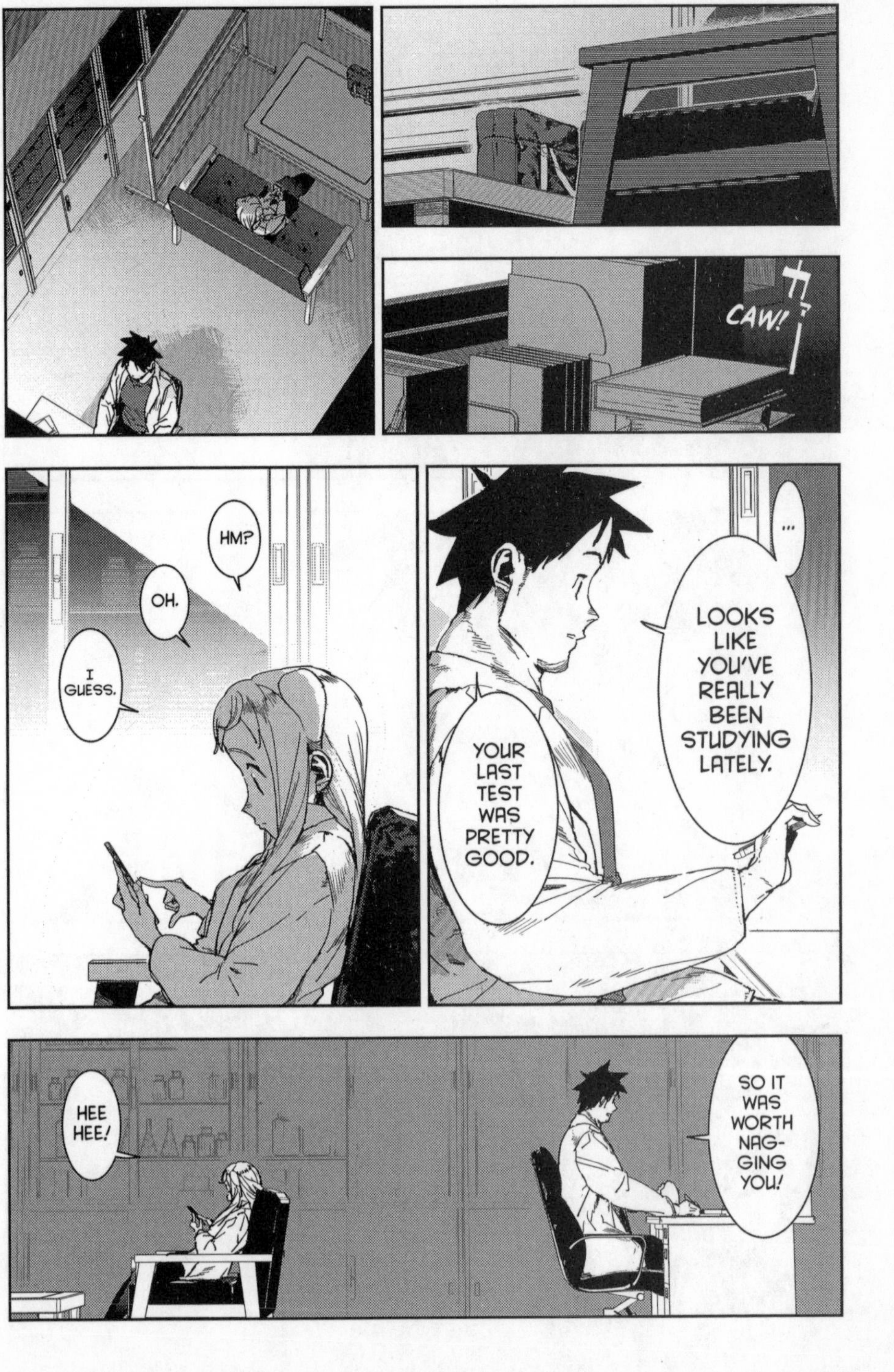
CAW!
...
LOOKS LIKE YOU'VE REALLY BEEN STUDYING LATELY.
YOUR LAST TEST WAS PRETTY GOOD.
HM?
OH.
I GUESS.
SO IT WAS WORTH NAG-GING YOU!
HEE HEE!

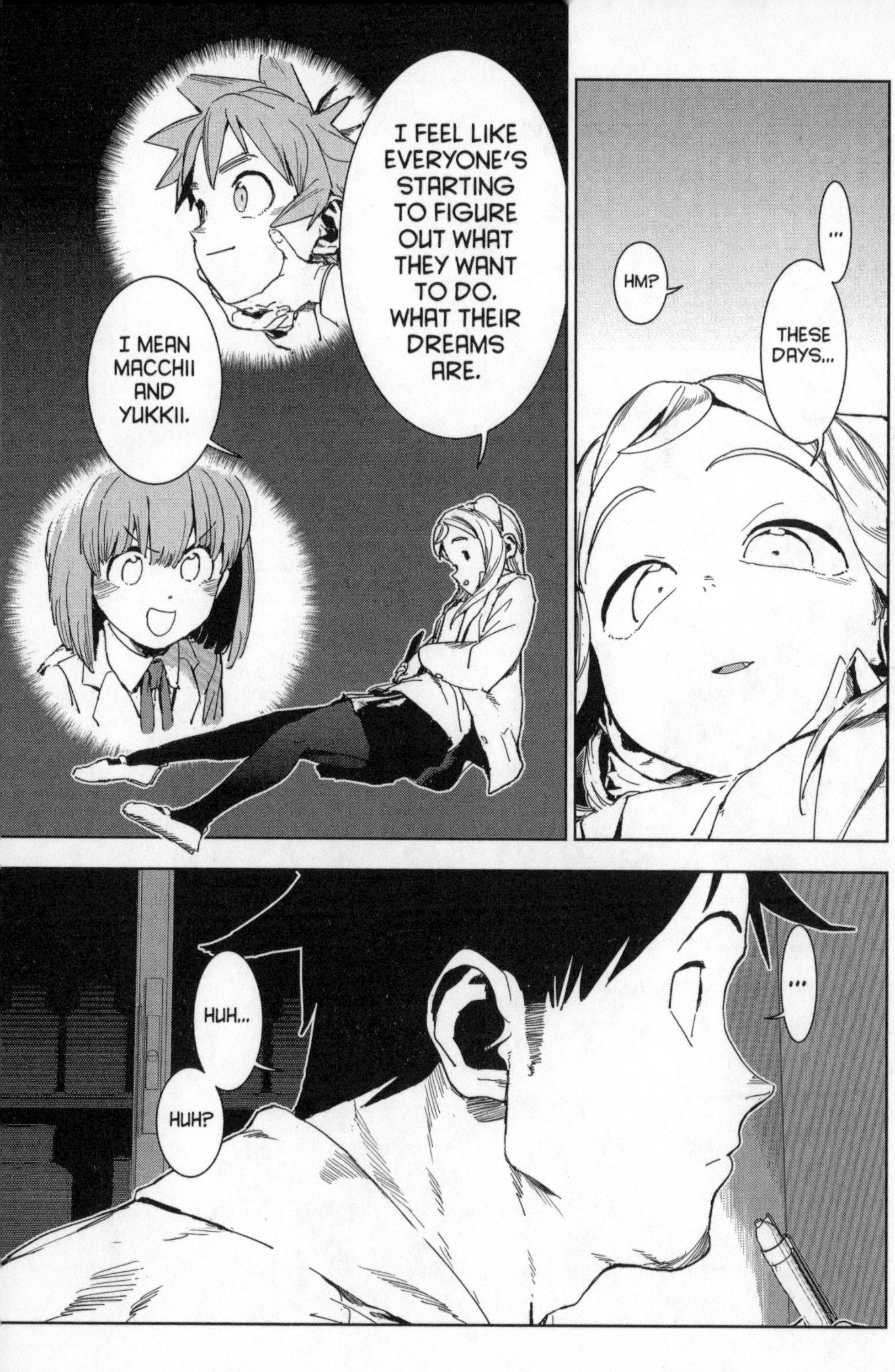
...
HM?
THESE DAYS...
I FEEL LIKE EVERYONE'S STARTING TO FIGURE OUT WHAT THEY WANT TO DO. WHAT THEIR DREAMS ARE.
I MEAN MACCHII AND YUKKII.
...
HUH...
HUH?

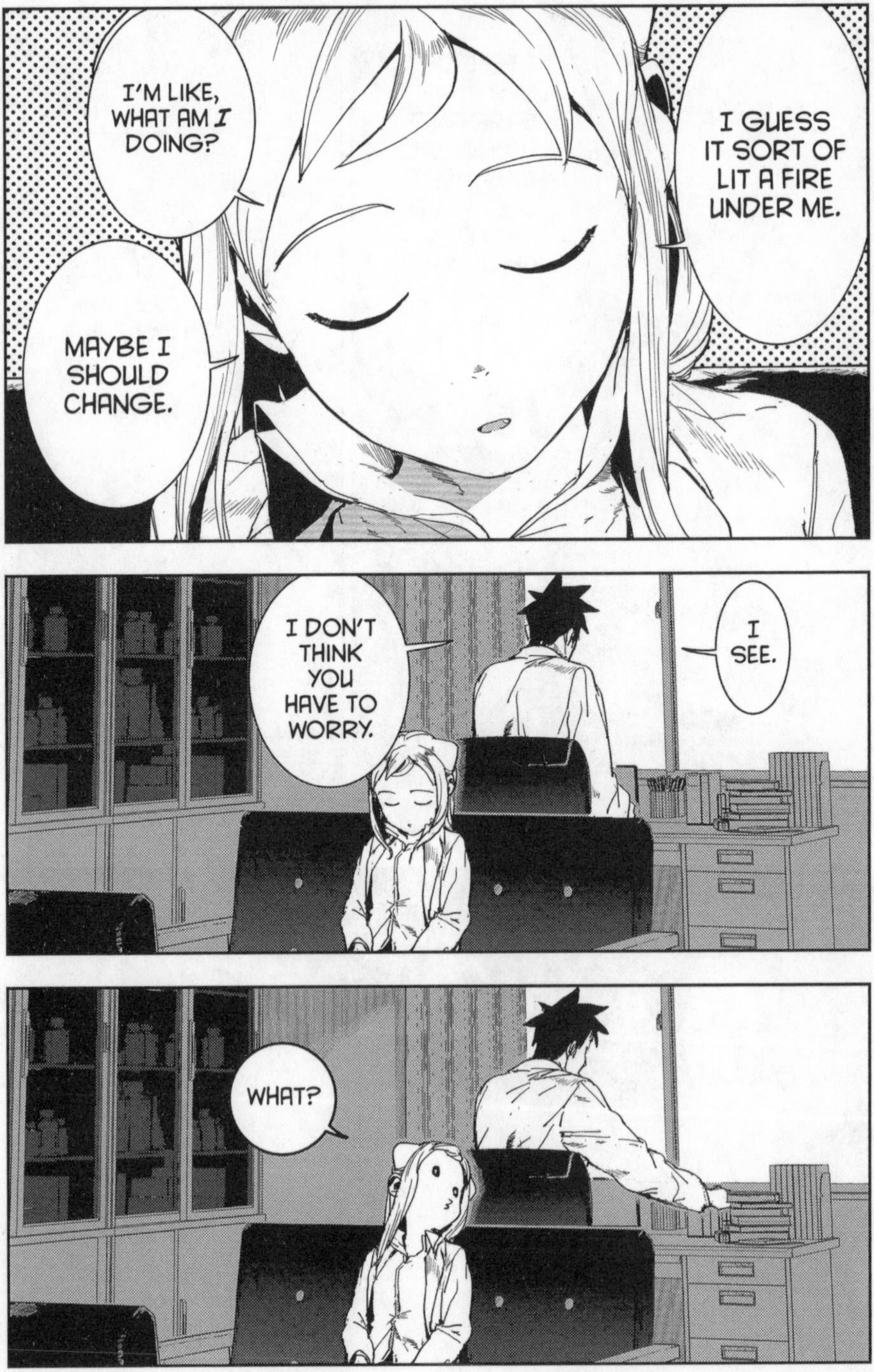
I GUESS IT SORT OF LIT A FIRE UNDER ME.
I'M LIKE, WHAT AM *I* DOING?
MAYBE I SHOULD CHANGE.
I SEE.
I DON'T THINK YOU HAVE TO WORRY.
WHAT?

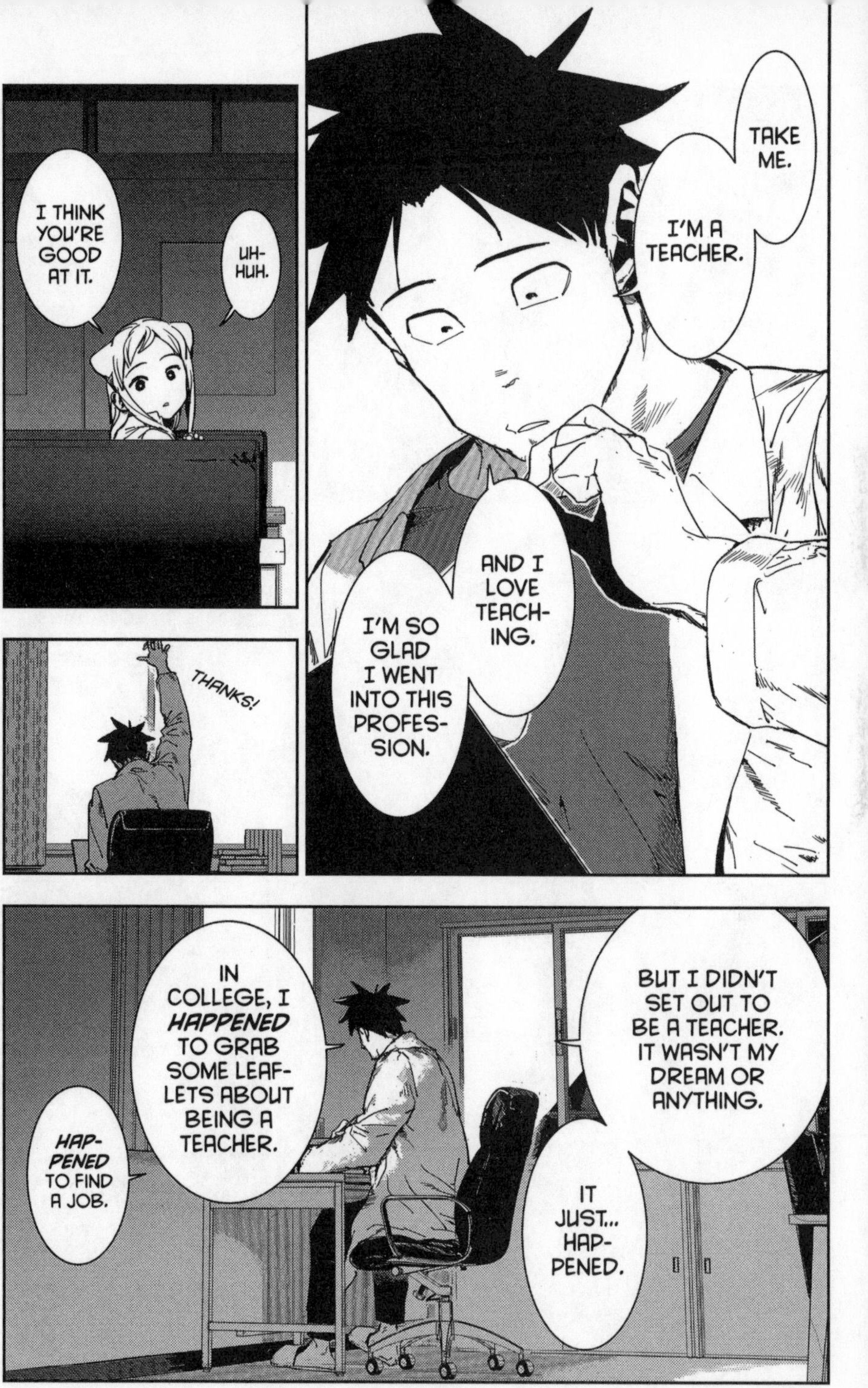
TAKE ME.
I'M A TEACHER.
AND I LOVE TEACHING.
I'M SO GLAD I WENT INTO THIS PROFESSION.
UH-HUH.
I THINK YOU'RE GOOD AT IT.
THANKS!
BUT I DIDN'T SET OUT TO BE A TEACHER. IT WASN'T MY DREAM OR ANYTHING.
IT JUST... HAPPENED.
IN COLLEGE, I *HAPPENED* TO GRAB SOME LEAFLETS ABOUT BEING A TEACHER.
HAPPENED TO FIND A JOB.

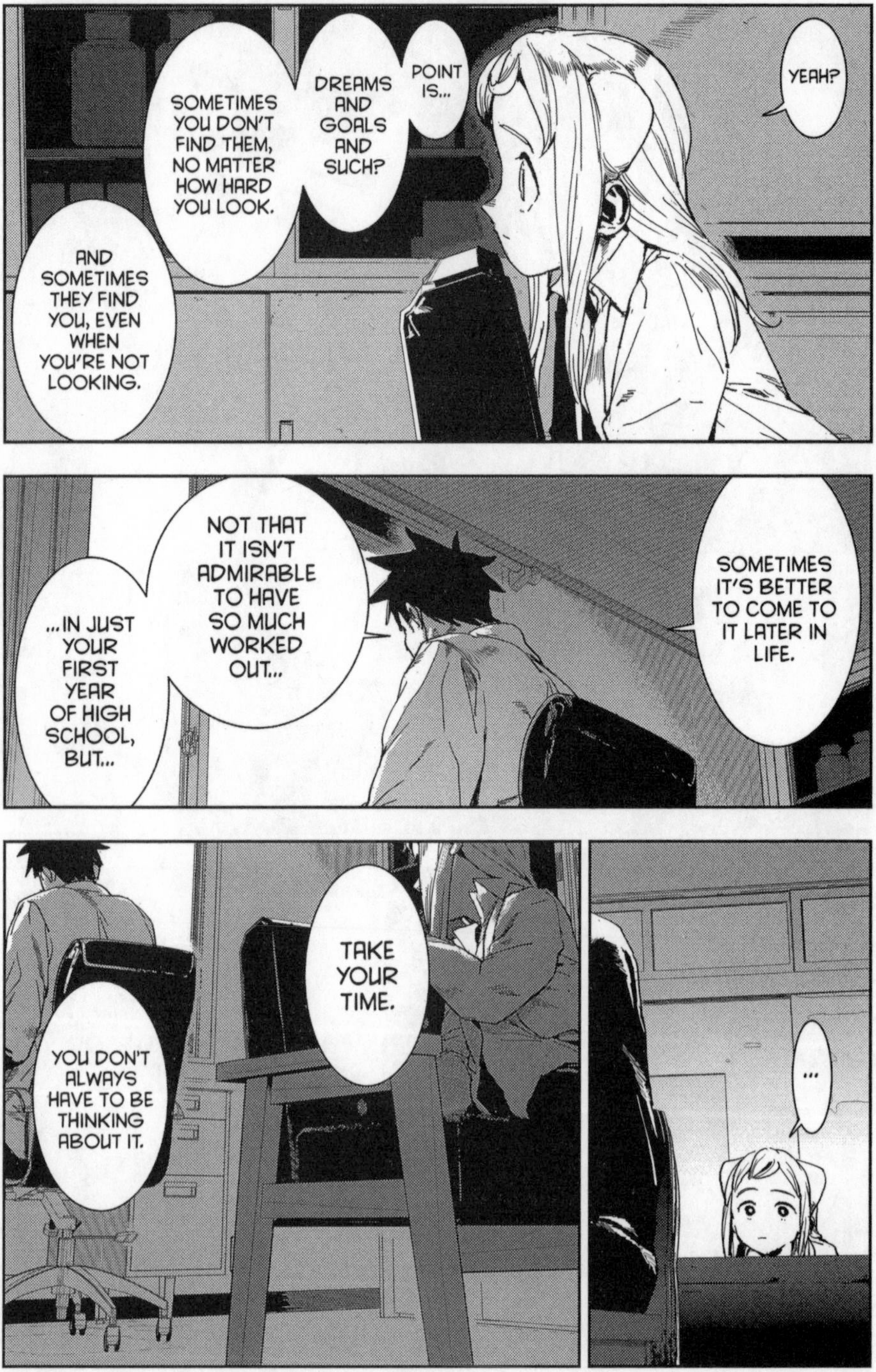
YEAH?
POINT IS...
DREAMS AND GOALS AND SUCH?
SOMETIMES YOU DON'T FIND THEM, NO MATTER HOW HARD YOU LOOK.
AND SOMETIMES THEY FIND YOU, EVEN WHEN YOU'RE NOT LOOKING.
SOMETIMES IT'S BETTER TO COME TO IT LATER IN LIFE.
NOT THAT IT ISN'T ADMIRABLE TO HAVE SO MUCH WORKED OUT...
...IN JUST YOUR FIRST YEAR OF HIGH SCHOOL, BUT...
...
TAKE YOUR TIME.
YOU DON'T ALWAYS HAVE TO BE THINKING ABOUT IT.

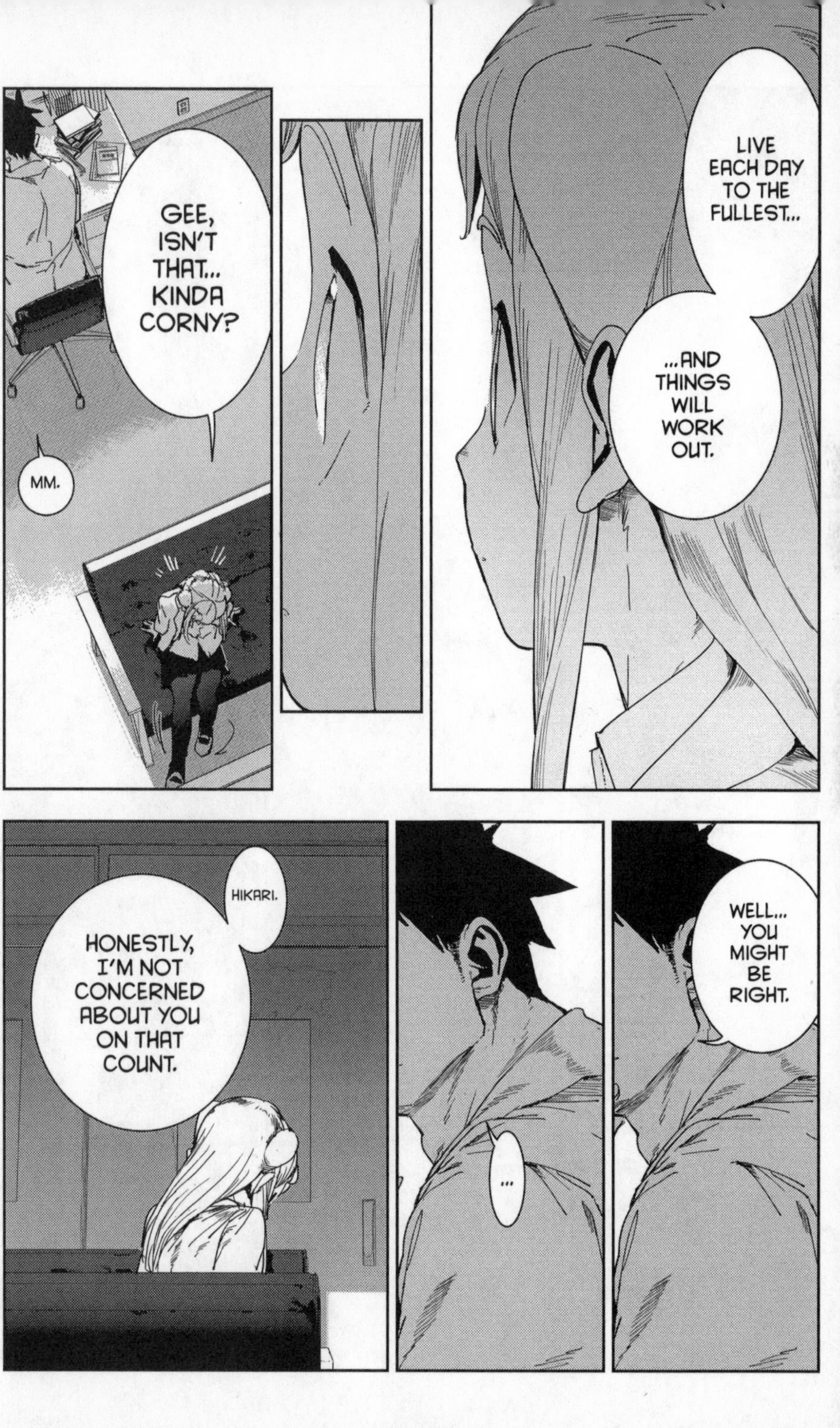
LIVE EACH DAY TO THE FULLEST...
...AND THINGS WILL WORK OUT.
GEE, ISN'T THAT... KINDA CORNY?
MM.
WELL... YOU MIGHT BE RIGHT.
...
HIKARI.
HONESTLY, I'M NOT CONCERNED ABOUT YOU ON THAT COUNT.

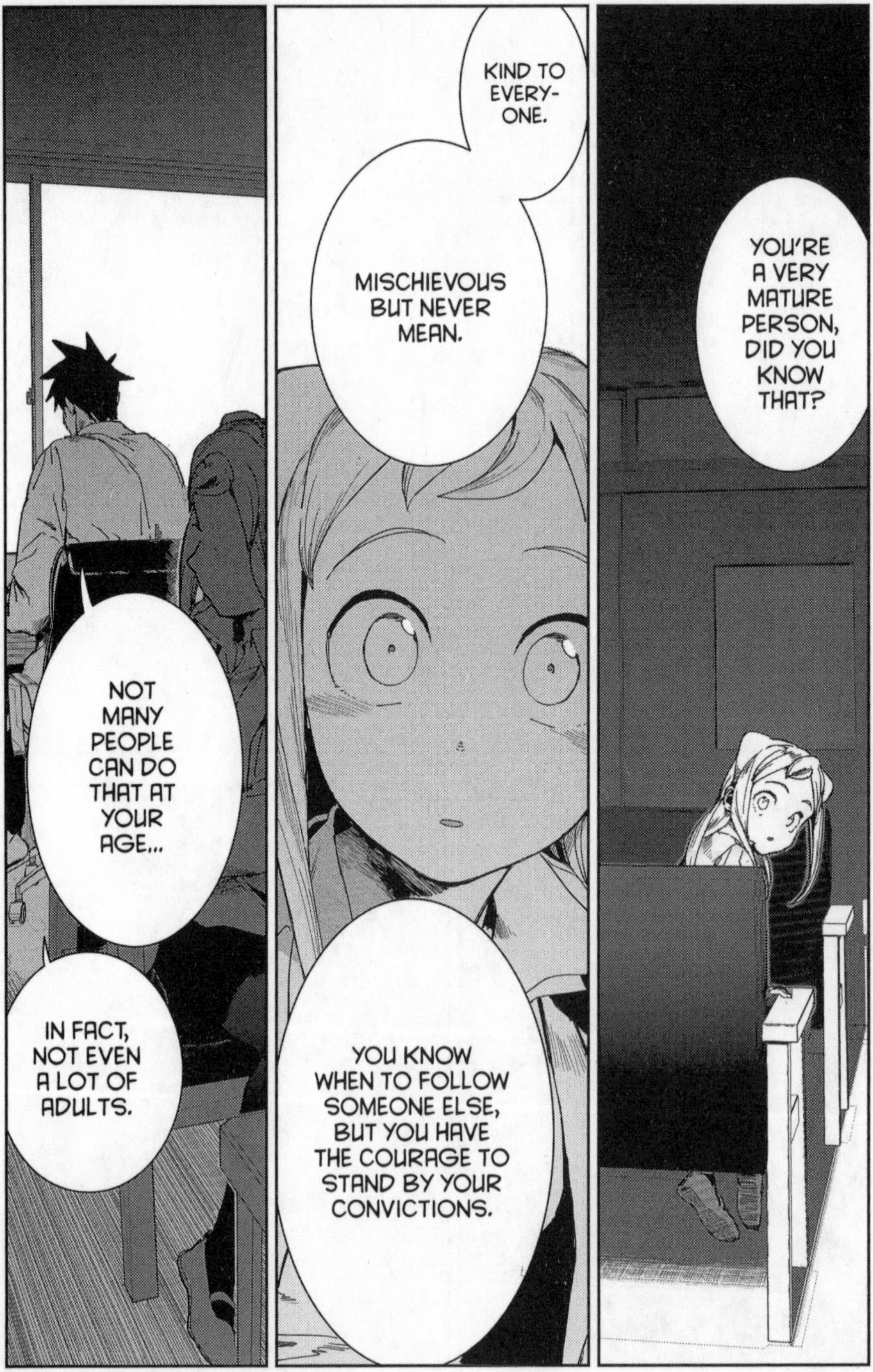
YOU'RE A VERY MATURE PERSON, DID YOU KNOW THAT?
KIND TO EVERY-ONE.
MISCHIEVOUS BUT NEVER MEAN.
YOU KNOW WHEN TO FOLLOW SOMEONE ELSE, BUT YOU HAVE THE COURAGE TO STAND BY YOUR CONVICTIONS.
NOT MANY PEOPLE CAN DO THAT AT YOUR AGE...
IN FACT, NOT EVEN A LOT OF ADULTS.

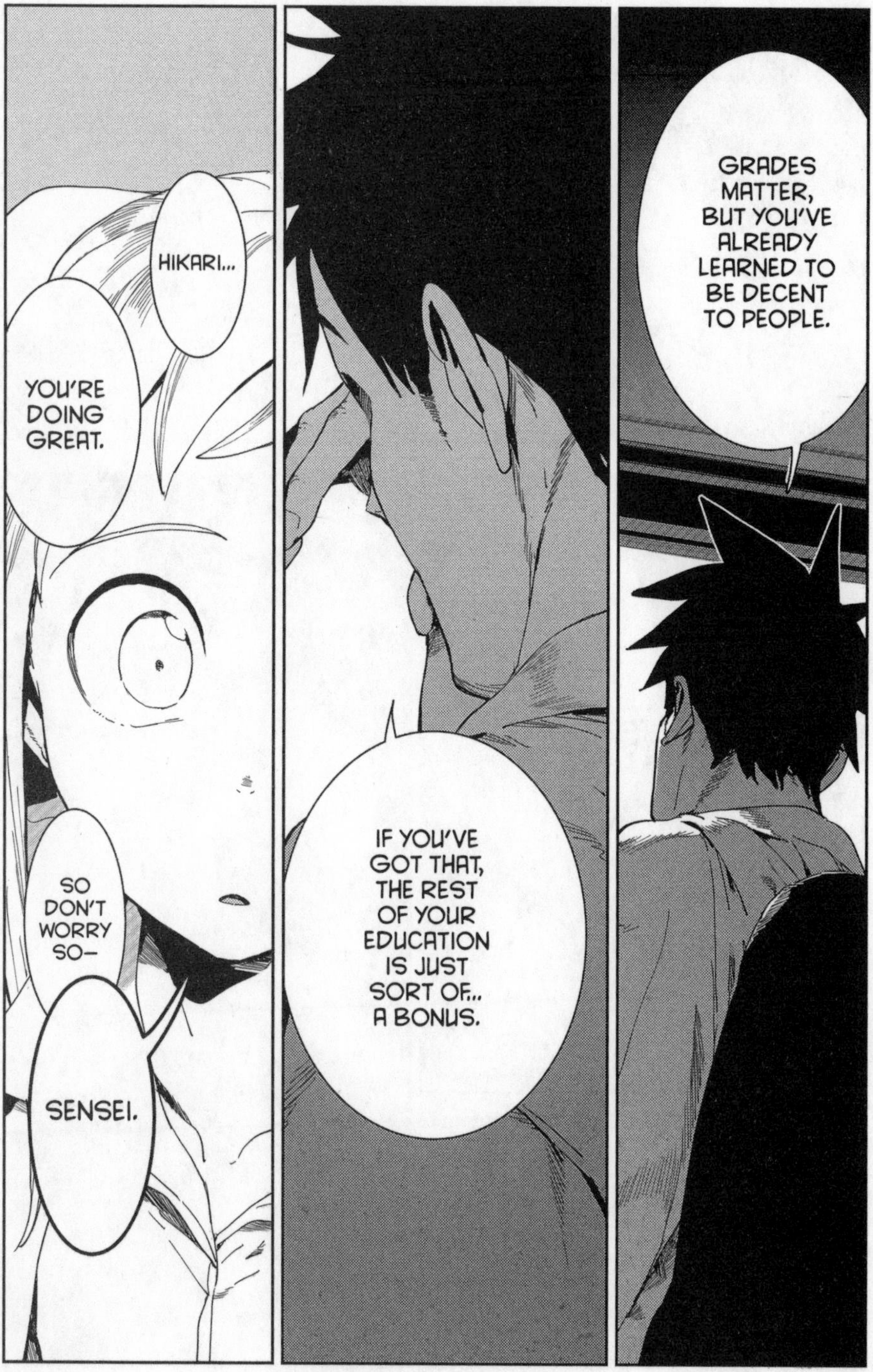
GRADES MATTER, BUT YOU'VE ALREADY LEARNED TO BE DECENT TO PEOPLE.
IF YOU'VE GOT THAT, THE REST OF YOUR EDUCATION IS JUST SORT OF... A BONUS.
HIKARI...
YOU'RE DOING GREAT.
SO DON'T WORRY SO—
SENSEI.

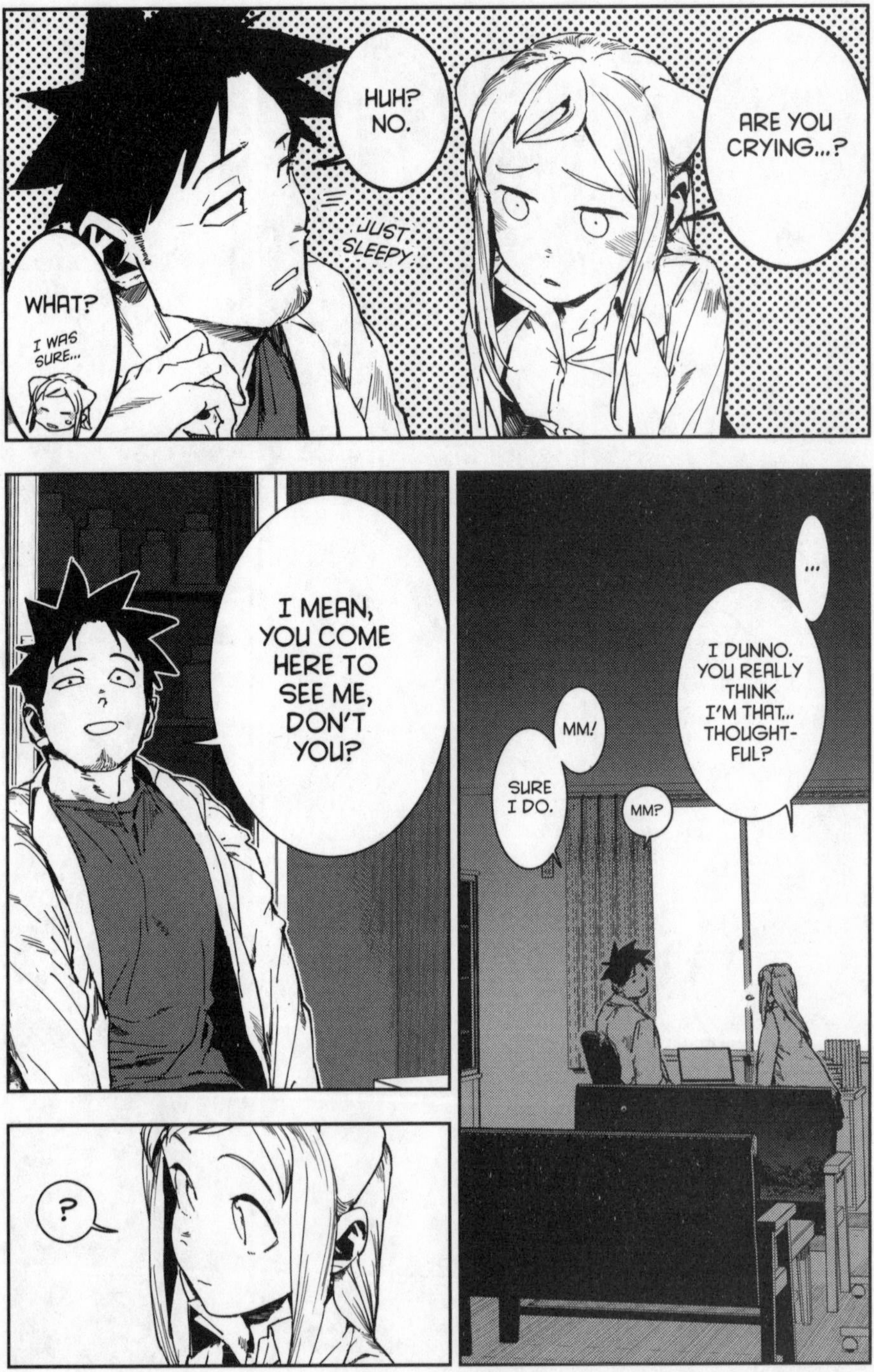
ARE YOU CRYING...?
HUH? NO.
JUST SLEEPY
WHAT?
I WAS SURE...
...
I DUNNO. YOU REALLY THINK I'M THAT... THOUGHT-FUL?
MM!
MM?
SURE I DO.
I MEAN, YOU COME HERE TO SEE ME, DON'T YOU?
?

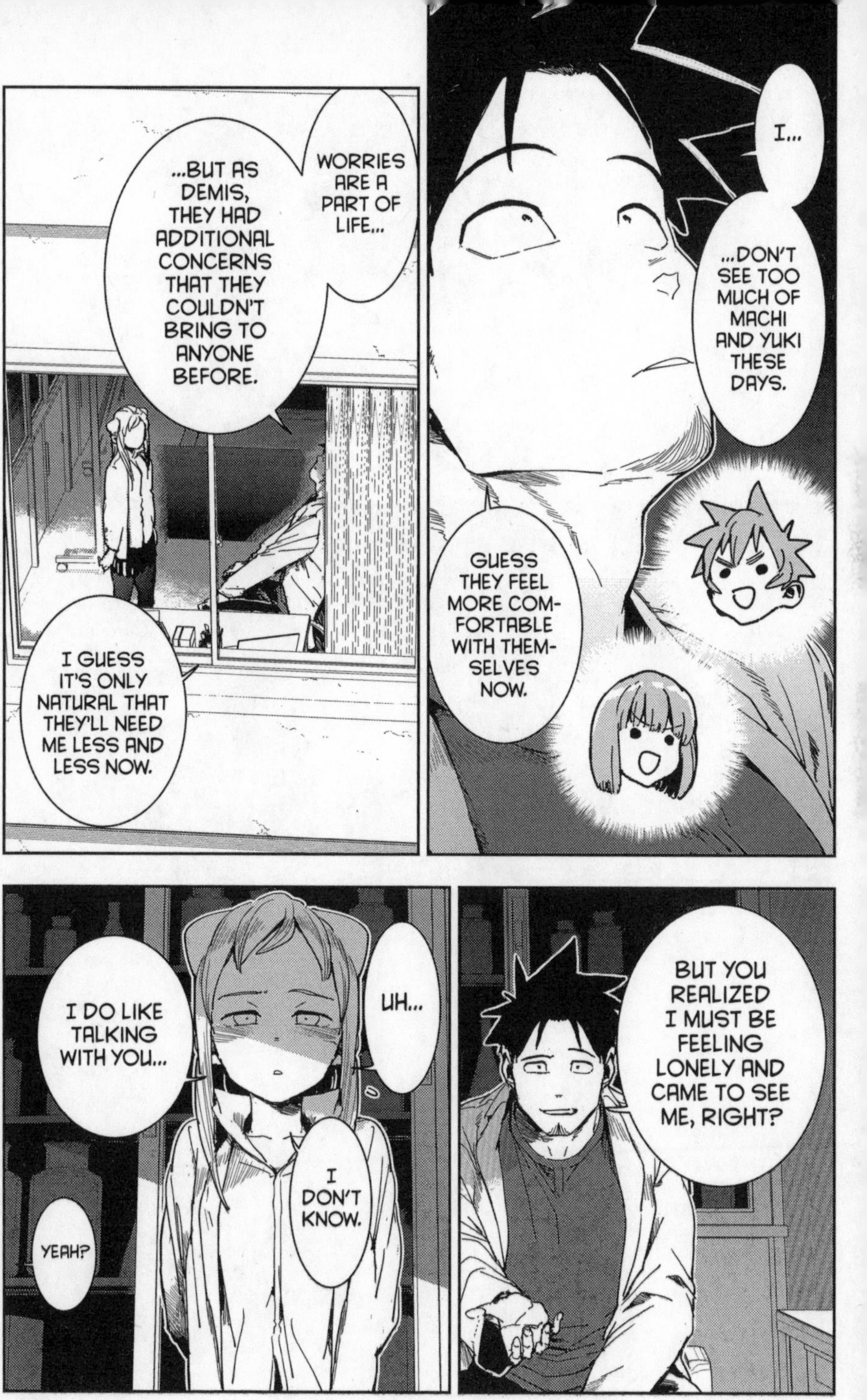
I...
...DON'T SEE TOO MUCH OF MACHI AND YUKI THESE DAYS.
GUESS THEY FEEL MORE COMFORTABLE WITH THEMSELVES NOW.
WORRIES ARE A PART OF LIFE...
...BUT AS DEMIS, THEY HAD ADDITIONAL CONCERNS THAT THEY COULDN'T BRING TO ANYONE BEFORE.
I GUESS IT'S ONLY NATURAL THAT THEY'LL NEED ME LESS AND LESS NOW.
BUT YOU REALIZED I MUST BE FEELING LONELY AND CAME TO SEE ME, RIGHT?
UH...
I DO LIKE TALKING WITH YOU...
I DON'T KNOW.
YEAH?

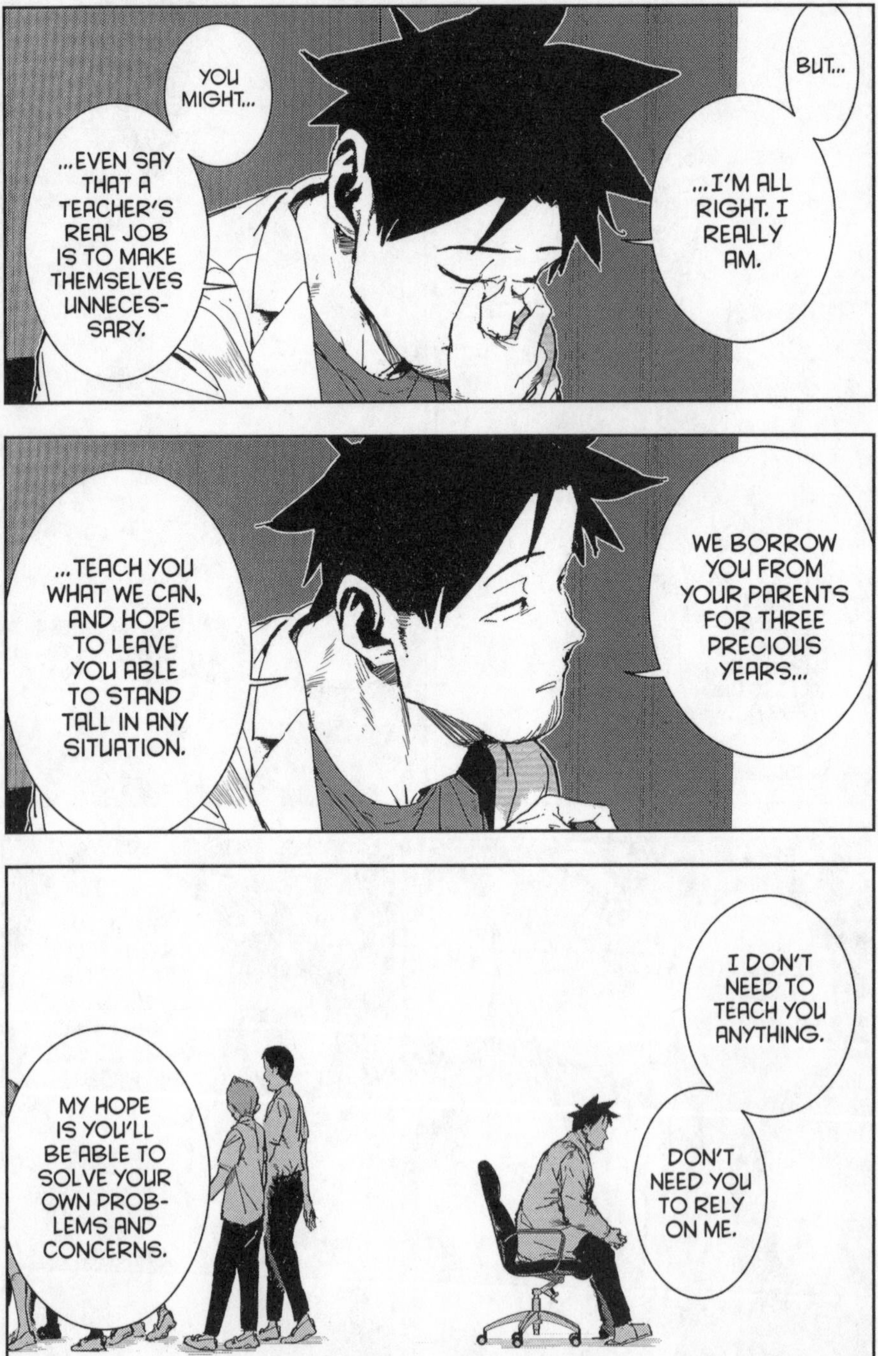
BUT...
...I'M ALL RIGHT. I REALLY AM.
YOU MIGHT...
...EVEN SAY THAT A TEACHER'S REAL JOB IS TO MAKE THEMSELVES UNNECES-SARY.
WE BORROW YOU FROM YOUR PARENTS FOR THREE PRECIOUS YEARS...
...TEACH YOU WHAT WE CAN, AND HOPE TO LEAVE YOU ABLE TO STAND TALL IN ANY SITUATION.
I DON'T NEED TO TEACH YOU ANYTHING.
DON'T NEED YOU TO RELY ON ME.
MY HOPE IS YOU'LL BE ABLE TO SOLVE YOUR OWN PROB-LEMS AND CONCERNS.

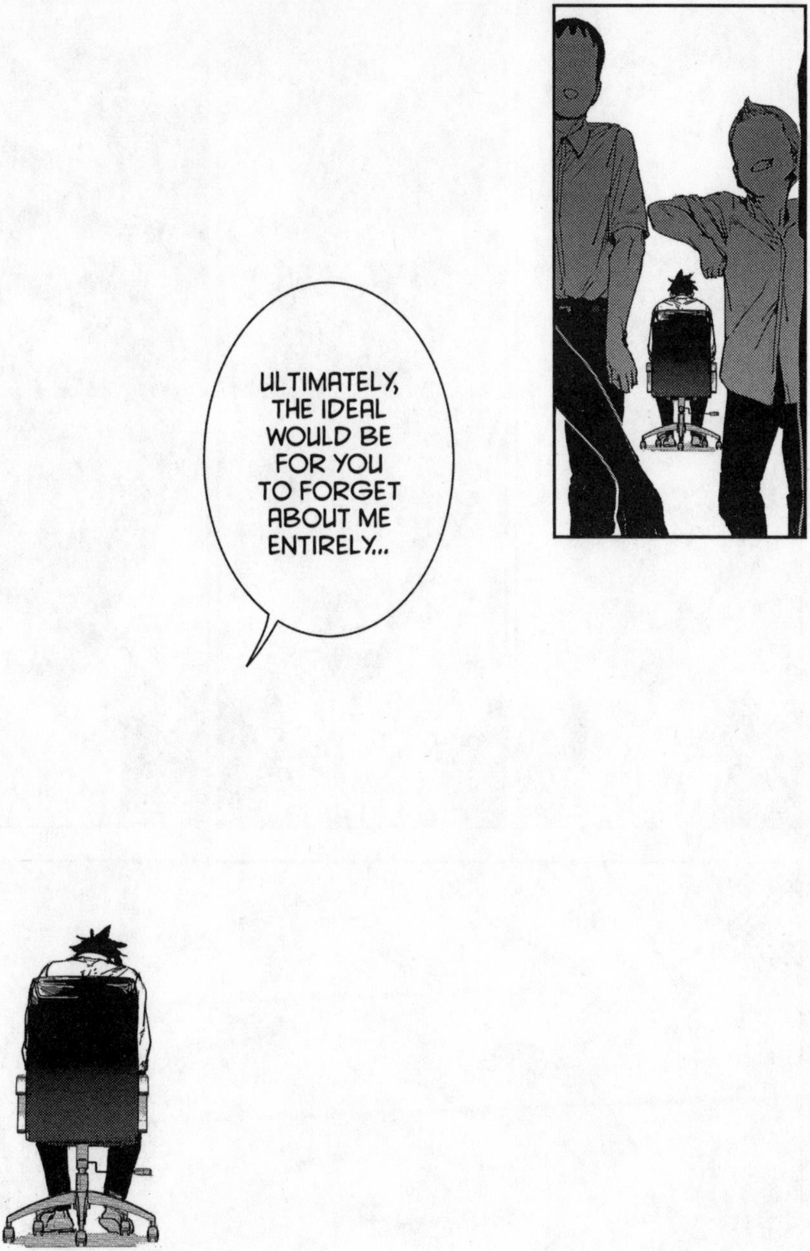
ULTIMATELY, THE IDEAL WOULD BE FOR YOU TO FORGET ABOUT ME ENTIRELY...

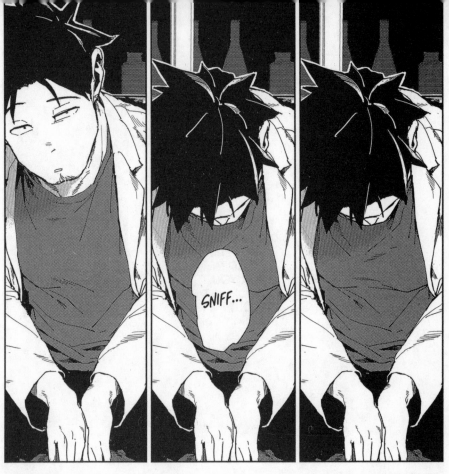

SNIFF...

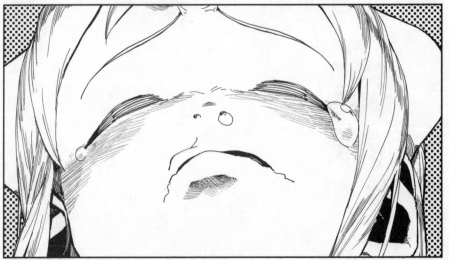

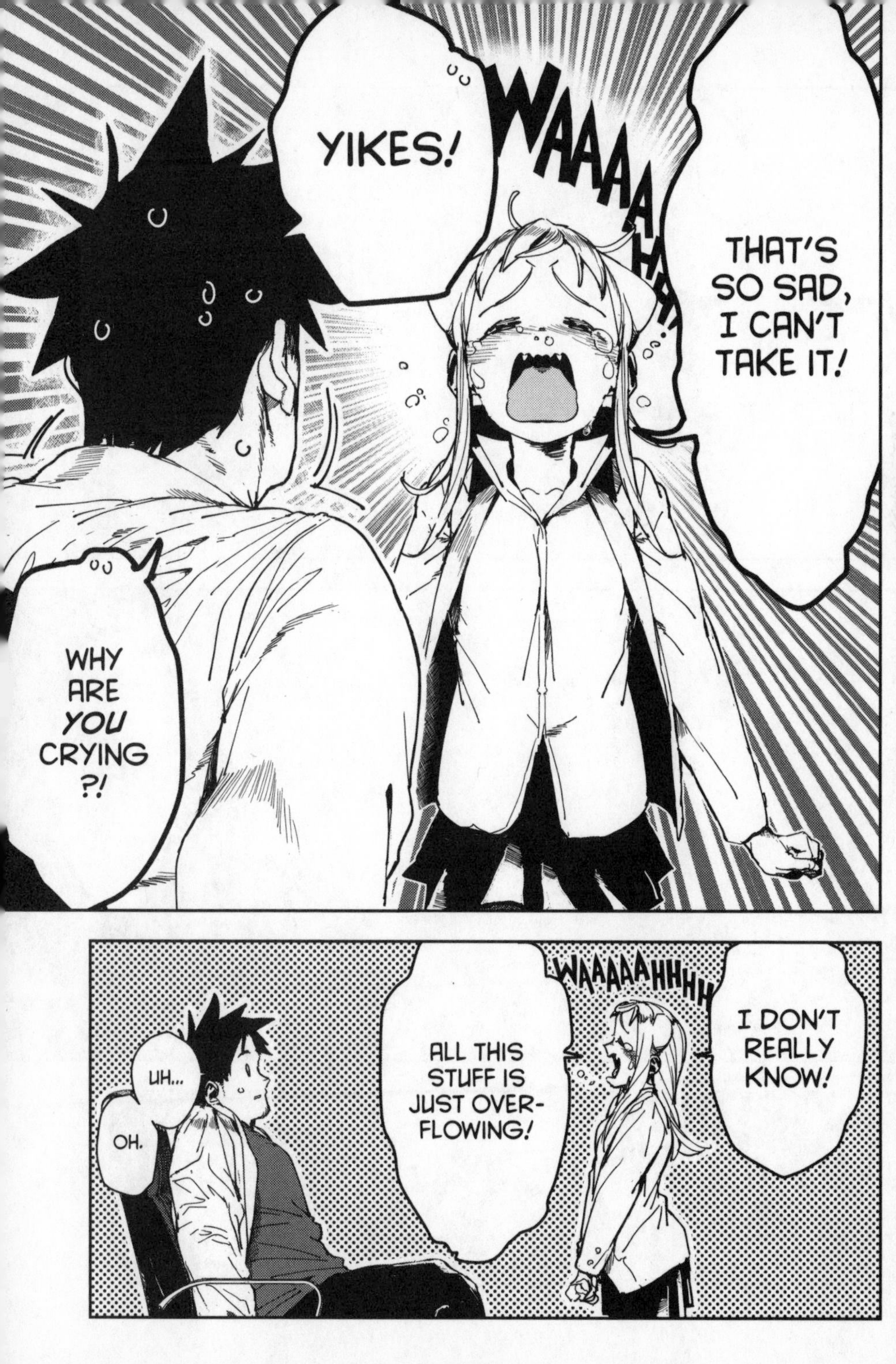
THAT'S SO SAD, I CAN'T TAKE IT!
WAAAAAHH!
YIKES!
WHY ARE *YOU* CRYING?!
I DON'T REALLY KNOW!
WAAAAAHHHH
ALL THIS STUFF IS JUST OVER-FLOWING!
UH...
OH.

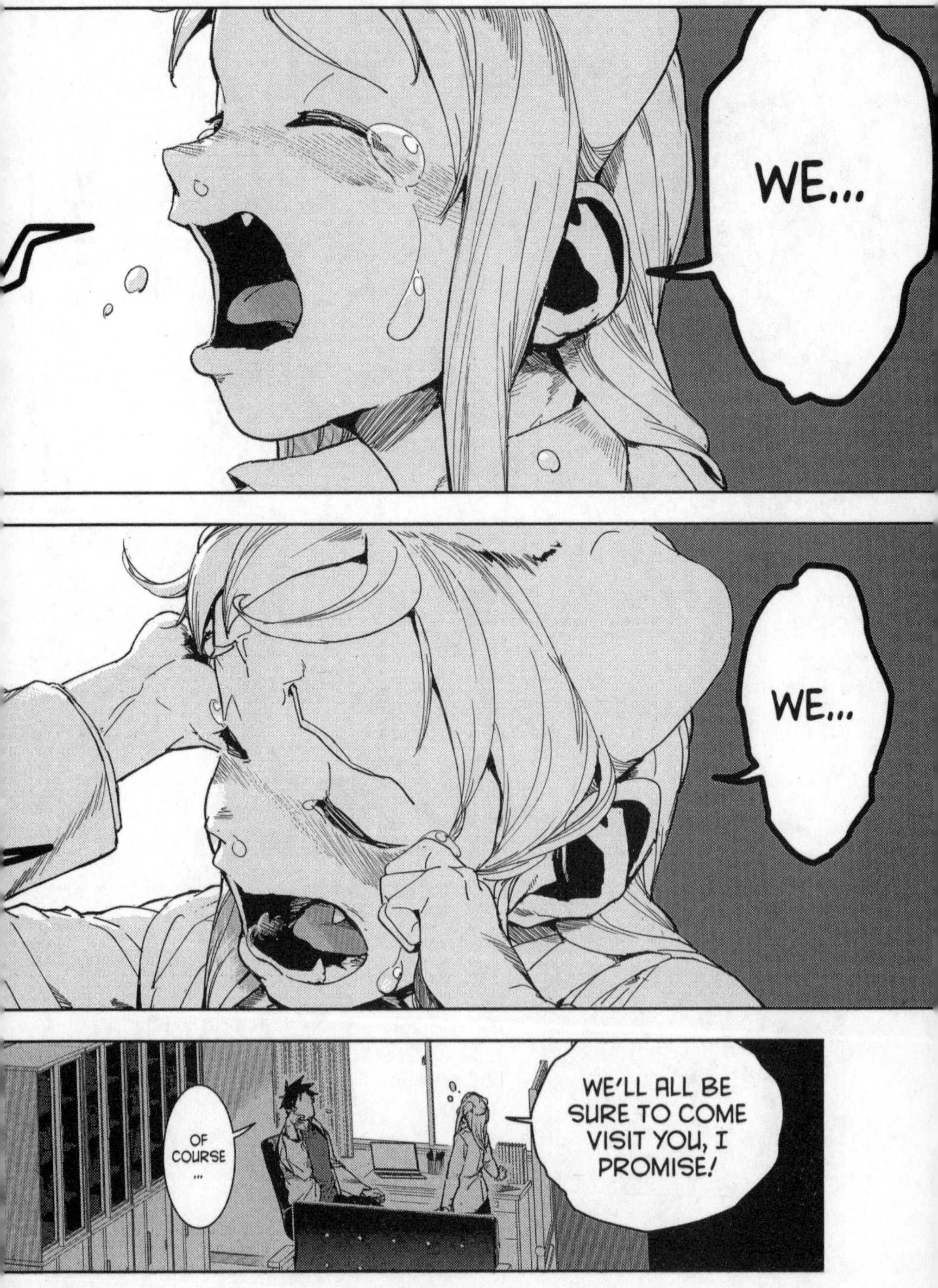
WE...
WE...
WE'LL ALL BE SURE TO COME VISIT YOU, I PROMISE!
OF COURSE ...

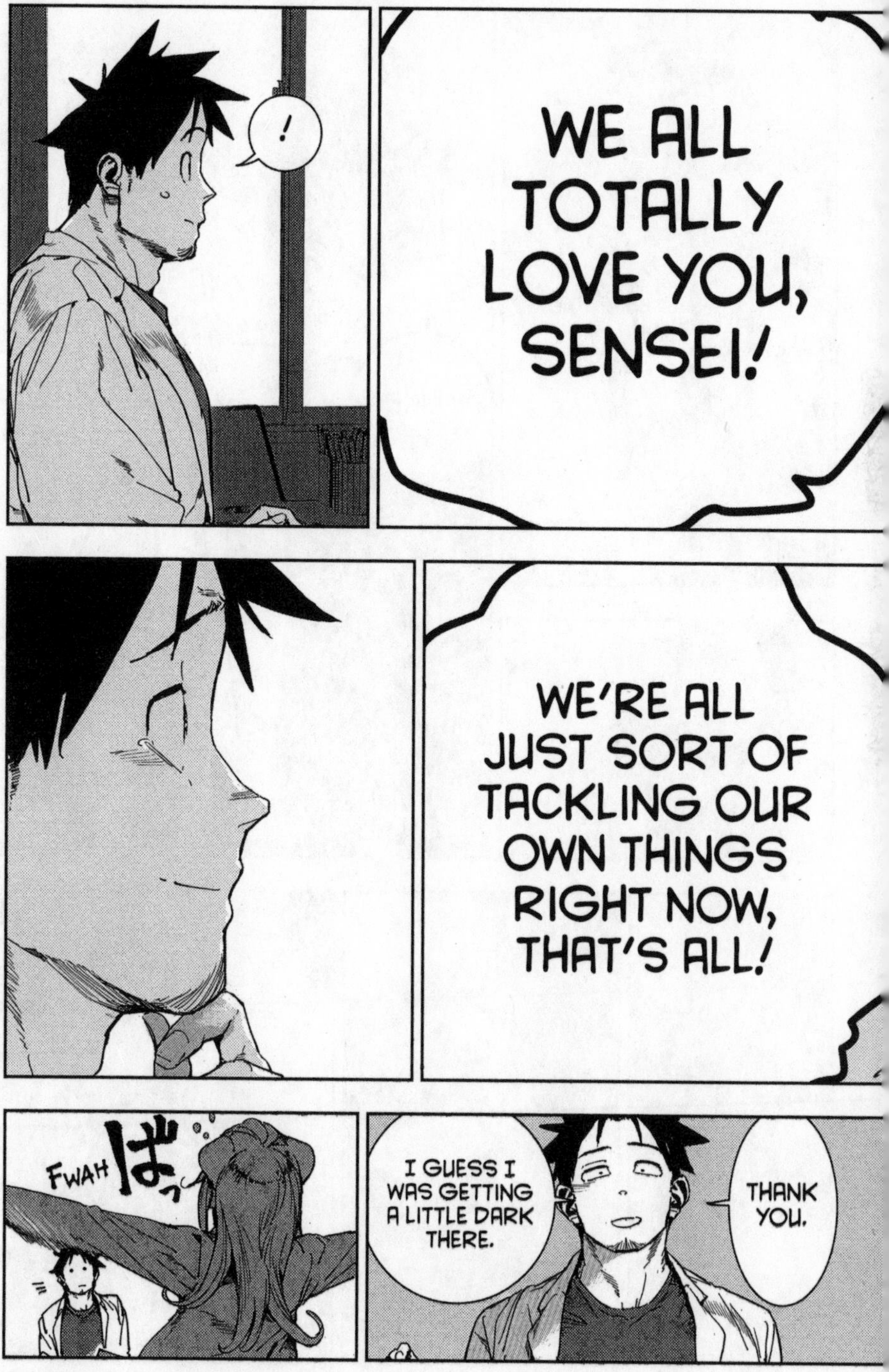
WE ALL TOTALLY LOVE YOU, SENSEI!
!
WE'RE ALL JUST SORT OF TACKLING OUR OWN THINGS RIGHT NOW, THAT'S ALL!
THANK YOU.
I GUESS I WAS GETTING A LITTLE DARK THERE.
FWAH ばっ

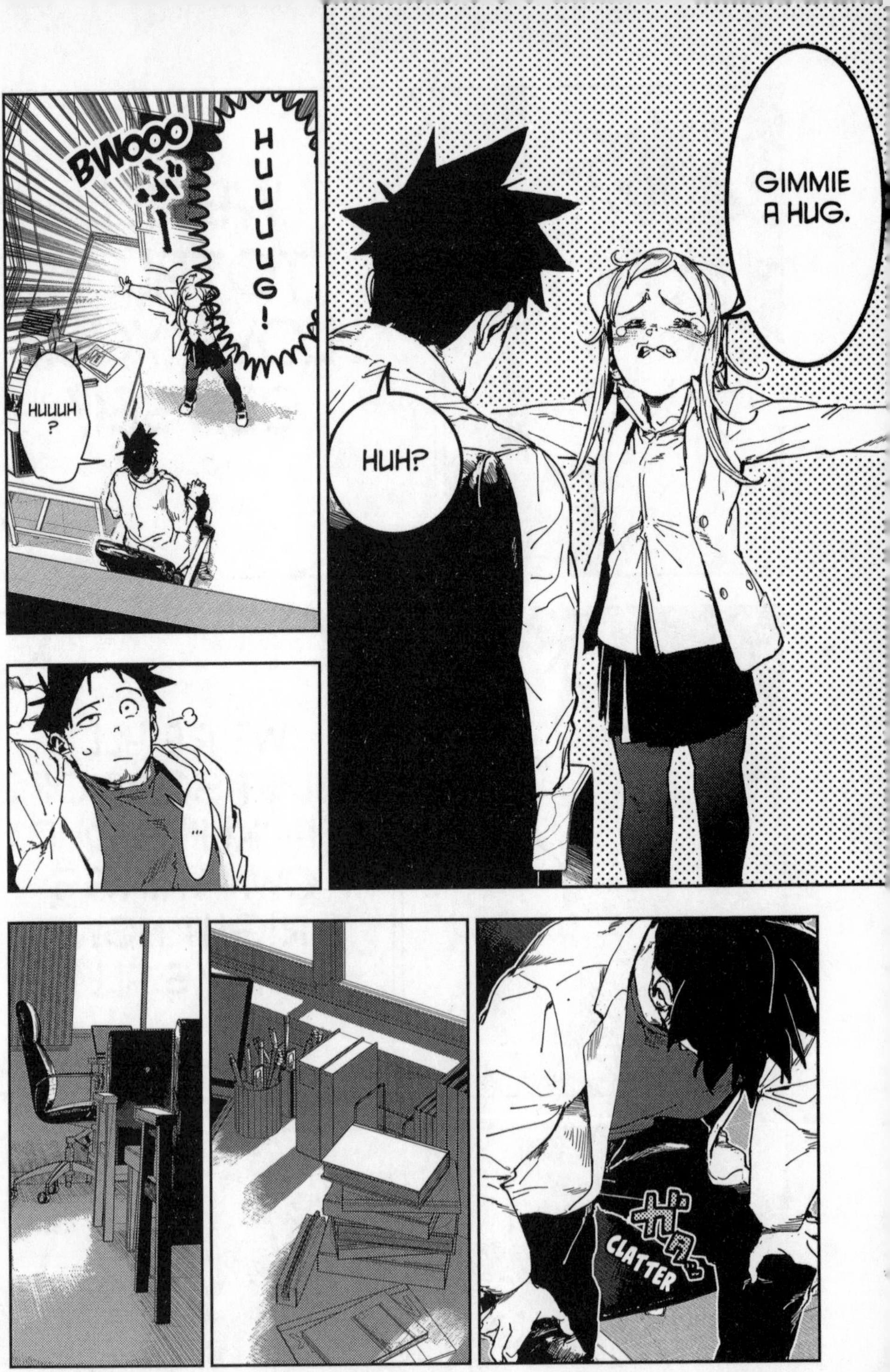
GIMMIE A HUG.
HUH?
HUUUUUG!
BWOOO
ぶー
HUUUH?
...
CLATTER
ガタ

SQUEEZE

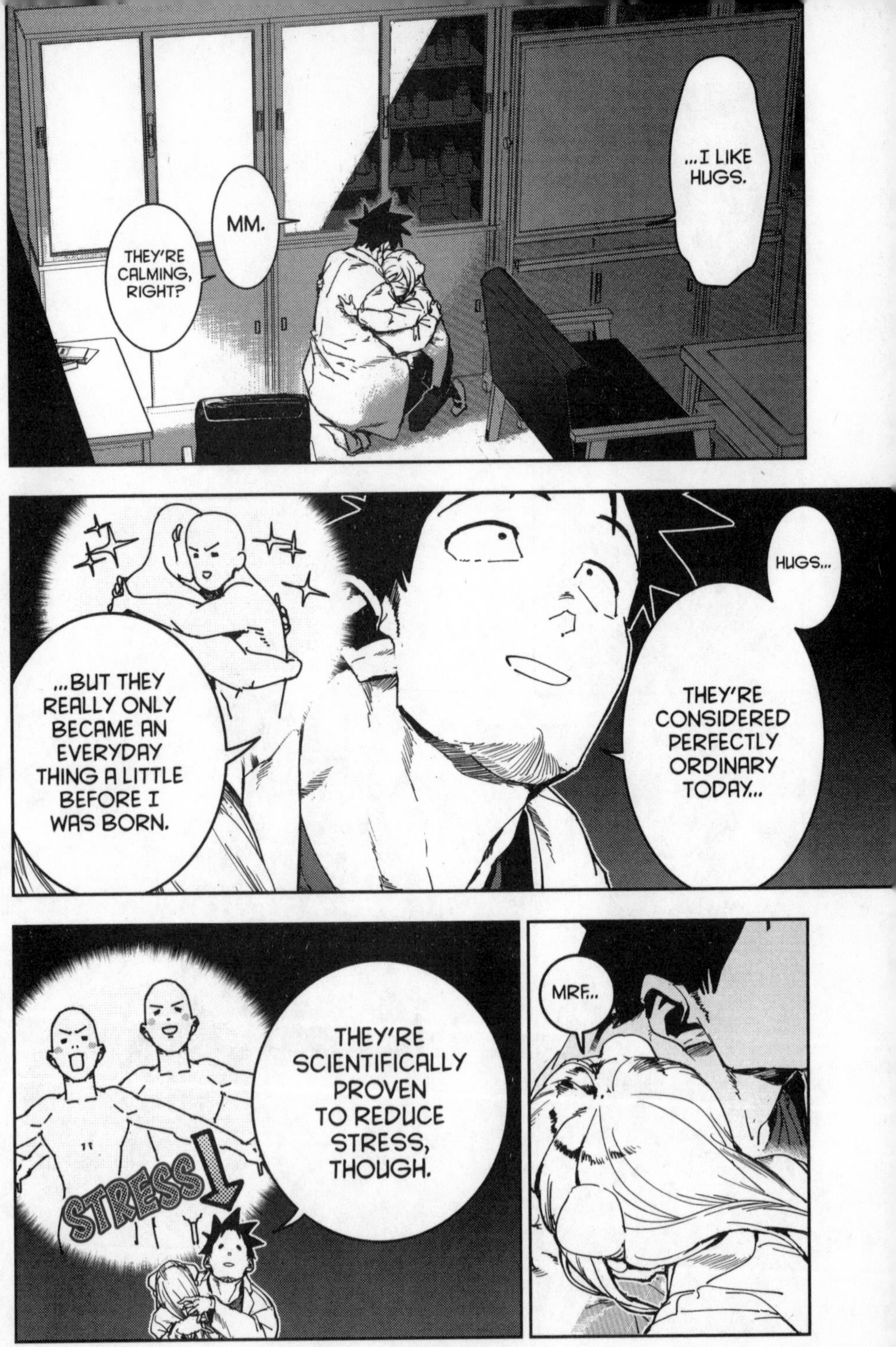
...I LIKE HUGS.
MM.
THEY'RE CALMING, RIGHT?
HUGS...
THEY'RE CONSIDERED PERFECTLY ORDINARY TODAY...
...BUT THEY REALLY ONLY BECAME AN EVERYDAY THING A LITTLE BEFORE I WAS BORN.
MRF...
THEY'RE SCIENTIFICALLY PROVEN TO REDUCE STRESS, THOUGH.
STRESS

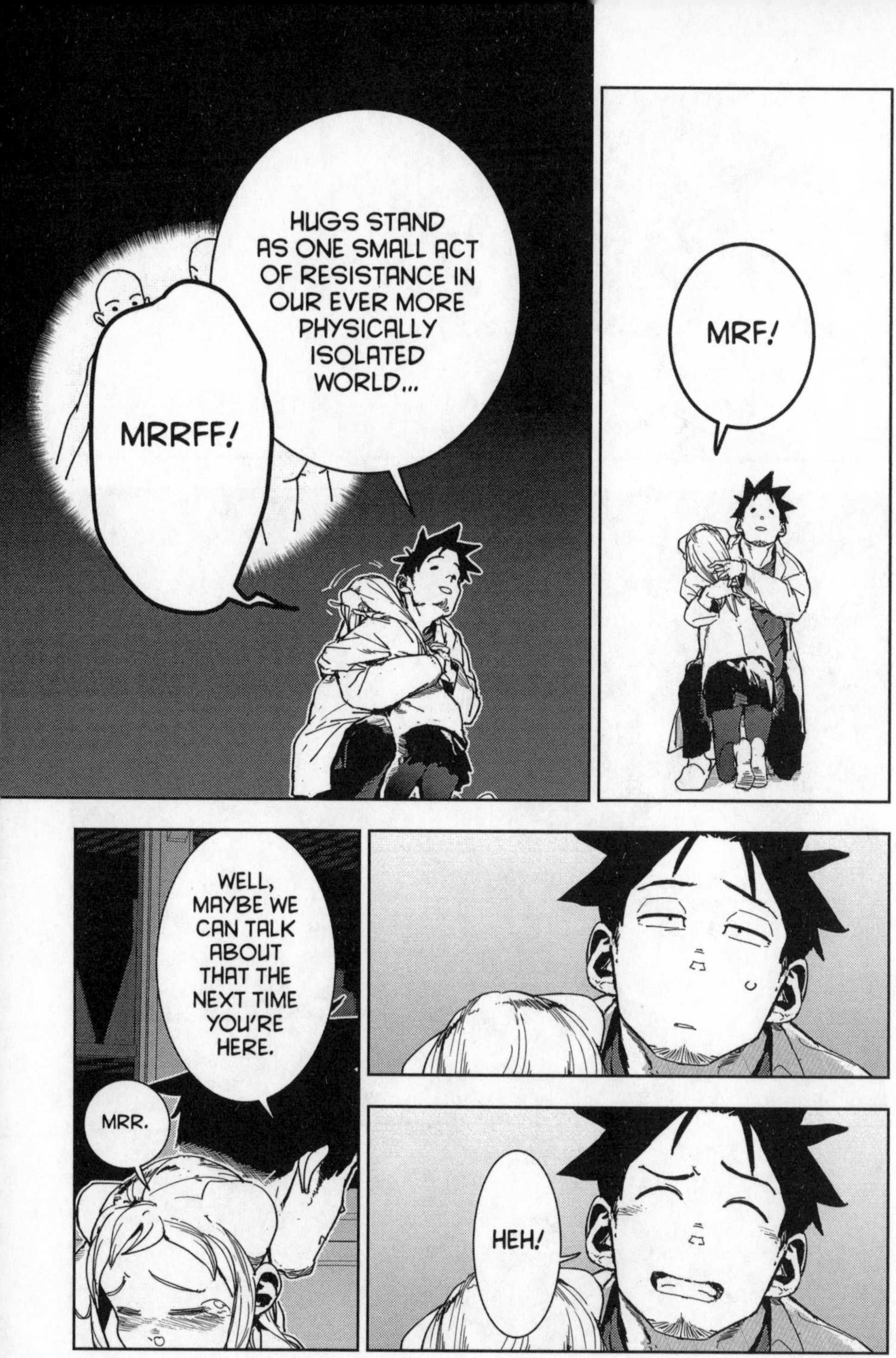
MRF!
HUGS STAND AS ONE SMALL ACT OF RESISTANCE IN OUR EVER MORE PHYSICALLY ISOLATED WORLD...
MRRFF!
HEH!
WELL, MAYBE WE CAN TALK ABOUT THAT THE NEXT TIME YOU'RE HERE.
MRR.

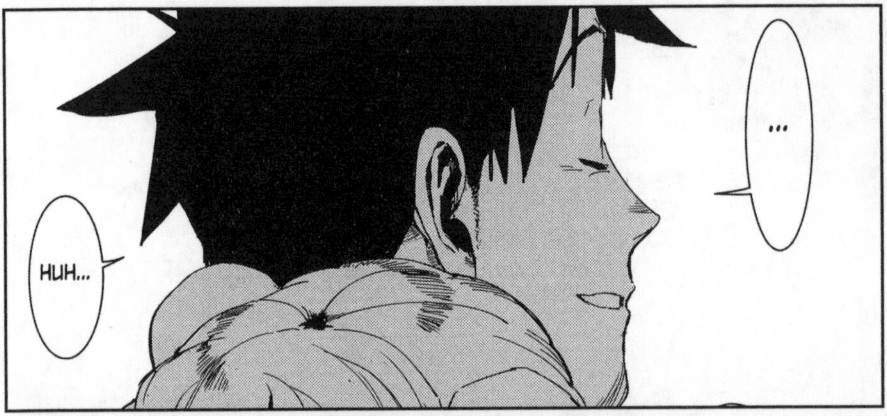
...
HUH...

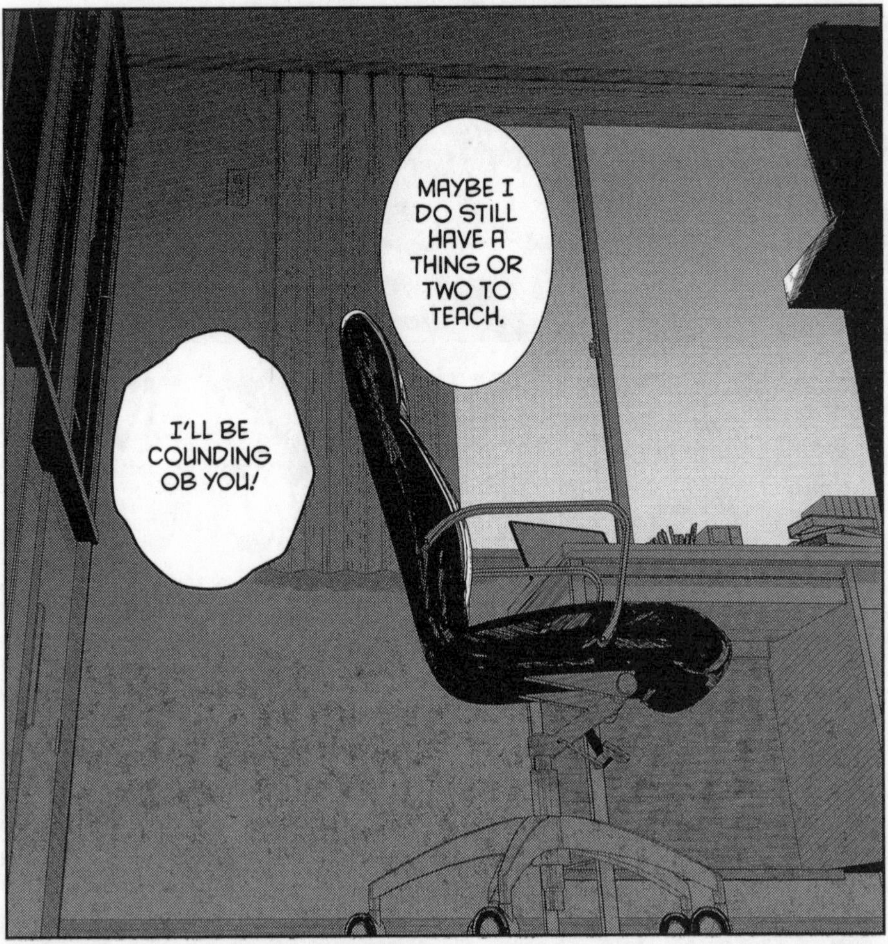
MAYBE I DO STILL HAVE A THING OR TWO TO TEACH.
I'LL BE COUNDING OB YOU!

HIKARI-CHAN, TERRIBLE NEWS!
YOU'VE BEEN SO DOWN LATELY THAT YUKI-CHAN HAS TURNED INTO A ZOMBIE!
MWAHAHA! I'M A ZOMBIE! MWA HA...
I DON'T GET IT, KYOKO.
IT'S HILARIOUS!

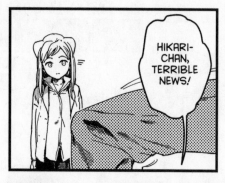

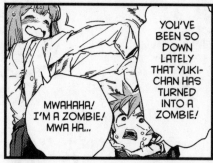

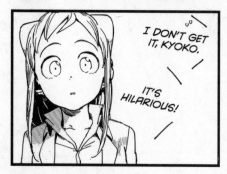

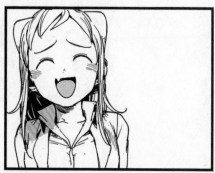

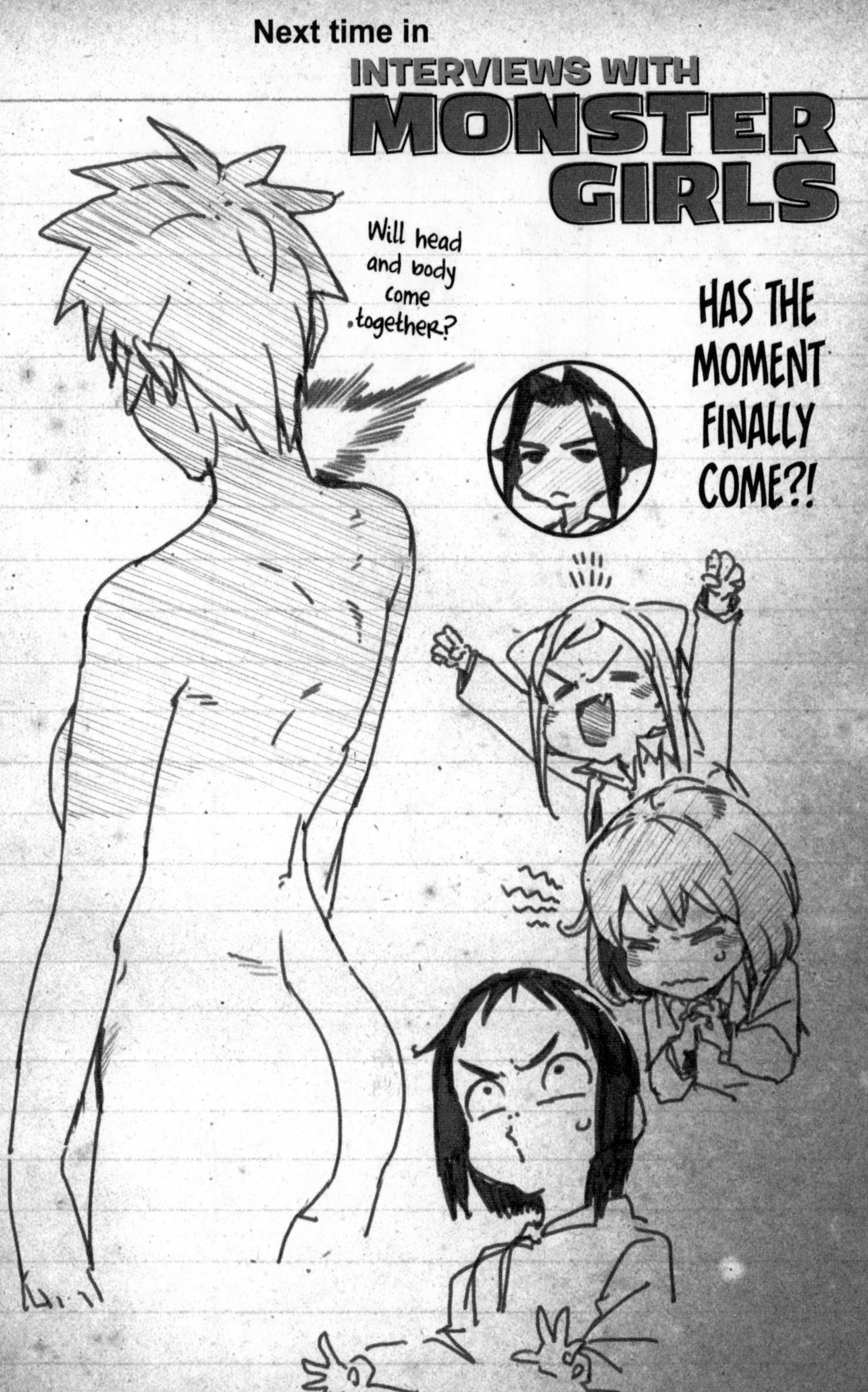
Next time in
INTERVIEWS WITH MONSTER GIRLS
HAS THE MOMENT FINALLY COME?!
Will head and body come together?

TRANSLATION NOTES

We Don't Even Have To Wear Our Uniforms, page 5
Usually, school students are expected to wear their uniforms any time they're on school grounds or when attending any school-related function, such as a club activity or meeting. Apparently this requirement is relaxed during summer break at Shibasaki High.

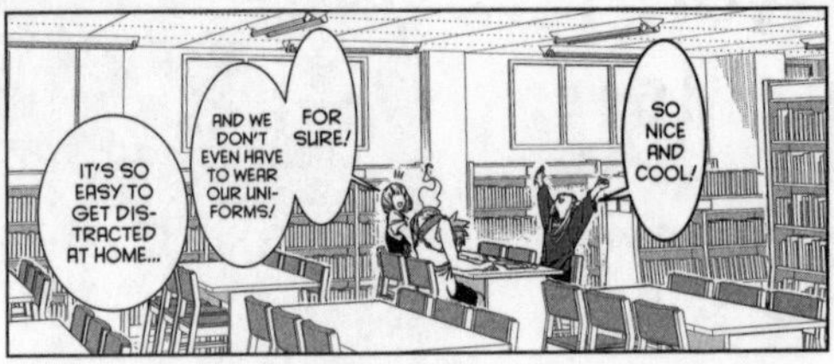
SO NICE AND COOL!
FOR SURE!
AND WE DON'T EVEN HAVE TO WEAR OUR UNI-FORMS!
IT'S SO EASY TO GET DIS-TRACTED AT HOME...

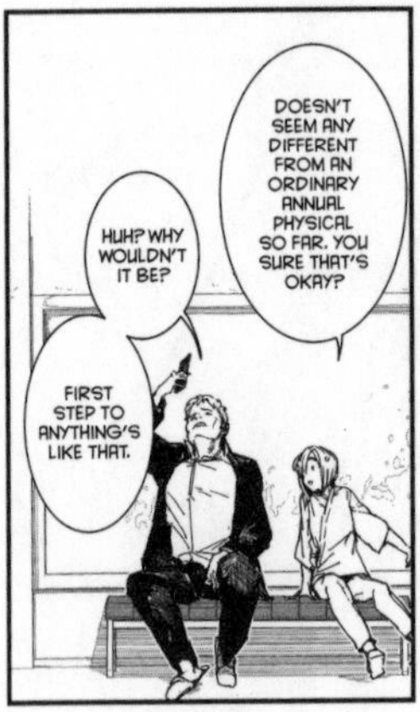
DOESN'T SEEM ANY DIFFERENT FROM AN ORDINARY ANNUAL PHYSICAL SO FAR. YOU SURE THAT'S OKAY?
HUH? WHY WOULDN'T IT BE?
FIRST STEP TO ANYTHING'S LIKE THAT.

Checkup, page 9
This scene mentions two different kinds of physicals. Kurtz initially mentions the *kenkou shindan* or "health checkup," a basic examination of an individual's health. Under Japanese labor law, kenkou shindan are provided annually and employees must undergo them. By contrast, on panel 5 of this page, Ugaki refers to *ningen dokku*. (The word *ningen* means "human"; *dokku* is usually seen simply as an abbreviation of this expression.) This is a much more thorough examination; the exact procedures vary from clinic to clinic, but include full bloodwork and possibly MRIs and other types of scans. *Ningen dokku* is not required by law, and as such, employers usually don't pay for it, but apparently Kurtz has access to it for free. (Perhaps it's one of the supports the government provides to demis.)

Teacher Visit, page 57
In Japan, it's not uncommon for teachers to visit students' houses to talk to their parents, particularly if the student is having trouble at school. The teacher is viewed as having authority in matters related to education and the school, which is part of why Hikari and Himari's parents react the way they do, showing deference in the face of the teacher's diatribe rather than arguing with her.

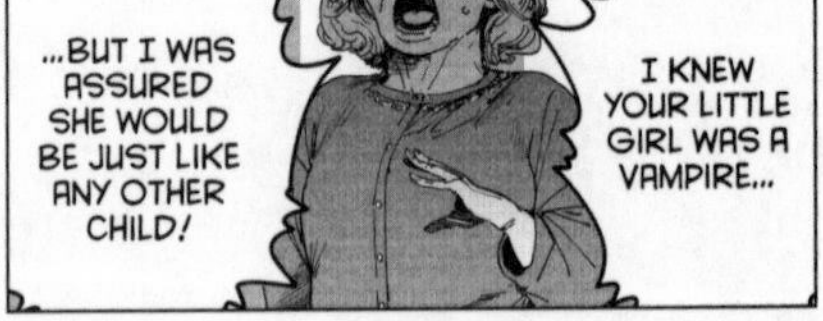
I KNEW YOUR LITTLE GIRL WAS A VAMPIRE...
...BUT I WAS ASSURED SHE WOULD BE JUST LIKE ANY OTHER CHILD!

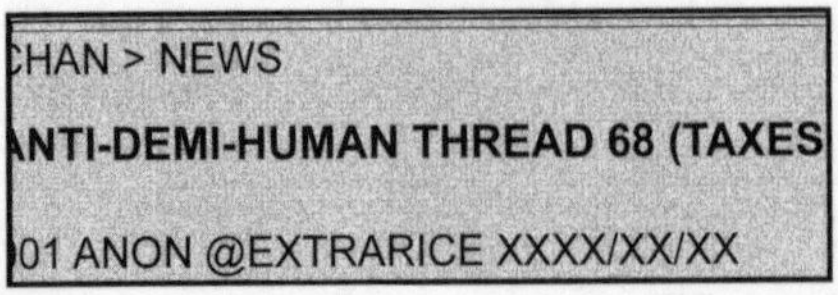
HAN > NEWS
NTI-DEMI-HUMAN THREAD 68 (TAXES
01 ANON @EXTRARICE XXXX/XX/XX

-Chan, page 87
The Japanese is *channeru*—the exact name of the site is obscured, but it seems to allude to 2chan (*ni channeru*), a major Japanese message board. Posts are almost entirely anonymous, as seen on this page, and can cover virtually any topic.

In Autumn, The Twilight, page 113

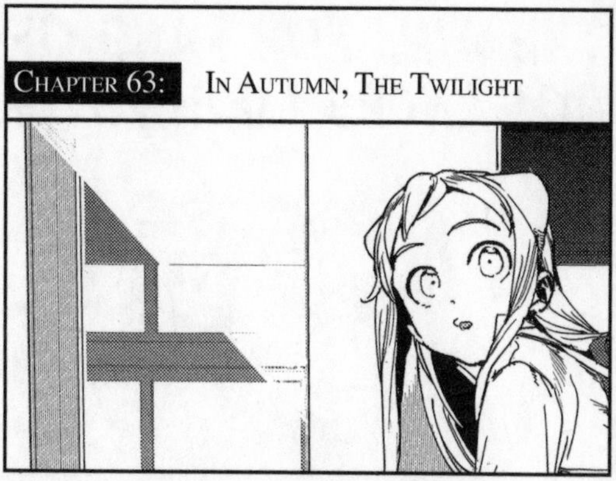
CHAPTER 63: IN AUTUMN, THE TWILIGHT

The title of this chapter is an allusion to *The Pillow Book of Sei Shonagon* (*Makura no Soushi*). Sei Shonagon was a lady of the Heian court in the late tenth century, and the *Pillow Book* is what amounts to her diary; in it, she records happenings at court as well as her thoughts, opinions, and a wide range of lists. The book begins with one simple, almost incomplete sentence that has become one of the most famous lines in Japanese literature: *haru wa akebono*, or "in spring, the dawn" (i.e., in spring, the dawn is the most beautiful time of day). She goes on to name the most beautiful part of the day in each season, describing some of the things that give it that distinction. "In autumn," she says, it's "the twilight. How moving when, with the sun just brushing the tops of the mountains, the crows make for their beds three and four and two at a time. Geese winging along, miniature in the distance, are striking. When the sun has sunk out of view, the sound of the breeze and the chirruping of insects touch the heart." If you're curious, Shonagon holds that in summer it's the nighttime and in winter the very early morning that are most beautiful.

A Zombie, page 135

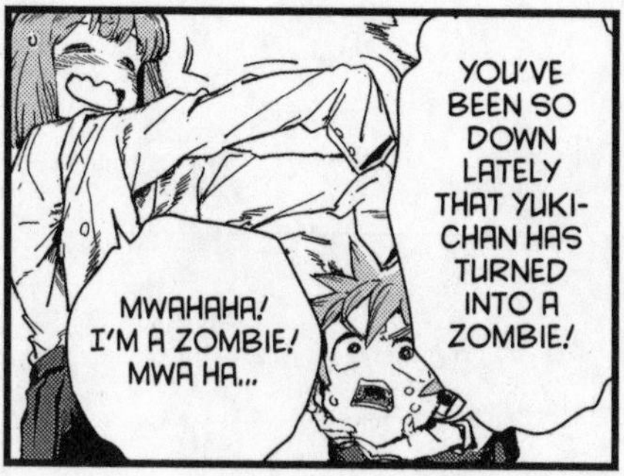
YOU'VE BEEN SO DOWN LATELY THAT YUKI-CHAN HAS TURNED INTO A ZOMBIE!
MWAHAHA! I'M A ZOMBIE! MWA HA...

In Japanese, Kyoko says Yuki has become a *kyonshii*, equivalent to the Chinese *jiangshi*. Sometimes called a "hopping vampire" for their characteristic way of hopping around instead of walking, these creatures are said to steal their victims' *qi* or life essence.

THE SWEET SCENT OF LOVE IS IN THE AIR! FOR FANS OF OFFBEAT ROMANCES LIKE *WOTAKOI*

Sweat and Soap © Kintetsu Yamada / Kodansha Ltd.

In an office romance, there's a fine line between sexy and awkward... and that line is where Asako — a woman who sweats copiously — meets Koutarou — a perfume developer who can't get enough of Asako's, er, scent. Don't miss a romcom manga like no other!

Something's Wrong With Us

NATSUMI ANDO

The dark, psychological, sexy shojo series readers have been waiting for!

A spine-chilling and steamy romance between a Japanese sweets maker and the man who framed her mother for murder!

Following in her mother's footsteps, Nao became a traditional Japanese sweets maker, and with unparalleled artistry and a bright attitude, she gets an offer to work at a world-class confectionary company. But when she meets the young, handsome owner, she recognizes his cold stare...

KC
KODANSHA
COMICS

One of CLAMP's biggest hits returns in this definitive, premium, hardcover 20th anniversary collector's edition!

CLAMP

Chobits 1

20TH ANNIVERSARY EDITION

"A wonderfully entertaining story that would be a great installment in anybody's manga collection."
— Anime News Network

"CLAMP is an all-female manga-creating team whose feminine touch shows in this entertaining, sci-fi soap opera."
— Publishers Weekly

Chobits © CLAMP-ShigatsuTsuitachi CO.,LTD./Kodansha Ltd.

Poor college student Hideki is down on his luck. All he wants is a good job, a girlfriend, and his very own "persocom"—the latest and greatest in humanoid computer technology. Hideki's luck changes one night when he finds Chi—a persocom thrown out in a pile of ~~trash. But Hideki soon discovers that there's much more~~ to his ~~cute new persocom than meets the eye.~~

KODANSHA COMICS

A SMART, NEW ROMANTIC COMEDY FOR FANS OF *SHORTCAKE CAKE* AND *TERRACE HOUSE*!

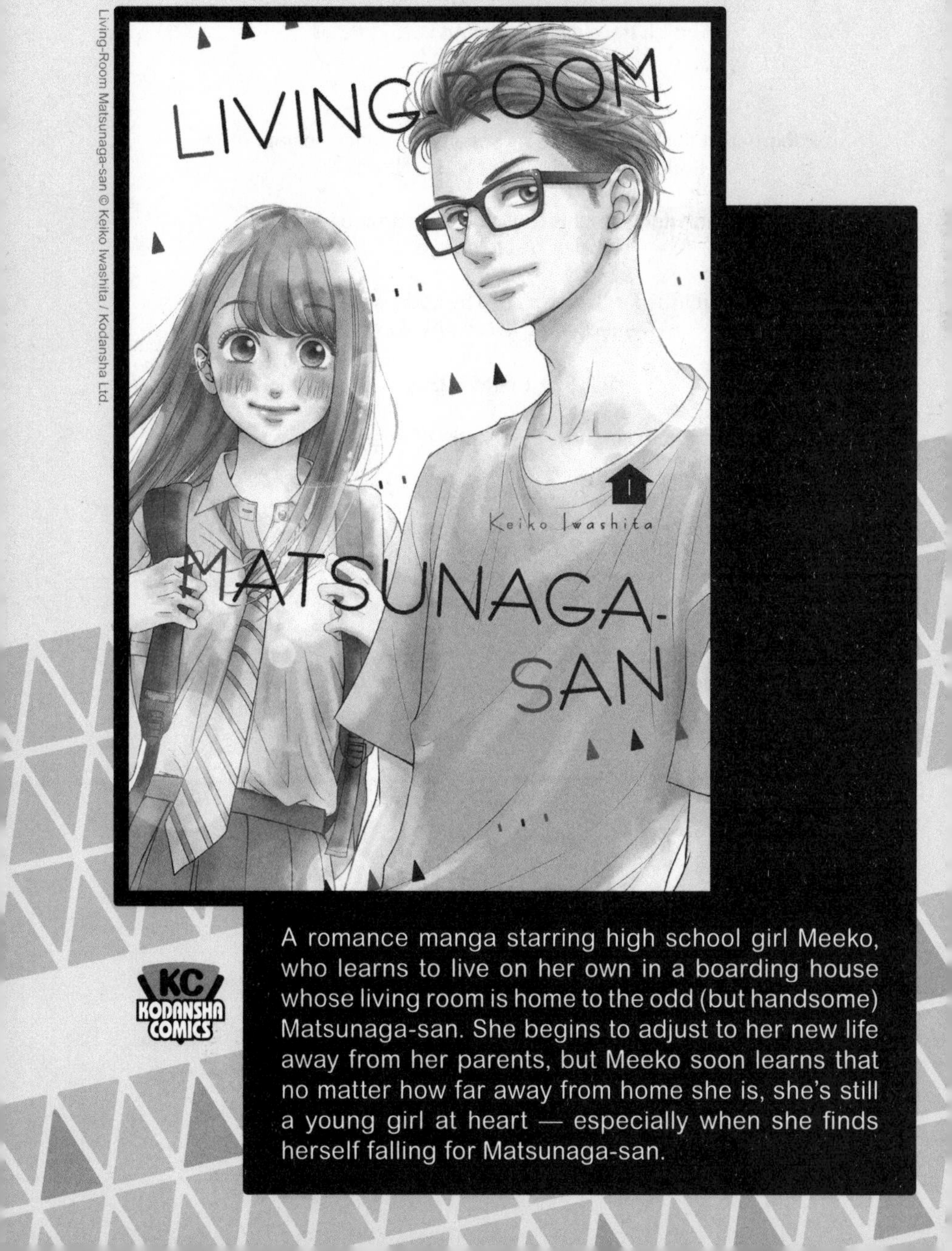
LIVING-ROOM
1
Keiko Iwashita
MATSUNAGA-SAN

KC KODANSHA COMICS

A romance manga starring high school girl Meeko, who learns to live on her own in a boarding house whose living room is home to the odd (but handsome) Matsunaga-san. She begins to adjust to her new life away from her parents, but Meeko soon learns that no matter how far away from home she is, she's still a young girl at heart — especially when she finds herself falling for Matsunaga-san.

A Kodansha Comics Trade Paperback Original
Interviews with Monster Girls 9 copyright © 2020 Petos
English translation copyright © 2021 Petos

Published in the United States by Kodansha Comics, an imprint of
Kodansha USA Publishing, LLC, New York.

Publication rights for this English edition arranged through
Kodansha Ltd., Tokyo.

First published in Japan in 2020 by Kodansha Ltd., Tokyo
as *Demi-chan wa Kataritai*, volume 9.

ISBN 978-1-64651-239-3

Printed in the United States of America.

www.kodansha.us

9 8 7 6 5 4 3 2 1
Translation: Kevin Steinbach
Lettering: Paige Pumphrey
Editing: Aimee Zink
Kodansha Comics edition cover design by My Truong
Kodansha Comics edition logo design by Phil Balsman

Publisher: Kiichiro Sugawara

Director of publishing services: Ben Applegate
Associate director of operations: Stephen Pakula
Publishing services managing editors: Madison Salters, Alanna Ruse
Production managers: Emi Lotto, Angela Zurlo